James Stewart

By the same author

THE MARX BROTHERS: THEIR WORLD OF COMEDY
THE WESTERN: AN ILLUSTRATED GUIDE
THE HOUSE OF HORROR
JOHN WAYNE AND THE MOVIES
(reissued as JOHN WAYNE)
BOGART

James Stewart

Allen Eyles

STEIN AND DAY/Publishers/New York

First published in the United States of America in 1984
Copyright © 1984 by Allen Eyles
All rights reserved, Stein and Day, Incorporated
Printed in the United States of America
STEIN AND DAY/*Publishers*
Scarborough House
Briarcliff Manor, N.Y. 10510

Library of Congress Cataloging in Publication Data

Eyles, Allen.
  James Stewart.

  Filmography: p.
  Bibliography: p.
  Includes index.
  1. Stewart, James, 1908-   . 2. Moving-picture
actors and actresses—United States—Biography. I. Title.
PN2287.S68E9 1984   791.43′028′0924 [B]   84-40252
ISBN 0-8128-2980-8

For Lesley, at last

Contents

Photographs

Acknowledgments

IT'S ALWAYS GRATIFYING TO TURN to friends and receive prompt and generous assistance. Not for the first time, that assiduous Irish film historian Pat Billings has dug into his files to provide all kinds of additions to the filmography (so that I could have the benefit of his corrections beforehand rather than afterwards!). In the United States, Alvin H. Marill (and, through him, John Cocchi) came up with some really elusive information—and a few tidbits I didn't think to ask for, while Pat McGilligan also helped. Here in Britain, Tom Vallance, Tony Sloman, Bernard Hrusa-Marlow and Clive Hirschhorn made a real contribution to my researches and Adrian Turner of the British Film Institute very kindly located a tape recording of James Stewart's appearance at the National Film Theater in 1971. Elaine Burrows efficiently organized viewings of some Stewart films from the National Film Archive. The research that went into this book would not have been possible without the British Film Institute's Information and Documentation section and the generous and tolerant access to its resources that was extended to me. I am grateful to CBS-Fox Video, distributors of *Bandolero!* and *The Green Horizon* for the opportunity to view video cassettes of these titles, and likewise to Warner Home Video for *The FBI Story*. The stills appearing in this book were all issued for publicity purposes and I thank the various companies directly or indirectly involved as well as the National Film Archive Stills Library for providing copies of some of them. When my fingers began hitting too many wrong keys on the typewriter, my wife Lesley generously added to her other work by re-typing the manuscript to present clean pages to a patient publisher. And, lastly, since I have once again contrived to write about a subject that really fascinated me, I can—and do—sincerely thank James Stewart for the pleasure he has given me over the years. It was hard work writing about his films but a delight to see many of them again.

1

The Old Dependable

O<small>N HIS SEVENTY-FIFTH BIRTHDAY</small> in 1983, they unveiled a nine-foot-high statue in Indiana, Pennsylvania, of the local boy who made good—Jimmy Stewart. Like its subject, it was larger than life.

For many of us, images that loomed large on a giant cinema screen will readily come flashing back—of Stewart as the man fighting a lost cause by talking until he drops, seeking to kill his wicked brother, bring food to desperate farmers, find a particular musical sound, resurrect a lost love, practice law in a wide-open territory, locate a missing son, or just cash a check in an unfriendly town; but also a shy, quiet-spoken fellow who carved napkin rings, couldn't tell a girl he loved her, but saw a magnificence in an icy heiress, and went around with a pooka named Harvey. . . .

The unforgetable moments are endless not only because of Stewart's great performing skills but because he had the good sense or good fortune to work with some of the best talents in the film business. In particular, there was his immensely rewarding association with the director Anthony Mann on *Winchester '73, Bend of the River, The Naked Spur, Thunder Bay, The Glenn Miller Story, The Far Country, Strategic Air Command, The Man from Laramie,* the films with Frank Capra *(You Can't Take It With You, Mr. Smith Goes to Washington* and *It's a Wonderful Life),* the work for John Ford *(Two Rode Together, The Man Who Shot Liberty Valance, Cheyenne Autumn* and a television film *Flashing Spikes),* and certainly not least the four films with Alfred Hitchcock *(Rope, Rear Window, The Man Who Knew*

Too Much and *Vertigo)*, long withdrawn from circulation but recently re-released to stimulate a new appreciation of Stewart's acting gifts.

James Stewart has never been a particularly ambitious actor. He has never wanted to stretch himself like his friend Henry Fonda. While he was in London playing live in *Harvey* for the umpteenth time, Fonda was at a nearby theater with a remarkable one-man show in which he portrayed Clarence Darrow. But the fact is I enjoyed them both equally but in different ways (while wishing they'd swap roles for a night to satisfy my curiosity). Fonda certainly suffered in movie popularity by chopping and changing his image but Stewart has never wanted to lose himself in a part to the same extent.

Unlike Fonda and almost all the major stars, Stewart never formed a production company to control his career. He could have become a director (almost all his rivals did), but he declined, with the exception of one television film, saying, "The job of acting is enough if you make it a full-time job. I've just felt that I would rather not wear too many hats."

Asked if he ever got tired of being typecast, Stewart once replied, "Those stars like John Wayne are stars because they have the ability to do just that, to keep their own natures intact through any script that might come along. And that's what audiences pay to see, I guess. Someone once came up to Spencer Tracy and asked, 'Aren't you tired of always playing Tracy?' and Tracy replied, 'What the hell am I supposed to do—play Bogart?' You have to develop a style that suits you and pursue it, not just develop a bag of tricks. I try to play Jimmy Stewart with deference to the character in the movie."

He has played famous people (Charles Lindbergh, Glenn Miller, Monty Stratton) and less famous people (a Chicago reporter, a convicted murderer) but even when they were on hand to advise him and to be studied, he never subordinated his own image to theirs—he merely leaned a little towards them. Another comparison with Fonda is useful: Stewart never starred as a full-blooded villain, yet Fonda did it for the sake of variety, once even playing Stewart's adversary *(Firecreek)*.

Yet in fact Stewart's range has been remarkably wide, from

cowboys to college professors, from stark westerns and tense psychological dramas to sophisticated comedies, and he covered far more ground than most of his legendary rivals. Cary Grant couldn't have handled his westerns and John Wayne was no good in drawing-room comedy. Joel McCrea had the range but never the same resonance. Perhaps only Gary Cooper (with whom Stewart was often compared in his early work) could fully match Stewart's variety of achievements (but did Coop ever sing?).

Stewart has been perceived by audiences as a decent guy, an average fellow. As his studio, MGM, put it in a 1940 official biography, "His type is as normally average as the hot dog and pop at Coney Island. He is good looking without being handsome, quiet without being a bore, ambitious without taking either himself or his job too seriously and unassuming without being dull. Stewart's growing appeal has sometimes been difficult to peg. He's no Gable and certainly has none of the qualities of a Valentino. A sixteen-year-old fan seems to have hit it when she wrote, 'I like you because you're like the boy next door.'"

As Stewart went on to greater success, he seemed to epitomize the ideal American—determined, resourceful, self-reliant, polite. Like the characters he played in such films as *Mr. Smith Goes to Washington* and *It's a Wonderful Life,* he was a small-town boy who worked hard and eventually made a success of his life. His private life reinforces this image. People in the film business have only complimentary things to say about him. The public has learned that he was a war hero, has been active in the boy scout movement, a staunch member of the Beverly Hills Presbyterian Church, a trustee of Princeton University. No scandal has ever been attached to his name. His one marriage has been long-lasting.

As a firm Republican, he has believed in tradition rather than change. "He projected America's favorite self-image: modest rectitude," said Anthony Quayle who directed him on his London stage appearance. "Jimmy is everything the British audience wants an American to be, but so rarely is."

He has the polite, small-town manner of talking slowly and listening carefully. He opens doors and lets ladies go first. He is a model of courtesy in interviews. He has cultivated the image of the man who speaks with hesitations, pauses and repetitions, hemming and hawing. And why not? People like it and expect it. On screen, Cary Grant sees him as pioneering the school of natural talk years before Brando and Dean: "He knew that in conversation people *do* often interrupt one another and that it's not always so *easy* to get a thought out."

One measure of Stewart's individuality is the ease with which he is imitated (though not necessarily well). "I suppose I must be the most imitated actor in the world," he acknowledges (though Jimmy Cagney might disagree). "Every mimic has a Jimmy Stewart impersonation in his ... uh ... repertoire." I had only to mention I was writing a book on Stewart's career to be greeted with grinning imitations ("Errr...ah...waal...you don't say!"). Writer John Culhane confessed in an affectionate tribute to Stewart in *American Film* that as a small-town boy he had copied the actor's lines and courting technique with Donna Reed outside the deserted house in *It's a Wonderful Life* and kissed quite a few local girls himself. Androids wanting to become human study the same sequence, too, according to Aaron Lipstadt's 1982 movie *Android* in which the title character uses it to try and understand love-making and mimics Stewart's gangling walk. Rich Little imitates Stewart as part of his comedy act in the United States and Rick Lenz has provided fetching impersonations of the young Jimmy in *Cactus Flower* (1969) and *Where Does it Hurt?* (1972) although he dropped any similarities of style when he actually appeared in the same film as the actor (*The Shootist*, 1976).

Stewart's great period of popularity in the 1950s may have been partly the result of more films being made in color, for it enabled him to make more of an impression with his startlingly blue eyes. The way they dart around in close-up as a dying Frenchman whispers in his ear in *The Man Who Knew Too Much*, or as he takes off for his historic flight in *The Spirit of St. Louis*, unable to see straight ahead, reinforce this notion which was advanced by Anthony Mann: "Have you noticed that all the great stars that the public love have clear eyes: Gary Cooper, James Stewart, John Wayne, Clark Gable, Charlton Heston, Henry Fonda, Burt Lancaster, Robert Taylor, Kirk Douglas ... ? The eyes do everything: they're the permanent reflection of the internal flame that animates the hero. Without those eyes, you can only aspire to second-string roles!"

Stewart has never been terribly concerned to analyze the characters he played. He was always willing to trust his director and co-operate to get any effect wanted. In an interview with Chris Wicking, Anthony Mann summed up Stewart as "a man who's devoted his whole life to acting and who's quite brilliant in what he does. He's very skillful and, once you start going with him, he's marvellous to work with, because he's always there; he's always anxious; he wants to be great . . . Within himself he has something more burning and exciting than when you meet him personally. And he'll say: 'Look, Tony, if you want me to be pulled through the fire, then I'll do it. If you want me to fight under the horse's hooves, I'll do it.' This is the kind of guy he is; he likes to have to do these things. And a lot of actors don't. . . . It's a curse when they don't learn; when they're not adept at the art of riding, fencing, swimming and the other things that are necessary, which they must learn if they don't know."

"He was good in anything," John Ford told Peter Bogdanovich. "Played himself but he played the character. . . . People just liked him." Frank Capra has spoken of an "indefinable personal integrity—awfully hard to make Jimmy look bad." He has enjoyed the respect and affection of audiences worldwide for more than forty years.

It's because Stewart made such a good impression that he could get away with portraying characters with some rather unsavory traits, especially in the Hitchcock films (the voyeur of *Rear Window*, the sick detective in *Vertigo*). Asked for his comments, Stewart declares, "I just didn't come to grips with it," or, queried about the "dark side" of Hitchcock, he replies: "I wasn't aware of it because I don't think it was there," and merely recalls the "completely relaxed" working atmosphere on a Hitchcock set. Similarly, asked if he helped enlarge on the obsessive characteristics of his western heroes, he replied, "I never really thought of it in that light—I wasn't conscious that that was happening." Now Stewart could have learned more sophisticated answers to tell people what they wanted to hear, so he seems to have a genuinely uncomplicated outlook. Whatever the case, Stewart proved a

[17]

marvellous vehicle for transmitting the ideas of some of Hollywood's most fertile minds.

In this book, I discuss the Stewart pictures and I refer to Stewart rather than the name of the character he portrayed because we remember the movies as stories in which Jimmy Stewart rather than the (usually) fictional character did this action or that. To be consistent, I refer to the other parts by the names of their actors too and hopefully save a lot of referring back to check on who played who.

2

A Small Town Boy

JAMES MAITLAND STEWART WAS born on Wednesday, May 20, 1908, at Indiana, Pennsylvania. It was then a rural community of about 7,500 people in an area of mining and farming about forty miles east of Pittsburgh. He was a first child, named after his paternal grandfather who had founded the local hardware store in 1853. The young Jimmy's father, Alexander Stewart, ran it under the name J. M. Stewart & Co. Four years after Jimmy's birth, a sister Mary was born; then, two years later in 1914, another sister, Virginia, followed.

Jimmy's parents were still young. They lived in a stucco house on a steep hillside that overlooked the town and went to church every Sunday. There his mother played the organ. She was active in the Ladies' Aid and one afternoon each week she played bridge. His father belonged to the volunteer fire department and would often be heard by his young son jumping out of bed when the fire whistle blew and descending the steps into town in his heavy boots. Jimmy became the firemen's mascot and they banded together to give him a uniform one Christmas. When he was a little older, he went along to some of the daytime fires and naturally dreamed of being a fireman when he grew up.

He was an adventurous and imaginative child. He caused an explosion in the basement of the house with one of his chemistry experiments. He sneaked into the big stockroom at the back of the hardware store and helped himself to hammers, nails and bits of wood to put together objects like his own version of an aeroplane.

[19]

One of his first Christmas presents had been a model aeroplane, beginning a life-long interest in aviation. Jimmy had one large model that he drove around on the ground for weeks, pretending it could fly. Then, on a dare, he took it up onto a roof and nearly broke his neck trying to fly off in it. With his father, he built little crystal radio sets and developed an interest in radio engineering.

When the First World War started, Jimmy played make-believe games of beating the Hun in the backyard. After America entered the war and his father enlisted in the Army, Jimmy stepped up his own patriotic efforts and wrote and performed a number of plays with titles like *To Hell with the Kaiser* and *The Slacker* (the story of a no-good who redeemed himself by joining up). These were presented to enthusiastic audiences of local children in the basement. The word spread and Jimmy had to stage one of his plays upstairs in the drawing-room before a group of adults. His one-man pageant was considered more comic than dramatic from the moment he appeared in an ill-fitting costume, and the spectators were unable to stifle their amusement.

After the war, many of the aviators were reluctant to give up flying and made a living traveling around giving stunt shows and rides in ramshackle aircraft. The appearance of one of these daredevils in Jimmy's vicinity had him saving every penny from working in the family store to make a trip into the wild blue yonder. It cost fifteen dollars for fifteen minutes—a considerable sum, but young Jimmy managed it and his father had too much respect for his efforts to deny him the chance. He did, however, take the family doctor along as a precaution. "Did it come up to your expectations, Jimmy?" asked the doctor on the way back. The boy was at a loss for words. "Yeah," was all he could say, "Yeah . . ." It confirmed his ambition to be a flyer.

Of his childhood, Stewart was later to say: "I can't recall anything unpleasant. Those things I remember best were getting my first long trousers when I was halfway through high school, vacationing in Atlantic City during the summer and not particularly liking school because I was only a fair student. It was a pleasant enough experience."

The interest in performing revived when Jimmy took up amateur magic. During summer breaks, when he wasn't helping out in the store he assisted a magician called Bill Neff. He also learned to play the accordion after his sister Virginia was given one (reputedly taken in trade by their father in place of cash from a customer). It proved too cumbersome for the girl to handle and went to Jimmy who became good enough to play it in the weekly concerts of the boy scout band.

From an early age, Jimmy was expected to follow in his father's footsteps and attend Princeton University. He left home for the first time to attend Mercersburg Academy and prepare for the day. At Mercersburg, Jimmy went out for football and became captain of the lightweight team. His long legs were a great help in track events where he excelled as a high hurdler and high jumper.

While at the academy, he became art director of the yearbook, *The Krux*. He also sang in the choir and the glee club, played the accordion in the school orchestra at entertainments, and wound up with a role in the senior play, *The Wolves*. When summer came, Jimmy returned home and worked at such jobs as pouring cement onto highways and hauling bricks for a construction company.

Then the young Mr. Stewart finally went to Princeton where he elected to major in electrical engineering. But his math wasn't up to it and so he tried political studies. He didn't like this much either, and after a course in descriptive geometry that called for the making of model bridges and buildings he settled down to becoming an architectural student.

In his spare time he took part in the university's Triangle Club shows and Theater Intime productions. In 1928, he appeared in a Triangle show written by Joshua Logan and Al Wade called *The Golden Dog* as a young accordion player in a number entitled "Blue Hell." The following year he played an accordion solo, "So Beats My Heart for You," in the annual Triangle Club musical that toured at Christmas. The next year he played the lead in *The Tiger Smiles*, singing along with Joshua Logan who wrote the operetta. Logan went on to become a celebrated stage and film director and recalled in his autobiography, "Stewart was gangling and hilarious singing and dancing 'On a Sunday Evening' which I had written for him. He winced as he sang my corny rhymes."

In Jimmy's senior year, the Triangle Club invited a leading lady

[21]

who had been in the University Players, a summer stock company at West Falmouth on Cape Cod in Massachusetts, to be their guest in the commencement play. The actress was Margaret Sullavan, who was loaned by producer Brock Pemberton from one of the touring companies of Preston Sturges' hit comedy, *Strictly Dishonorable*.

She appeared in a play called *The Artist and the Lady* and Stewart was the stage manager. An immediate friendship sprang up between them. Margaret Sullavan went on to rapid fame and fortune in Hollywood and was not to forget Jimmy Stewart.

At Princeton, Joshua Logan was Jimmy's best friend and was totally committed to the theater as a career. Logan graduated a year ahead of Stewart and joined the University Players.

Stewart graduated with a B.Sc. degree in architecture in 1932. With the Depression biting hard and few buildings being erected, prospects were somewhat dubious. He was undecided about the future but applied for a scholarship so that he could take a post-graduate course and study for his master's degree. He could have filled in the summer vacation helping out in the family hardware store but he accepted an invitation from Logan to spend it at West Falmouth. It was simply a break before he looked for a job or went back to Princeton.

3

Broadway and Busking

T HE OFFER WASN'T THAT PROMISING. There was a little tea-room attached to the theater in West Falmouth and Logan suggested that Stewart perform on the accordion there and occasionally fill a small role on stage. "I was the worst accordion player," claims Stewart. "I just emptied that tea-room—and they got rid of me."

He moved over to looking after props and was given a small part in the University Players' opening production in June 1932. It was a revival of Booth Tarkington's 1923 comedy *Magnolia* and Joshua Logan, who directed the comedy, recalled that Stewart was "howlingly funny in it as a lanky Southern slob." He then appeared in a new production of a play by Laurence E. Johnston, *It's a Wise Child*, that had featured Humphrey Bogart on Broadway in 1929. Logan declared that "he proved to be a fine actor— honest and talented."

Princeton came up with the offer of a scholarship and Stewart thought about it carefully before making a decision. "Mary and Virginia were growing up right behind me," he said. "Mary was scheduled for an art course at Carnegie Tech. Virginia was going to Vassar. If I went back to Princeton, my tuition would cost nothing, but I would need money for food and clothes. I'd be an added expense. Dad didn't seem to worry about it, but I did. Money at home wasn't limitless. I knew that and I felt I had had my share. I wrote the trustees expressing my appreciation for the scholarship, and I wrote Dad telling him what I had done." (That

[23]

wasn't quite the end of Stewart's connection with Princeton: in the late fifties, he was to be elected to the board of trustees himself.)

A Broadway producer, Arthur J. Beckhard, interested the University Players company in working for him. For openers, he staged a biographical drama about a well-known temperance agitator, *Carrie Nation,* with his wife Esther Dale in the principal role under the direction of Blanche Yurka, best remembered for her later career as a screen actress. It did a trial week at West Falmouth which gave Beckhard the confidence to take it to Baltimore and then to Broadway where it opened on October 29, 1932 and, despite downbeat reviews, staggered through thirty-one performances. This not only provided James Stewart with his Broadway debut in the part of Constable Gano, providing some light relief, but it also marked the New York debut of Logan as well as Myron McCormick and Mildred Natwick (both later character players in movies).

Beckhard had a new comedy, *Goodbye Again* by Allan Scott and George Haight, in the works. It was tried out in Falmouth and opened on Broadway at the Masque Theater on December 28, 1932 to wild acclaim. One of the hits of the show was Jimmy Stewart, playing a three-line three-minute role as a chauffeur in the first act for thirty-five dollars a week. His slowly-drawled exit line, "Mrs. Mainwaring's going to be sore as hell," brought the house down. As it settled into a run of over 200 performances, Jimmy and fellow player Myron McCormick and Joshua Logan (the company manager and assistant box-office cashier) rented a third-floor flat in a seven-story building on West 63rd Street near Central Park West in what was mainly a brothel. It was a community flat and others who stayed there included Burgess Meredith and Charles Arnt. Another who found it a refuge was a young out-of-work actor called Henry Fonda, who had been a star at the University Players before Stewart went there and whose marriage to Margaret Sullavan, now a big name, had come unstuck. Those who worked paid the rent for those who were "resting." There was a bedroom with twin beds, a living room with two battered studio couches and a bathroom, while a huge kitchen stove sat in the hallway.

[24]

"We drank, laughed, listened to good jazz, rotated our sleeping arrangements so as to leave the living-room couches to those who had dates," recalled Joshua Logan.

Jimmy Stewart was the only one of the group who wasn't dead set on a career in the theater. "Acting is no job for a man," he would declare. "You work two hours a night, *when you work*; and you sleep all morning and maybe all day because you have nothing else to do." But for him the jobs kept turning up.

In the summer of 1933, he took the midnight train from Grand Central Station to Boston where the great Jane Cowl was to star in *Camille*. On this occasion, he was merely to be stage manager. Miss Cowl was a grand actress of the old school who milked her death scene for all it was worth. Part of Stewart's job was to stand in the wings and ring down the curtain when she had finally passed away. One night she was on stage dying, the audience was hushed, and Stewart became aware of thudding noises behind him. He rushed off to investigate and found a drunk throwing stones onto the roof of the theater. Moving him on, Jimmy rushed back to the side of the stage, listened and could hear absolutely nothing. Terrified by the thought that he had missed his cue, he brought down the curtain only to find that Miss Cowl had not yet fully expired. Hidden from the audience, the actress rose in anger from her bier and stalked over to him. "Do you know what you've done!" she exclaimed, her finger pointing at him. "You've ruined my performance, ruined it *completely*!" The upshot was that James Stewart took the next train back to New York.

Word of his incompetence seemingly failed to follow, as he was engaged to be both stage manager and bit-part performer with Blanche Yurka in *Spring in Autumn*, which opened on October 24, 1933 for a forty-one performance run. He played the role of Jack Brennan.

From then on, Stewart worked solely as an actor. His knowledge of the accordion came in useful when he obtained a part that required one to be played on stage. By now, he and Henry Fonda had moved into rooms at the Madison Square Hotel where they spent their spare time assembling model airplanes. Both were engaged for a comedy called *All Good Americans* by the satirist S. J.

[25]

Perelman (collaborating with his wife Laura) and it made fun, for the umpteenth time, of Americans on the loose in Paris. When Jimmy found that he was required to throw the accordion out of the window in one scene, he couldn't bear the thought of mal-treating it in that way and was allowed to use a banjo instead. It was a $50-a-week part. The play opened on December 5, 1933 but ran only thirty-nine performances. (MGM made it into the film *Paris Interlude* in 1934.)

When the play closed early in the New Year, there was a last night party and Stewart took along his accordion. At about three in the morning, somewhat the worse for wear from drink, he and Fonda started out across Times Square for the subway home. Then, as Stewart recalls: "Hank dared me to start playing the accordion to see if I could draw a crowd. It was bitter cold and there wasn't a soul in sight. I've never been one to turn down an honest dare so I said, 'There's only one way to find out and that's to start playing.' Well, I began playing some of my repertoire: 'Ragtime Cowboy Joe,' 'Dinah,' 'Wait 'Til the Sun Shines Nellie' and part of 'Rhapsody in Blue.' Four or five people appeared and stood around listening. I played another number and some more people came up. What made the recital such a triumph was that one of the poor souls requested a particular song, 'Shanty Town.' I could play the hell out of that song. Then some of the others started giving requests and I was playing up a storm and singing too. The next thing I saw Fonda passing the hat. We got thirty-six cents.

"About four in the morning, I felt somebody hit me on the back of the leg with something hard. It was a cop with a nightstick and he was furious. I wouldn't exactly call it disturbing the peace, except that's what *he* called it. He said, 'It takes me three or four hours to get all these drunks off the streets and asleep in door-ways and you come along and start that noise!'"

That was the end of Stewart's busking career but it did suggest a possible alternative career in case of a rainy day. He was still not that impressed by acting. "When I joined in the final curtain call," he said, "I'd see people in the audience wondering who I was and what I was doing up there." There were also his first brushes with the movies. He was screentested by Fox but turned down.

[26]

He did find some film work, however. "I did a two-reel short made for Warner Bros out of curiosity because I didn't believe they paid $50 a day. I found out that they did and that I wasn't being kidded." It was a Big V comedy called *Art Trouble* which starred Harry Gribbon and was shot in New York.

Fortunately, he was to bag a really substantial part in an important play, *Yellow Jack* by Sidney Howard. His old roommate Myron McCormick was also in the cast. *Yellow Jack* was a sombre drama about the heroic manner in which a cure for the deadly yellow fever was sought in Cuba at the turn of the century. To sustain the mood, the two-hour play ran without intermission; but even with shoals of praise from the critics it was hard to persuade audiences that it was worth spending money on. It opened on March 6, 1934 and closed after a respectable seventy-nine performance run.

"I tried out for the part of the Irish soldier but was told my brogue was too poor," Stewart has recalled. "So I got in touch with an old Abbey player, Frank Cullinan, and rehearsed with him in the lobby of the old Lincoln Hotel. When the actor who got the part fell ill, I was able to step into it." The role was that of Sergeant O'Hara, a marine who volunteers his services as a guinea-pig to test a possible cure. (When MGM filmed the play in 1938, Robert Montgomery played O'Hara.) It was the first time Stewart's name went up in lights but this was not the cause of his comment, "I think that was the turning point of my work on the stage"; rather it was the thrill of working with the notable director Guthrie McClintic who made Stewart appreciate that the theater was a sensitive craft and that it was as worthwhile a task to move audiences as to design buildings. He now became dedicated to making acting his life's work. MGM's chief talent scout, Billy Grady, was one of those who watched the show and was sufficiently impressed to start a file on James Stewart.

In the summer of 1934, Stewart joined the Locust Valley Company on Long Island's fashionable North Shore and played in a variety of plays at the Red Barn Theater. It was more useful experience, and in a couple of the productions he worked with a young director called Anthony Mann.

On Stewart's return to New York, Guthrie McClintic had

another part for him, in the new play *Divided by Three* by Margaret Leech and Beatrice (Mrs. George S.) Kaufman which opened on October 2, 1934. He played a son who leaves home on finding that his mother (Judith Anderson) is an adulteress. Notices were mixed and the run lasted only thirty-one performances. Billy Grady noted: "This kid has finally arrived. Unaffected and sincere in everything he does." Also in the cast was Hedda Hopper. She had been working at MGM as an actress and studio aide. She has related how she was so impressed that on returning to Holly-wood the following February she advised MGM to put Stewart under contract.

When MGM did screentest him in New York (sending the film on to the Culver City studios), it was a scene from *Divided by Three* that Stewart performed.

Stewart appeared for another notable Broadway director, George Abbott, in the farce *Page Miss Glory*, playing a shifty small-time promoter who submits a composite photograph, built up from the best features of famous movie actresses, in a beauty competition and on winning has to produce a woman who looks like the picture. The play opened on November 27, 1934 and ran to sixty-three performances. Warner Bros snapped it up and Pat O'Brien had Stewart's role in the movie adaptation which came out in 1935.

In March, his good friend Henry Fonda, who had made a big hit on Broadway with *The Farmer Takes a Wife*, went off to Hollywood to make the film version at Fox. A month later, on April 16, 1935, Stewart made the last of his thirties' stage appearances and it helped shift his sights towards the movie capital. The production was called *Journey by Night* and it died after seven performances. He had the starring role as a Viennese bank clerk who becomes an embezzler and a murderer out of love for a prostitute. The notices were lethal. "He is as Viennese as a hamburger," pronounced one critic. "James Stewart wanders through the play like a befuddled tourist on the Danube," declared another. It taught Stewart the dangers of straying beyond his range. "It was only because I was down to my last bean that I went into *Journey by Night*," said the actor. "It was vile. But it paid me one hundred good American dollars a week. I spent seventy on a suit I had to wear in it. I could use that suit—and how. And thirty dollars in my pocket was a darn sight more reassuring than only one had been."

MGM still wasn't sure what to do with someone like Stewart. He went West by train for more elaborate screentests. Then it was back East—to wait. Eventually a cable came from Billy Grady: "Report to Hollywood—part available with three months' option on your services."

4

Mr. Stewart Goes to Hollywood

BILLY GRADY HAD BEEN APPOINTED casting director at MGM and was now based in Hollywood, making monthly return trips back East to keep up with the new plays. He wanted to use Stewart. Even though MGM had "more stars than there are in the heavens," it didn't have anyone quite like the gawky, gangling Jimmy Stewart with his slow, hesitant drawl. The problem was how to get him started.

Grady kept his eyes open and spotted a small movie called *The Murder Man* in production on Stage 18. There was a minor part of a police reporter called Shorty which had yet to be cast. Producer Harry Rapf was looking for a pint-sized actor but Grady persuaded his good friend, Tim Whelan, who was directing the movie, to put Stewart in the role. He was 6 ft. 3 ins. and weighed 130 lbs. Rapf didn't see the humor of putting such a beanpole of an actor in the part and complained to studio boss Louis B. Mayer. Meanwhile, Stewart was summoned and arrived in Hollywood by plane on Saturday, June 8, 1935. He roomed with Henry Fonda.

"I signed a contract with Metro-Goldwyn-Mayer without even looking at it—it was impossible to read," recalled Stewart years later. "The contract was for three months: I found out later that it was one of those contracts with an option for a further three months and so on. In other words, they got you for life. Mine was terminated by the war. Not that I wanted to get away. It was great fun." (In fact, MGM's options ran to seven years at most.) He started at something like $350 a week.

Nobody remembers *The Murder Man*. It was only significant for marking Spencer Tracy's first starring vehicle at MGM after several leads at Fox. He played the newspaperman who kills one of the men responsible for his wife's suicide and rigs the evidence so that the other baddie takes the rap for the crime. No fuss was made about the screen debut of the twenty-seven-year-old James Stewart. He wasn't even listed on the posters or promoted in the press book. He was just a supporting actor.

Stewart remembers Tracy's friendliness. "I told him to forget the camera was there," Tracy once said. "That was all he needed. In his very first scene he showed he had all the good things." Stewart, however, winces at the thought of his performance: "I was all hands and feet—didn't seem to know what to do with them."

At least Louis B. Mayer, viewing the rushes, backed Grady and allowed Stewart to keep the part. But for many weeks the studio had nothing else for him to do but work out in the gym. As he was being paid, he found a flying instructor and started to take lessons at Mines Field, soon learning to fly solo. Later, he bought a little fabric-covered airplane which he used to fly home to Pennsylvania, navigating by following the railroad tracks.

Eventually MGM came up with a second role and exercised their three-month option so that he could play in the new Jeanette MacDonald and Nelson Eddy operetta, *Rose Marie*. It was the key supporting role as the man who complicates the romance between the pair. Stewart played John Flower, the boastful weakling kid brother of Jeanette MacDonald. She is the Canadian opera star who has a soft spot for him even though he has been put in prison. When he escapes, killing a Mountie, and is wounded himself, she rushes off into the wilderness to help him. There she encounters Nelson Eddy's Sergeant Bruce of the Royal Mounted who is also looking for her brother.

When Jeanette finally reaches Stewart's hiding place in a backwoods hut, she gives him money and tells him, "You're all I have left in the world. You'll be good, won't you?" "I'll give it a fling," responds Stewart, thinking only of making for China and new excitement. But he is arrested by Nelson Eddy and subsequently executed, which seems to put the dampers on Eddy's chances of winning MacDonald's affections. Fortunately, time heals the wound . . .

It was a meaty assignment for Stewart, playing this wild-eyed, reckless kid, and the kind of part in which he could be noticed. He received favorable comment in most of the reviews, while the critic of the London *Observer* really went out on a limb: "And finally there is a new screen actor, one Mr. James Stewart, who plays the small part of the hunted young brother with considerably more than average promise. Mr. Stewart is very tall, dry in manner, and rather like our own Raymond Massey. I think you will like him, and I am sure you will hear more of him. The Mounties are not the only people who will be out to get this man."

But even before critics and audiences could respond to his performance in *Rose Marie,* his friend Margaret Sullavan had interceded on his behalf. She had become a major star over at Universal and was about to make *Next Time We Love* but the studio was stuck for a leading man after the idea of using Francis Lederer had been discarded. Sullavan was insistent that Stewart should be tested.

"Jimmy Stewart? Who's he?" was the studio's response, allowing the actress to respond, "Haven't you seen Jimmy Stewart in pictures yet? Well, he's a great actor from the New York stage. He's had years of experience and he recently came out to Hollywood, where they've been trying him out in small parts first."

Universal gave in and borrowed Stewart from MGM for tests. To put him at ease, Sullavan performed the scenes with him and their rapport was unmistakable. Besides, who else could they use? They even had to borrow Ray Milland from Paramount to fill out a key supporting role.

Next Time We Love was a soggy tear-jerker in which Sullavan played a promising Broadway actress and Stewart played the newspaperman Chris Tyler whom she marries. They want to preserve their own individuality so that, when Stewart is posted to Rome, he goes alone, determined not to interfere in his wife's career; she stays behind partly so that she can continue acting but also for the sake of her unborn child and a desire not to hinder her husband. Later assignments keep him abroad and they grow accustomed to living apart with occasional reunions. Eventually,

[33]

Stewart contracts a serious illness from a germ picked up in China and goes to Europe for treatment. Sullavan now regrets the time they've spent apart and goes with him, telling him "Next time we live, we'll have time for each other," as she helps him onto the train at a small Swiss railway station for the sanatorium where he might just regain his health.

It was a film played from the woman's angle with Stewart crying in the scene where he has to go off and leave his young wife and baby behind, but it retains a freshness from the tender playing of its two leads. Stewart recalled, for Margaret Sullavan's daughter Brooke Hayward, how the actress kept their performances fresh. "When you'd play a scene with her, you were never quite sure, although she was always letter perfect in her lines, what was going to happen. She had you just a little bit off guard and also the director. I've always called what your mother would do planned improvisation—she could do just moments that would hit you, maybe a look or a line or two, but they would hit like flashes or earthquakes; everybody'd sort of feel it at the same time. It's a very rare thing."

Margaret Sullavan was a stubborn woman. Ten days into production, she refused to come into the studio until sections of the script were rewritten to her satisfaction. The film took much longer to shoot than it should have done, starting in October 1935 and finishing just after Christmas. The delays meant that Stewart couldn't take up a part that had been assigned to him at MGM, the juvenile lead opposite Maureen O'Sullivan in *The Voice of Bugle Ann*, a film that relied on veteran star Lionel Barrymore and some cute bugle hounds for its principal appeal. Eric Linden took Stewart's place.

Once *Next Time We Love* was in the can, Universal made up for lost time by premiering it only a month later at Radio City Music Hall. (Nationally, it proved to be a flop, drawing worse attendances than *The Voice of Bugle Ann*.) Margaret Sullavan retired to Palm Springs for a week's rest but Jimmy Stewart reported back to MGM and was immediately assigned a supporting role in *Small Town Girl* which had just gone into production. He also did a memorable bit in a Jean Harlow film shooting at the studio, *Wife vs. Secretary*, and tested for a role in *The Good Earth*.

Small Town Girl had Stewart playing second fiddle to Robert Taylor. He was Elmer, the boyfriend of Janet Gaynor's small-town shop assistant, Kay Brannan. Boston surgeon Taylor sweeps her off her feet and marries her while drunk. He then takes a lot of time coming to his senses and realizing that he does love her and not the snobbish socialite played by Binnie Barnes. He comes dashing back to Hicksville to snatch her away from Stewart a second time. Even in such a thankless part, Stewart retained the enthusiastic support of the London *Observer* whose critic remarked, "In case somebody wants to see really distinctive acting, there is Mr. James Stewart in one of those small-time, small-town parts that are the salt of any film he essays."

Wife vs. Secretary was an MGM comedy with a title that put the plot in a nutshell. It pitted Myrna Loy's spouse against Jean Harlow's secretary with Clark Gable as the prize, the husband and boss. Stewart was Harlow's boyfriend, Dave, who gives her up when she refuses to stop working and marry him. But he is around to take her back, on his terms, after she almost breaks up Gable and Loy's marriage by her innocent actions and realizes that marriage is more important than a career . . .

Stewart was hardly noticeable with Gable and Harlow in such sparkling form on their fifth picture together. He himself was starstruck by Harlow. "Now there was a girl! She had a personality that really measured up to that 'blonde bombshell' nickname. My part took just three hours filming one evening. I'd never met Harlow before and suddenly on to the set came this stunning girl with that stupendous figure and a dress so low-cut you had to bend down to pick it up. And me? I was just a guy from Pennsylvania. We had to do a scene with some conversation and at the end of it I had to embrace her. I think she may have subdued her acting a bit because we were only rehearsing, but not the kiss! It was—oh, everybody out! I'd never been kissed that way before in my whole life. I mean, boy, when Harlow kissed you, she *kissed* you. Know what I mean? And if you were made of flesh and blood, you responded. When it was over, the man said, 'You'd better do it once more.' She made some changes in the way she said her lines. Then she kissed me again—in just the same way. Hollywood being what it was, we did the scene over and over

[35]

again. By the time we actually filmed it, I was a very exhausted actor."

The Good Earth had been giving MGM casting problems for some time. For the film version of Pearl S. Buck's saga of Chinese peasant life, the studio had lined up Paul Muni to star, then considered the idea of an all-Chinese supporting cast, discarded it, and looked through its roster of contract players for possibilities. James Stewart was far too tall but he reckoned that his skinny frame suggested him for a test as he looked as though he might have been through a famine. So make-up wizard Jack Dawn put a "bald cap" on Stewart's head, yanked up his eyelids with spirit gum, trimmed his eyelashes, and sent him off for a try-out with Paul Muni. As Frank Westmore relates in The Westmores of Hollywood, "The first thing Muni said when he saw Stewart was, 'That's one hell of a tall Chinese.' So they dug a ditch for Stewart to walk in when he was near Muni. That didn't work because Muni, striding next to the gangling Stewart, tripped and took a header into Jim's ditch."

Stewart spent three days testing for the part of Ching, the good friend of the Muni character, but his disguise didn't fool anyone and Louis B. Mayer ordered a stop. "They gave the part to a little Chinese fella," reported Stewart. (His name was Chingwah Lee.)

Despite this setback, Stewart could hardly complain that he wasn't being seen by audiences. He ended up being in no less than eight of the studio's 1936 releases as well as appearing in Universal's Next Time We Love. His work for MGM ranged from turning up in a Chic Sale short to his very first starring role in Speed.

The short was Important News and he was almost unrecognizable in glasses and a very odd haircut as a printer's apprentice or "devil" in support of veteran actor Chic Sale (who was the small-town newspaper editor bravely deciding that an impending frost is of more importance to his readers than a gangland killing).

Speed was a quick response to Malcolm Campbell breaking the world's automobile speed record in Bluebird at Bonneville Salt Flats on September 3, 1935. MGM decided to cash in on the public interest in land speed records and arranged with Chrysler Motors to use their testing grounds, cars, buildings and other equipment.

Director Edwin L. Marin was assigned to it and shot background footage in Detroit of cars being tested in November 1935 before going off to make another film for MGM. Who was to play in the film didn't really matter and wasn't decided until Marin was ready to resume work on it in 1936.

Jimmy Stewart was picked to play Terry Martin, auto engineer and test driver of the Falcon, the car in which he experiments with a new high speed carburetor. (According to publicity, Stewart actually drove the specially designed car at speeds up to 140mph.) Mona Barrie played his girlfriend, a worker in the publicity office who is really the company president's daughter but keeps it a secret as she wants to be treated no differently from anyone else. Weldon Heyburn played a fellow engineer who clashes with Stewart over both work and the girl, and Ted Healy provided comic relief. The film featured a sequence at the Indianapolis Speedway in which Stewart crashes the car, enabling Mona Barrie to use her influence to have another one built. This Stewart drives at Muroc Lake, smashing all records on the mile run but being injured, not fatally.

The film lasted a little over an hour, which was about as much as audiences could be expected to tolerate of its simple plot. With its exploitable title, *Speed* was useful for propping up a dreary A feature, as well as for testing Stewart's appeal as a leading man. Run as a main feature, it did feeble business.

Stewart's next, *The Gorgeous Hussy*, needed someone like Jean Harlow, for whom it had originally been written, to liven it up. Instead, Joan Crawford seemed stiffly out-of-place in this period costume affair playing Peggy O'Neal, the innkeeper's daughter whose friendship with President Andrew Jackson (Lionel Barrymore) is misunderstood. The combination of Crawford and Robert Taylor failed to ignite the box-office while the expensive production also brought in Melvyn Douglas and Franchot Tone as well as Stewart to compete for Crawford's favors. She wasn't sufficiently wicked nor passionately feminist enough to make their enthusiasm credible. Stewart, sporting generous side whiskers, plays an early American newspaperman on Capitol Hill who remains a sympathetic friend even after he knows he hasn't a chance with Crawford. He was, according to the advertising, "a

[37]

rough and tumble young blade . . . he loved a fight, a kiss in the moonlight . . . and particularly the 'gorgeous hussy.'"

Testing the Stewart abilities to the utmost, the young contract player was thrust into *Born to Dance*, a musical built around the talented discovery of *Broadway Melody of 1936*, Eleanor Powell. He sang in several ensemble numbers and even shook a leg alongside Eleanor Powell, but his big moment came crooning the melodic Cole Porter number "Easy to Love" in the park with Miss Powell. "He sings far from well, although he has nice notes in his voice, but he could play the part perfectly," was how Porter assessed Stewart's abilities on testing him. Nearly forty years later, Stewart had the chance to introduce the number in the compilation film *That's Entertainment!* and rightly remarked, "They reckoned the song was so great even I couldn't hurt it."

After the Thin Man, MGM's first follow-up to its original *The Thin Man* and the studio's big Christmas attraction of 1936, gave Stewart third billing after Myrna Loy and William Powell as Nora and Nick Charles. A long but amiable mystery picture with some excellent interludes featuring Asta the wire haired terrier chewing up clues and the like, it does have a memorable conclusion thanks to James Stewart.

He plays the shy, likeable young man who has quietly continued to love a woman who has gone off and married a bounder. Stewart is even prepared to pay the wretch to go away so that she can get a divorce and marry him. He is therefore a suspect when the man is murdered. Stewart may have been helped, if publicity releases are to be believed, by not knowing the outcome of the picture as it was claimed that the last four scenes were withheld from the cast and director until the last moment.

As it turns out, William Powell's sleuthing reveals that appearances can be deceptive and that James Stewart is the murderer! As he is exposed in the obligatory gathering-of-all-the-suspects scene, the ingratiating, hesitant persona dissolves before our eyes admirably as his features twist and cameraman Oliver Marsh gives him ghoulish lighting (his eyes in dark hollows, the boniness of his face emphasized). Stewart pours out the hatred he has felt for both the girl and the man she married which inspired him to kill and frame her for his crime. "I did it, you hear!" he foams, "And I'm glad, glad, glad!" It's a very nice Jekyll-into-Hyde transformation that's more effective today than it was in 1936 when Stewart's good guy image had yet to be established. It also gives George Zucco's phoney doctor, who has earlier labeled the Stewart character a mental case, a richly amusing moment observing "Heavens! I was right."

5

Working to Contract

"I WAS A CONTRACT PLAYER. IT WAS a full-time job. You worked a six-day week, fifty-two weeks a year. If you weren't making tests with new people the studios were thinking of signing, you were in the gym working out to keep in shape. Taking voice lessons. Going out and exploiting pictures you weren't even in. Beating the drum for motion pictures." That's how Stewart looked back on it in 1979, adding, "You didn't pick your movies. You did what you were told. Your studio could trade you around like ball players. I was traded to Universal once for the use of their back lot for three weeks."

It was a hectic time. Stewart claims he was at one time working on five pictures at once. "Each morning I had to check which one I was working on that day and what part I was playing. You did small parts in big pictures and big parts in small pictures. It was the best training ground in the world, like a huge repertory theater."

There were frustrations, like never seeing Greta Garbo even though she worked on the same lot. He and Henry Fonda shared a Mexican-style farmhouse in Brentwood with an elderly couple to look after them. There were plagued by wild cats (the house-keeper filled the bathtub in her quarters with milk for them) and Stewart was tantalized by having Garbo as a next-door neighbor. He lurked around behind a signpost hoping to glimpse her but felt even more frustrated when she put up an eight-foot high wall around her property. He and Fonda thought up a scheme to tunnel under the wall into her front yard and rise up in front of her declaring, "This is so unexpected."

Stewart seems to have felt none of the irritation that Fonda did as a captive of the studio system, forced to make films at 20th Century-Fox he didn't want to. Stewart's prospects were somewhat limited at MGM in any case, with Clark Gable, Robert Taylor, Spencer Tracy, William Powell, Robert Young, Melvyn Douglas, Robert Montgomery and Franchot Tone all competing for star roles. He had to be glad for the scraps. At least he was beginning to distance himself from other newcomers at the studio like John Beal, Alan Curtis and Eric Linden.

But it was a real problem knowing what he was best suited for. As Ted Allan, one of the studio's leading portrait photographers, told John Kobal: "Two years after Stewart had been with the studio, we still didn't know what the hell to do with him. Was he a comedian, or a romantic leading man? We tried photographing him outside, leaning over fences, working with a shovel, with a tennis racket—but while that worked with Robert Taylor in helping to make him more athletic, it didn't work with Stewart. There was no problem in making him look handsome—he had great eyes and a generous mouth, but in the time I worked with him, I wouldn't have guessed he'd become a star."

In fact, MGM was so clogged with talent that it took other studios to give him big breaks. One of these occurred when Tyrone Power dropped out of the re-make of *Seventh Heaven* at 20th Century-Fox and the studio had to come up with a replacement in a hurry. MGM loaned them Stewart—the part may not have been ideal but it was a starring role, opposite the young French actress Simone Simon who took top billing.

The film was set in Paris at the time of the First World War and Stewart played the French sewage worker Chico (but didn't attempt an accent). He's badly miscast as a boastful, wildly ambitious character who keeps declaring "I'm a very remarkable fellow" without ever proving it, but he does make Chico more acceptable by conveying an underlying earnestness. The man longs to be promoted to cleaning the streets and breathing fresh air and longs also to find an intelligent, attractive wife. Simone Simon is the girl he rescues from a brutal guardian and from the police. They live together in his seventh-floor garret in Montmartre which becomes heaven to them as happy, contented lovers. "Don't ever leave me—or like a candle I'll go out," he tells her. He is called up into the Army and pledges to be with her in spirit at the same hour each night until he can return in person. After a long delay, he does come back, having lost his sight but not his optimism. "They can't keep me blind," says Stewart, "because—I tell you—I'm a very remarkable fellow." What Charles Farrell and Janet Gaynor had made so palatable only ten years before via titles didn't work nearly so well with the greater realism of sound. Stewart's American accent jarred with Simon's French one and the atmosphere seemed phoney.

Stewart returned to MGM but it was to be more than six months before he went before the cameras again. He did do another familiar story with a French background, *Madame X*, opposite Ann Harding, but this time it was for "Lux Radio Theater," broadcast on June 14, 1937. In fact, he worked quite a bit on radio and was often heard on the MGM-Maxwell House "Good News" program, which was an hour-long production promoting the two companies' products.

In August 1937 MGM finally told Stewart to put on a mustache for a top supporting role in an Edward G. Robinson picture, *The Last Gangster*. The mustache didn't suit him at all and the film was little better. Robinson is the crime czar put behind bars; Stewart is the newspaperman who befriends the gangster's European wife (Viennese actress Rose Stradner) and her young son. Stradner gets a divorce and marries Stewart who adopts her boy. Ten years later, Stewart is a respected newspaper editor and Robinson is a free man wanting revenge on the couple who've taken his kid. But when Robinson sees the happy environment they've created for the boy, he relents and, having been shot by another racketeer (the outcome of a hidden-loot subplot), he dies clutching his boy's school medal. MGM insisted on sentimentalizing the subject—Robinson was better off back at Warner Bros.

And Stewart was better off in *Navy Blue and Gold*, which was shot almost concurrently with *The Last Gangster*. Here the studio made a determined effort to sell him and Robert Young as stars. It was the story of three buddies at the Annapolis Naval Academy who come from different walks of life—there's Tom Brown's wealthy Dick Gates, Robert Young's brilliant but lazy Roger Ash,

[43]

and Jimmy Stewart's poor but eager Truck Cross, a former fireman on a navy cruiser, who played center on the fleet's championship football team. He is really the son of a cashiered officer and has entered the Academy under an assumed name. He is suspended when this comes out but reinstated after an inquiry that clears his father's reputation.

The prominent American critic Howard Barnes had a backhanded compliment to pay Stewart: "Although he has been denied Robert Taylor's beauty and has been endowed with none of the strong, silent intensity of Gary Cooper, he breathes life into his character.... It is due to his expert rendition of a rather preposterous part that a rather preposterous show becomes generally exciting."

This wasn't the first time that Stewart had stimulated comparisons with Gary Cooper. When *Born to Dance* came out, Alastair Cooke had declared, "There is James Stewart, trying to be ingenuous and charming like Gary Cooper but many tricks and years behind!"

By the time of *Navy Blue and Gold,* he was closing the gap because to another and more important observer he did recall Coop. Seeing Stewart playing his "sensitive, heart-grabbing role.... I sensed the character and rock-ribbed honesty of a Gary Cooper, plus the breeding and intelligence of an ivy league idealist," said one of Hollywood's greatest directors, Frank Capra, who would soon be making use of him. As Donald C. Willis observes in his book on Capra,"... Stewart has one big scene, and he's more than up to it. In it his character defends his father's reputation, and, in the middle of nothing, Stewart creates a moving scene. He's at once defensive, unsure of himself, angry, inspired; and he single-handedly salvages one scene from an otherwise thoroughly dispensable movie. You can see what Capra saw in him." Preview audiences, too, saw something in this film's Jimmy Stewart and marked their cards approvingly; an impressed MGM extended his contract.

The next role they gave him was a major one, even if the film was more of a prestige attraction than a sure-fire hit. *Of Human Hearts* was a somber drama of frontier life in pre-Civil War days with Walter Huston as the circuit preacher who is determined

[44]

that his son, played by Stewart, shall follow in his footsteps and who opposes the boy's idea of becoming a doctor. Stewart is closer to his mother, played by Beulah Bondi. It was her second time in a film with Stewart (the first was *The Gorgeous Hussy*) and the first of five occasions when she would portray his mother (she was sixteen years older than he). Here she scrimps and saves to provide him with money to buy books and educate himself.

An argument with his father over being forced to wear the cast-off clothes of parishioners makes Stewart leave home and take up studying medicine in Baltimore. On his father's death, his mother sells all her possessions to provide him with more money. The boy becomes so absorbed in his career that he neglects even to write to her. While serving in the Civil War with distinction as a surgeon, he is summoned to the White House where President Lincoln (John Carradine) lectures him on the subject of filial ingratitude and he rushes home to make amends. There he is also reunited with his childhood sweetheart (Ann Rutherford).

It was a complex part that Stewart handled masterfully under the guidance of director Clarence Brown. It required a stubborn streak that Stewart knew how to bring out as well as an inner sensitivity. Huston matched him in obstinacy. In perhaps the key moment of the film, audiences knew why Stewart struck out at his father and why he allowed himself to be knocked to the ground in retaliation.

At MGM, Stewart could only hope to obtain stooge roles in comedies, playing dull and dependable "other men" with names like Elmer, who usually lost the girl. It was director George Stevens who gave Stewart his big break in comedy, enabling him to demonstrate his humorous abilities as a leading actor, by borrowing him to star opposite Ginger Rogers in *Vivacious Lady* at RKO. Jimmy was the well-bred Peter Morgan, an associate professor of botany at the university where his father (Charles Coburn) is president and where his grandfather was president previously—so that we know what direction Stewart's life is supposed to take.

When he ventures from the sheltered groves of academe into a New York nightclub to round up a friend (James Ellison), he encounters Ginger Rogers' nightclub singer, Francey Larache.

He is mesmerized by her, and likens the feeling to when he was run over by his father in an automobile as a boy. There is a lightning romance and marriage. On the train back to the university, Jimmy frets on how to break the news to his parents and to his blueblood fiancée (Frances Mercer), picked for him by his dad. Complications amusingly ensue: Jimmy brings his father out to meet Ginger, only to find her brawling with Frances Mercer. Jimmy's mother (Beulah Bondi—for the second time) has a weak heart (or so she pretends) and news of Jimmy's marriage must be kept from her until it can be broken gently.

There is a running gag about the failure to consummate the marriage. On the train there is nowhere to sleep so they have to sit in the observation car. At the university they are kept apart by the snooping of Franklin Pangborn's apartment manager and by the presence of students everywhere. Only at the very end of the film are the couple alone in a train compartment with a bunk that falls down of its own accord to welcome them.

Vivacious Lady is pleasant enough, but slight and unsatisfactory. We are not shown what persuaded Ginger to marry Jimmy or what an experienced showgirl like her sees in his gauche professor—the touching naivete and innocent charm that Stewart was to express as a common soldier in his next film are not part of his character here. Why they marry so quickly is not explained (we don't even see the ceremony), nor is Ginger's patience at the delay in telling his parents (who have to know sooner or later). It adds up to rather thin situation comedy, flatly dialogued and dully staged. The only strength of the film lies in the personalities of its two stars: Ginger Rogers (at her most attractive here) and James Stewart (likeable but weak). His most memorable scene comes when he concocts a potent brew in the laboratory and turns up drunk to take his class, becoming emboldened enough to resign from the faculty before falling off the dais onto the floor. Drunk scenes are difficult to play really effectively but Stewart gets away with playing this one to the hilt.

Whereas *Vivacious Lady* could have been much improved, his next film back at MGM turned out a lot better than anyone had a right to expect. *The Shopworn Angel* was the first of four films Stewart made in 1938. As further evidence of the way he was being regarded as a new, younger Gary Cooper, he was given the role Coop had taken in the 1928 version. Joan Crawford considered it but Margaret Sullavan finally took the part which Nancy Carroll had performed memorably ten years before, and obviously her rapport with Stewart in *Next Time We Love* was another good reason for putting them together in *The Shopworn Angel*—and perhaps she demanded him again!

Jimmy played the naive young soldier Bill Pettigrew, who has left the plains of Texas and is in New York on his way to fight in Europe. He meets a fast-living gold-digging showgirl (Sullavan) who helps him make an impression on his comrades by pretending they're good friends. She has a wealthy lover, a draft-dodging playboy (Walter Pidgeon), and leads a selfish, complacent life. When Stewart thinks she's ill (she has a hangover), he brings her flowers and sweets. She comes to enjoy being idolized by him and he reawakens her to the simple pleasures—sharing an ice-cream soda, enjoying an evening out at the fairground (taking the 100-ft. slide and looking into distorting mirrors). Eventually she marries him, quickly, in an army chapel before he goes overseas rather than destroy his happiness; and besides, she has come to love him. A sentimental, shamelessly contrived story, it nevertheless becomes warmly memorable under H. C. Potter's direction, thanks especially to the work of Margaret Sullavan with that touching fragility one senses behind her tough exterior. As for Stewart, the entire shy, awkward, gangling, sincere, charming personality that made him a pre-war star is now in place. As in *Vivacious Lady*, Stewart is weaker than the feminine lead. He was becoming a specialist in immature figures who needed looking after by more sophisticated women. It is easy to see why he was regarded as appealing most strongly to older women in the audience, arousing their mothering instinct.

You Can't Take It With You was the film version of the George S. Kaufman and Moss Hart Broadway hit comedy. Frank Capra produced and directed it at Columbia from a screenplay by Robert Riskin. It concerns an eccentric clan, poor but happy, led by Lionel Barrymore's Grandpa Vanderhof, living in a private Shangri-La in the middle of New York, a house where "everybody does exactly what he wants to do." Capra arranged to borrow Stewart

[47]

from MGM and he received third billing, behind Jean Arthur and Lionel Barrymore and ahead of the fourth star, Edward Arnold, who played his father.

Jimmy's role was that of Tony Kirby, the newly appointed vice president of his father's bank which is planning to create a huge munitions monopoly. Jean Arthur portrayed Alice Sycamore, the only member of the zany household who goes out to work. She is Stewart's stenographer and he's an unaffected, charming, considerate boss, even if he has always been spoilt and had everything he wanted. Now he wants Jean Arthur but he is too shy to tell her directly. He begins by informing her that he has told his mother that he will marry her. Jean Arthur says that this is news to her. "You didn't ask me," replies Stewart and adds, as their conversation progresses, "You know, if you scratch around under the surface here, you'll find a proposal lying around." She is worried about the impression her madcap family will make on Jimmy's staid, upper-crust parents but she gives in because she loves him. Finally, he admits it too: "One little detail I forgot to mention—I love you, Alice." In this brilliantly written scene, Stewart is soft-spoken, shy, yet forceful in a way he's never been before. He's not a sap. He retains dignity.

Under Jean Arthur's tuition, the Stewart character learns to loosen up and relax. The pair enjoy themselves learning a new dance craze, the Big Apple, from a bunch of youngsters. There is also a richly amusing scene in a nightclub where Stewart displays his mastery of comic playing and timing. It begins with his declaration to Jean Arthur, "Every time I think how lucky I am, I feel like screaming . . ." and then, with a great deal of physical activity with his arms, he describes how he can feel a scream working its way up towards his mouth—a performance so vivid and spirited that Jean Arthur covers her ears and she yells instead, disturbing the entire establishment. Stewart's so good we know exactly what makes her respond the way she does. There is more amusement as he nimbly tells the diners that she saw a rat and the pair depart under cover of the panic this causes.

Jean Arthur sets about making her crackpot family behave themselves for a visit from Jimmy's parents. But Stewart is so enchanted by their ways that he deliberately brings his parents on the wrong evening. They are appalled at the wild antics they see and a rich series of social disasters ends with an explosion in the basement where Jean Arthur's father makes fireworks. Everybody, including Stewart's parents, is arrested for disturbing the peace and put in jail.

Eventually, the father sees the error of his ways. There's more satisfaction in making fireworks for general merriment than in making munitions to blow everybody up.

Stewart's position is similar to that in *Vivacious Lady* where he had to introduce equally stuffy parents to a woman of unsuitable background. But the scenes at the Vanderhof house have a strained eccentricity that is no longer very amusing (and note how it is the black servants who make it all possible, quietly cooking the meals and doing the other chores). It's the intimate scenes between Stewart and Jean Arthur that remain enchanting and fresh.

You Can't Take It With You won the Academy Awards for Best Picture of 1938 and for Best Direction by Frank Capra. It was a considerable boost to Stewart's career to be in such a well received film and it paved the way for his two later collaborations with Capra in much more memorable undertakings.

Back at MGM, the production heads were still having difficulties deciding what to do with their star, so they were happy to loan him out on a two-picture deal to David O. Selznick who wanted him to co-star with Carole Lombard in *Made for Each Other*. It was an attempt to interest audiences in Lombard as a dramatic performer rather than a comedienne, an experiment the actress was keen to make. "Carole Cries!" headlined a poster for the film, in competition with "Garbo Laughs!" in *Ninotchka*.

Steward played Johnny Mason, a young attorney. His initial situation is again similar in some respects to that in *Vivacious Lady*: he has gone away from home and married on impulse—now he has to break the news to his employer (Charles Coburn), whose daughter (Ruth Weston) he was expected to marry, and to his possessive, disapproving mother (Lucile Watson). Coburn, who played Stewart's father in *Vivacious Lady*, plays the father figure here, while Lucile Watson clutches her heart and faints at the news of her son's marriage just as it was feared Beulah Bondi would do in the earlier film.

The first part of the film is comic in tone. There is Stewart with his fully developed hesitancies and stutters explaining to Coburn, "I had a few hours to spare ... and so I ... uh ... had a ... just a few hours ... *I got married!*" There is a disastrous dinner party at which Stewart learns that Coburn is depriving him of an expected partnership in the law firm. And there is an amusing sequence where Stewart rehearses demanding a pay rise but eventually finds himself agreeing to a cut in pay.

The Stewart character is another weak one. He doesn't stand up to his insufferable mother; he gives up his honeymoon to help his career (in vain, as it turns out); he has to be pushed by Lombard into demanding the pay rise and, having failed, returns home drunk at 7 A.M. He is more appealing as a father, delightedly yelling out his wife's name in court when he realizes she is telling him that she is pregnant (she covers his mouth to try and silence him); fainting at the sight of the baby ("Is this mine?"); and crying over the phone (though not actually seen doing so) trying to persuade a pilot to fly a serum 2,000 miles through foul weather to save the pneumonia-stricken infant after the film has suddenly turned into a stark drama.

The baby's illness brings the couple back together again after Stewart had decided that he's no good for her and that their marriage just hasn't worked out. (Things have become so bad Lombard has had to give up their cook and is looking for a job herself.) Sneak previews showed that the original routine recovery of the infant wasn't strong enough an ending for the film and so the shameless contrivance of the distant serum was brought in to produce an artificially tense climax. The crisis does provide Stewart with the backbone to march into his boss's bedroom in the middle of the night to ask for the money to pay the pilot and its happy resolution illogically enables Stewart to go on and become a partner in the law firm and lecture the others on how it should be run. This last scene reinstates the humorous atmosphere of the film but does nothing to rescue it from being a mess. Oddly, Lombard's role is not as prominent as one might expect, although the concerns of the film with marriage and baby mark it out as being aimed at the woman's market. Stewart is only saved from seeming a feeble sap to the male half of the audience by playing the part so much for comedy.

Once *Made for Each Other* had finished with Stewart, MGM had a part waiting for him supporting Joan Crawford in *The Ice Follies of 1939*. Miss Crawford's career was crumbling and the film can either be interpreted as an insult to her abilities or as an attempt to popularize her by extending her range. For Stewart, though, it was a total waste of his talent, though the spectacle of Crawford and him on skates has a certain novelty appeal. Sonja Henie had made films with skating displays into big hits and MGM thought they were on to a sure thing engaging the International Ice Follies Group with stars to back them up. The musical sequences were the highlights of the film and the story a dismal afterthought. It was the old one about lovers separated by their careers (which Stewart had gone through with Margaret Sullavan in *Next Time We Love*).

In this film, Jimmy Stewart's Larry Hall does a skating act with Lew Ayres' Eddie Burgess, and Stewart's actress wife Mary (Joan Crawford) joins the act to sing on skates with them. The going is tough and Crawford decides to strike out on her own to make more money: she wins a contract with Monarch Studios, pretending she is unmarried (there is a "no marriage" clause in the agreement), and becomes a big star in Hollywood. Stewart remains in the East trying to put on an Ice Follies show. Crawford has only a half-hour to spare him in Central Park when she comes to New York on a personal appearance tour and later decides to give up her career.

But Monarch is clever: it signs up Stewart to produce an Ice Follies movie in Hollywood starring his wife and Lew Ayres for a happy ending all around, celebrated by a big Technicolored ice ballet sequence representing an extract from Stewart's first film as a producer. "Everyone was out of their creative minds when they made *Ice Follies*. Me, Jimmy Stewart and Lew Ayres as skaters ... preposterous," Joan Crawford later reminisced to Roy Newquist. "A dancer I am, a skater I'm not ... it was a catastrophe. The public thought so, too."

[51]

Fortunately for Stewart, he had another picture with Frank Capra at Columbia in the offing but that was taking time to shape up. It was now early 1939. MGM had been talking about putting him into a film called *Hands Across the Border* with Robert Taylor but the script never turned out right; he was also announced to play the part of a wealthy Eastern collegiate in *The Glamor Girls* but that assignment ultimately went to Lew Ayres. Instead, MGM found a decent screwball comedy for Stewart to do, opposite Claudette Colbert (brought in from Paramount).

It's a Wonderful World gave top billing to Miss Colbert of course, and it came a little too late in the eccentric comedy cycle to register strongly. It now has the handicap of being eclipsed in Stewart's career by the similarly titled and much better known *It's a Wonderful Life*. Stewart's role was that of Guy Johnson, a former star football player who, rather than become a store salesman, opts for chaperoning an irresponsible, ageing Broadway million-aire playboy (Ernest Truex). The latter is framed for murder and Stewart earns a year in jail for trying to help him evade the law. Stewart breaks loose to follow up a clue and kidnaps the poetess (Colbert) who witnesses his escape. The night they spend handcuffed to each other in an orchard recalls *The 39 Steps* with Robert Donat and Madeleine Carroll unwillingly linked together. Here Colbert proves such a scatterbrained strain that Stewart has to sock her on the jaw. The other highlights of his perform-ance are his disguises—an inept impersonation of a Boy Scout leader in pebble glasses and an imitation of an actor with stage fright during a revival of *What Price Glory*. Pleasant as it was to filmgoers of 1939, it bore no comparison to the two films that Stewart next made on loan-out: *Mr. Smith Goes to Washington* and *Destry Rides Again*.

6

The Breakthrough

"I T WAS EITHER COOPER OR STEWART, and Jim was younger and I knew he would make a hell of a Mr. Smith—he looked like the country kid, the idealist—it was very close to him. I think there's no question but that this picture shaped the public image of him, of the real Jimmy Stewart." That was Frank Capra talking to Peter Bogdanovich. *Mr. Smith Goes to Washington* was unquestionably the breakthrough film. Stewart was still being billed after the leading lady, the longer-established Jean Arthur, but his was the star role (as even the title indicated) and she was supporting him.

The part was an extremely difficult one to play successfully: to be so naive convincingly, simple but not simple-minded. Gary Cooper actually came from Montana as Mr. Smith does but would probably have played the character as a continuation of Vermont's Longfellow Deeds in a sequel to *Mr. Deeds Goes to Town;* he would have been too old and too reserved to play the part as Stewart does. For Stewart had a more open, sensitive, outgoing way about him. He wasn't afraid to register extremes of emotion—from pain to elation—and to throw himself into a part. There are not many actors who could, without losing face, play the scene where Stewart, falsely denounced in the senate as a corrupt figure, decides to get out of town, visits Lincoln's tomb with his packed suitcase and sits on it in the shadows, head in hands, sobbing.

Stewart portrayed Jefferson Smith, the idol of Montana's youth—head of the Boy Rangers and the man behind their *Boy's*

Stuff newspaper. When one of the state's senators dies, Stewart is appointed by the crooked party machine as a suitable dupe to complete the dead man's term of office. For them, he's "the simpleton of all time—a big-eyed patriot—knows Washington and Lincoln by heart—collects stray boys and cats . . ." To keep an eye on their stooge, there is Jean Arthur's cynical secretary, Saunders, and the corrupt senior senator, Joseph Paine (Claude Rains), a figure revered by Stewart, a close colleague of his dead father, a man who could become President.

In the world of politics and power, Stewart is like a duck out of water. He wears crumpled shirt and tie to a banquet where the others are in evening dress. He takes a crate of homing pigeons with him to Washington to carry messages back to his Ma (Beulah Bondi, her third time as Stewart's mother). At his first press conference, he is coaxed into making bird calls and mocked in press photographs when he does so. His solution to the reporters' sophisticated mockery is a sock on the jaw, making him momentarily heroic with his dishevelled hair and seething anger, even though they're right and he's wrong.

A reporter has warned him, "The wild life around here is a little different to what you're used to—it wears high heels." Stewart proves tongue-tied with all strange women. He keeps dropping his hat and knocks over a lampstand while telling the senator's daughter (Astrid Allwyn) about his pigeons and finally rushes away (later he even drops his hat when she talks to him on the phone). But all this shyness vanishes when he gets on to a subject that grips him, like the importance of liberty or the joys of nature, as when he's talking to Jean Arthur. "Liberty is too precious a thing to be buried in books, Miss Saunders. Men should hold it up in front of them every single day of their lives and say, 'I'm free, to think and to speak.' My ancestors couldn't. I can, and my children will." It's interesting that the Stewart character should assume that he will have children, ignoring the real problem posed in his case of getting married first. Of course, the film is really about the maturing of Stewart—not only eventually winning Jean Arthur as a wife but, more importantly (in view of the world situation in 1938), learning not to take freedom for granted and to defend it against all odds.

[54]

Stewart is very human in his nervousness on the floor of the Senate as he presents the bill for his boys' camp, leaping to his feet and yelling "Mr. President!" at the first suitable moment, having everyone laugh, then finding it difficult to keep his papers sorted, but being applauded when he's finished. His enthusiasm and sincerity have affected Jean Arthur and she reveals that he is being used and that Claude Rains' fellow senator is on the take. Because the bill is on land needed by the party machine for its own purposes, Stewart is falsely accused of having a financial stake in its outcome in order to get the bill quashed. Stunned by the well-organized smear, he has no fight left in him until rallied by Jean Arthur.

The climax of the film is his filibuster on the floor of the senate to prevent his fellow senators from voting on his expulsion, using "the American privilege of talking your head off—free speech in its most extreme form." He is encouraged by the vice-president, presiding over the chamber: the casting of friendly, avuncular Harry Carey, Sr. with his simple outdoor image from cowboy films was an inspired move to smooth over the improbability of such support, which persists even when Stewart seems about to give up his marathon talk session. Another inspired touch is to have Stewart whistle at one point, causing the other senators to look up, enabling him to explain that he only wanted to see if they still had faces—a way of lightening the sequence that is completely in character.

The odds are stacked ferociously against Stewart. The Montana newspapers suppress his accusations and attack him instead; when the children take up his cause through *Boy's Stuff*, they are physically maltreated by party thugs. Public opinion is whipped up against him and bags of hostile mail are brought into the Senate. Even the Senate page boys, who've become Boy Rangers, turn in their badges.

But still Stewart's Jefferson Smith won't give in. That is the marvellous thing. He stands up to the most gruelling test of character imaginable. "You think I'm licked," he cries hoarsely, faced with the mountain of critical letters. "You *all* think I'm licked. Well, I'm *not* licked and I'm going to stay right here and fight for this 'lost cause' and if this room gets filled with lies like

[55]

these . . . Somebody'll listen to me." He finally collapses from exhaustion. But somebody has listened. "Every word that boy says is true," admits the corrupt fellow senator from Montana, now conscience-stricken.

The film's triumph of faith over cynicism is still wonderfully moving. The filibuster seems to be achieving nothing in the end except to put off the moment of surrender. It doesn't matter that it's possibly holding up other vital legislation, that it's a dubious democratic tool just as capable of being used in a bad cause (Stewart does check to see if there's any other way of addressing the people in his state), that there is no evidence to convince the other senators of his case. It doesn't matter because we in the audience, having inside knowledge of his innocence, applaud any means of establishing it, assuming that the filibuster will do the trick without knowing how, otherwise it wouldn't have been introduced into the film. Only the harming of the children makes us momentarily wonder whether Stewart's stand is worth it— and the film is careful to establish he doesn't know about it.

Stewart could hardly have asked for a more impressive setting to demonstrate his acting skill. The huge set of the senate chamber was an exact studio reconstruction with Stewart standing amid a sea of ninety-six desks. He is helped to convey a heroic image by the angle from which he is often photographed—from below, with his head obscuring the corner of the gallery behind him so that the lines of the balcony front lead in towards him. He was also helped to fake hoarseness in his voice, very difficult when he had to project his words across the senate. Frank Capra recalled the answer in his autobiography: "Twice a day Jimmy's throat was swabbed with vile mercury solution that swelled and irritated his vocal chords. The result was astonishing. No amount of acting could possibly simulate Jimmy's intense pathetic efforts to speak through real swollen chords." It is an early example of Stewart's willingness to put up with any kind of physical hardship to make his work more believable (another had occurred in *Next Time We Love* when Stewart irritated his eyes with cigarette smoke to make them sore and weepy in the days before glycerin for the many takes of a scene where he had to say farewell to his wife and baby). In spite of all this help, Stewart still had to *act* haggard and his performance here is a *tour de force*.

The real volatile passion of the film is Capra's with its giddy see-saws of emotion. The people are easily lead to applaud one moment, boo the next. It is skillful drama that the Stewart character—a *boy*, as he is so often called—has to go to such lengths to win through, but worrying to reflect how nearly the dark forces of corruption came to winning the day and a chance to put their man in the White House. A more realistic film would have centered on the corrupt senator Paine rather than a boy senator who believes the world needs more boys' camps, but that would have deprived us of the chance to cheer an exceptional hero.

Stewart's work was recognized by the New York film critics who named him the year's Best Actor. He was nominated for an Academy Award, as was Clark Gable for *Gone with the Wind*. They were considered equal favorites to win but, in a year when Selznick's epic otherwise cleaned up, Robert Donat beat them both as the schoolmaster of *Goodbye Mr. Chips*. Others who lost were Laurence Olivier *(Wuthering Heights)* and Mickey Rooney *(Babes in Arms)*. *Mr. Smith* was also up for Best Picture, Best Director, Best Supporting Actor (Claude Rains), Best Screenplay (Sidney Buchman) and numerous other categories but Capra had done so well the year before with *You Can't Take It With You* that he was never likely to repeat his success. *Mr. Smith*'s only Oscar came for Best Original Story (Lewis R. Foster).

Directed by George Marshall, *Destry Rides Again* was a breezy addition to the western boom of 1939 led by *Jesse James, Union Pacific* and *Stagecoach*. This one was a parody of the genre and the secret of its success was that it would have made a good straight western: it had a strong story, neat construction and skillful characterization. Universal used the script to re-launch the career of Marlene Dietrich after a two-year gap during which she had been regarded as box-office poison, unable to draw flies. Stewart was a useful man to borrow since he wouldn't mind taking second (but equal) billing to her and might attract the newer generation of cinemagoers. Besides which, he was ideal for the part. Dietrich and he were a well-balanced pair: she exotically foreign and sexy, he homespun and ultra-American.

As in his previous film, he played a character set down in the midst of political corruption and a man whose father died opposing crime. In the wide open town of Bottleneck, there is another appointment to an unexpired term of office to be made by a crooked boss, but in this film it goes to the town drunk, Wash Dimsdale (Charles Winninger). Made sheriff, he decides to outwit the boss and call in James Stewart's Tom Destry as his deputy. Dressed in a suit, holding a parasol and a canary for a woman passenger alighting from the stage, Stewart makes a terrible initial impression, just as he did arriving in Washington as Jefferson Smith with his pigeons. But here Stewart has the chance to play a much more assured character, a shrewd figure who dominates events and who only appears to be simple.

"Are you sure your name is Destry?" asks a disbelieving fellow passenger on the stage, knowing his reputation for having cleaned up Tombstone. "Folks is always asking me that," replies Stewart, busily whittling napkin rings as the coach lurches back and forth and warning against first impressions. His voice remains calm and pleasant even when he is provoked or angry. After the chief villain (Brian Donlevy) tries to force a shoot-out, Stewart outwits him by revealing that he doesn't carry guns, causing Donlevy to burst into laughter. Stewart then says, quietly, "One of us might have got hurt and it might have been me. I wouldn't like that—*would I?*" Those last two words are spoken in a kind of teasing, firm way with a big, open, disarming smile on his face that puts Donlevy off taking the matter further.

Marlene Dietrich's saloon singer Frenchie is in with the bad guys and Stewart questions her indirectly about hot coffee she spilled to distract a gambler from noticing his cards being switched. "Hot coffee in your lap—you don't know what's going to happen—*do you?*" he asks when she's serving him with coffee, mock-pleasant as he watches her reaction to his probing question, again in charge of the situation.

Stewart is determined to bring the villains to book legally, by guile rather than gunplay, and his methods seem to be working until the sheriff is shot in the back while guarding the jail. As the old man dies in Stewart's arms, Stewart's eyes dart back and forth mirroring his rage—he is no longer composed but a man of fury who straps on his six-shooters and leads the honest citizens to wipe out the villains.

The only real match for Stewart is Marlene Dietrich. She meets humor with humor by handing Stewart a mop and bucket in the dance hall as suitable instruments for cleaning up Bottleneck since he doesn't carry guns. They are drawn to each other because he can see the good girl beneath her make-up just as she can see through his cover, but she makes the fatal mistake of saving his life by luring him away from the jailbreak. She tries to make amends and rallies the womenfolk to march in and break up the battle between the townspeople and the badmen in the saloon. She puts herself in the way of a bullet intended for Stewart and dies in his arms, leaving him free to marry the sensible, suitable but tepid cattleman's sister (Irene Hervey).

Indicative of their having to remain apart, Stewart and Dietrich never quite kiss. Stewart toys with her in his arms before commenting on her excessive make-up (the sign of a bad woman) and they are about to kiss when the sound of gunfire at the jail interrupts them; and at the end of the film she is too badly wounded to do more than rub her hands on his lips as he tries to stop her slipping down to the floor. (Off-screen, things may have been different. Of Marlene Dietrich, producer Joe Pasternak told Charles Higham: "She took one look at Jimmy Stewart and she began to rub her hands. She wanted him at once! He was just a simple guy; he loved Flash Gordon comics—that was all he would read. So she did something incredible—the most incredible thing I ever saw. She locked him in his dressing-room and promised him a surprise. The surprise was that she presented him with a doll, which she had had the whole studio art department come in over a weekend and make up for him—a life-size doll of Flash Gordon, correct in every detail! It started a romance!" As far as reading tastes go, Charles Higham reports that Stewart gave Dietrich a present of John O'Hara's novel *Butterfield 8*, published in 1935.)

Quite apart from providing her with some memorable songs, especially "See What the Boys in the Back Room Will Have," and a lively scrap with Una Merkel, the film also favored Dietrich in other small ways to build up her part. As she dies, her face is towards the camera while Stewart's features are prevented from being a distraction since they are hidden in shadow by the brim of his hat; and she manages to linger in spirit to the very end of the film as a small girl strums a banjo and sings one of her songs, "Ragtime Cowboy Joe," at the end, bringing fond memories to Stewart's face. Had Dietrich survived, there would have been no contest for his affections. Irene Hervey wouldn't have had a chance.

This was a rare occasion when not only were Stewart and his leading lady ideally matched but the script gave them strongly interacting parts of equal weight. In a lesser key, this was true of his next film back at MGM, Ernst Lubitsch's *The Shop Around the Corner*, the best of the four films he did with Margaret Sullavan. The characters they play spend too much of the time getting on each others' nerves to register very strongly together; but, on its rather slight level, the film is a total success. The bitter-sweet romantic comedy cast the pair as workers in a leather shop in Budapest—he the head salesman, she a beginner. Each of them is carrying on a pen-pal correspondence that blossoms into love—sight unseen, that is—not knowing that in fact they're writing to each other. They correspond on "cultural subjects" because, as Sullavan puts it in one of her letters, "We have enough troubles in our daily lives. There are so many great and wonderful things to discuss in this world of ours, it would be wasting these precious moments if we told each other the vulgar details of how we earn our daily bread." Halfway through the film Stewart discovers the truth and wrestles with the problem of how to break the news to her that he is the "Dear Friend" she worships, since she regards him with contempt as a fellow employee: "It's difficult to explain a man like him to a man like you."

A subplot has to do with Stewart being wrongly suspected of having an affair with the wife of his employer (Frank Morgan) but the role is somewhat limiting because the character is not really that intricate. Stewart plays the Hungarian without any attempt at an accent, but that doesn't really matter. What matters more is that Stewart is deprived of the detailed American cultural context in which his image is most resonant. We don't care so much about the dreams and aspirations of a fairly nondescript Budapest store manager.

Stewart was to remember *The Shop Around the Corner* for the greatest number of takes he ever did on a movie—forty-eight—in a scene with Margaret Sullavan. As he told her daughter Brooke Hayward: "We were in a little restaurant and I had a line: 'I will come out on the street and I will roll my trousers up to my knee.' For some reason I couldn't say the line. Your mother was furious. She said, 'This is absolutely ridiculous.' There I was standing with my trousers rolled up to the knee, very conscious of my skinny legs, and I said, 'I don't want to act today; get a fellow with decent legs and just show them.' Your mother said, 'Then I absolutely refuse to be in the picture.' So we did more takes."

Sullavan, Stewart and Frank Morgan went straight on to appear together in *The Mortal Storm* at MGM, all playing Germans in this melodramatic but forceful condemnation of the Nazis and their anti-Semitism. As much as the American accents, it was the cramped Alpine village setting created largely on the Culver City sound stages that made the German atmosphere very artificial, more mythic than real. Fortunately, the right director was on hand to concentrate on the human relationships. Frank Borzage was noted for his sensitive, unabashedly emotional approach to drama.

Stewart portrayed Martin Breitner, a horse doctor of peasant background. He loves Margaret Sullavan's Freya, the daughter of Frank Morgan's Professor Roth, who is engaged to Robert Young's Fritz Marberg. Young and the professor's two stepsons (Robert Stack and William T. Orr) are delighted at the news that Hitler has become Chancellor of Germany but Stewart anticipates the persecution and war that will result from Hitler's rise to power. We see him refusing to join in a martial song glorifying Fascism in the tavern and going to the defense of an elderly teacher picked on by the Nazis for not singing. The professor's stepsons leave home because he is a Jew and his house becomes a danger spot. Stewart comes to believe he has a chance with the daughter but he has to take a fugitive teacher over the mountains into Austria and stay there himself. He disappears for a long stretch of the film, leaving the main emphasis on the misfortunes of the professor, sent to his death in a concentration camp.

Stewart then comes back into the picture to rescue Sullavan and take her on skis over the high mountain pass. They are chased by a patrol under the leadership of Robert Young. Both are shot but Stewart manages to carry Sullavan into town where she dies in his arms. "Oh, no, Freya," he sobs, his voice shivering with emotion as she is lost to him. Here once again Stewart lets all the stops out to convey intensity of feeling.

Yet Borzage's films are full of lovers whose earthly tragedies are conquered in the next world. Finding each other so late, Stewart and Sullavan have had no time for the little things lovers say or do ("We'll have our whole lives to say them") but the fervency of their attachment ("Nothing will ever part us again") suggests a love stronger than the death of Margaret Sullavan which follows on so closely. Her demise at least has the effect of disturbing her former fiancé, the fanatical Nazi who shot her, and causes one of the professor's stepsons to fall out with the other; and it seems less of a tragedy if it is only to be regarded as a temporary misfortune to be overcome in the rest of eternity. Borzage doesn't emphasize their spiritual future but instead ends the film by recalling the happier past when the professor's family was one.

David O. Selznick had never got around to making the second film with Stewart under the deal he struck with MGM. Instead, he passed Stewart on to Warner Bros. to star in *No Time for Comedy* in settlement of their loan of Olivia de Havilland for *Gone with the Wind* (for which he also made a cash payment).

It was a serious piece of miscasting in a role for which Laurence Olivier had proved ideally suited on the stage, when the S. N. Behrman comedy had been directed by Guthrie McClintic. It is very hard to believe in Stewart as Gaylord Esterbrook, the author of light, amusing society comedies who is persuaded that he ought to tackle deeper, more weighty subjects in such grave times.

There was an attempt to make the role more suitable for the actor. He is introduced as a country bumpkin who has had a surprise hit satirizing Park Avenue. Back home he was always chasing fire engines, never missed a good blaze, and always wanted to become a volunteer fireman—reminiscent of Stewart's own childhood, as well as Gary Cooper's Longfellow Deeds in *Mr. Deeds Goes to Town,* with his eccentric passion for leaping on fire engines. So the character is made into another small-town innocent who's easy prey for women. Rosalind Russell portrays the leading lady who proposes to the callow playwright on a park bench at 4 A.M. and is accepted. Genevieve Tobin is the more wicked patroness of the arts who persuades him to abandon writing his shallow but popular pieces in favor of something more significant. Stewart conveyed the right degree of naiveté to succumb believably to Tobin's determined advances, but his character is unconvincing and uninteresting and the film as a whole a bore. Naturally, Stewart's attempts to produce important work are a disastrous flop and he returns to his true metier. Just what could be done with that idea was shown the following year with Joel McCrea in Preston Sturges' *Sullivan's Travels* as a film director who learns there is nothing to be ashamed of in writing comedy and making people laugh.

7

The Oscar Winner

THE ROLE WAS THAT OF THE thirty-year-old author-turned-scandal sheet reporter, Macaulay Connor, in *The Philadelphia Story*. It turned out to be the best thing that happened to him at MGM but he wasn't the automatic choice for the part.

Katharine Hepburn had made a huge success in the stage play, written especially for her by Philip Barry, and wanted to use it to make a big comeback in Hollywood where she was regarded as temperamental and a weak box-office draw. She knew she would need strong support and MGM was the ideal place for her with its big roster of male stars. When the studio took on her and the play as a package, she asked for Clark Gable and Spencer Tracy as co-stars. However, it was obvious that her role of the spoiled heiress Tracy Lord was the best in the picture and she had to settle for lesser names.

Cary Grant, with whom she had co-starred previously in three films, was an obvious solution. He was offered top billing and a choice of the two top male parts. James Stewart was readily available under his studio contract, was suggested to Hepburn who approved, and took the remaining part and third billing. Neither Joseph Cotton nor Van Heflin, who had played the Grant and Stewart roles on stage, were then known to cinemagoers and so were totally ineligible. For director, George Cukor was another obvious choice, having made six films with Hepburn before.

At the beginning of the picture, Stewart's Macaulay—Mike—Connor arrives at the Lord estate in Philadelphia with Ruth

Hussey's photographer Liz Imbrie to report on Katharine Hepburn's second marriage, to John Howard's coal millionaire George Kittredge, for *Spy* magazine. Neither likes the assignment but times are hard—Stewart's book of short stories didn't bring in enough to live on, while Hussey is a thwarted painter. Hepburn's first husband, Cary Grant's C. K. Dexter Haven, is also around.

Hepburn takes an interest in Stewart, looking out his work in the local library, being impressed and offering him a hunting lodge on the estate where he can do some serious writing in peace. He becomes intoxicated by her, visiting her ex-husband and, freed from inhibitions by liquor, telling Grant that she's "one in a million," "a radiant, glorious queen"—something that Grant well knows.

Stewart tells her that she shouldn't marry Howard as he gets to know her better and they dance around a swimming pool late at night, high on champagne. "There's a magnificence in you, Tracy, that comes out in your eyes, that's in your voice, in the way you stand there, in the way you walk," Stewart tells her softly, earnestly. "You're lit from within—bright, bright, bright. There are fires banked down in you, hearth fires and holocausts. And you are made of flesh and blood—that's the blank surprise of it. You're the golden girl, Tracy, full of love and warmth and delight." Stewart gives these lines a fervor that makes them moving while their extravagance is understandable coming from the writer he is—they also draw on that naive worship of women that was part of the Stewart image from earlier films, as he is really sensing her potential rather than responding to what she has been—an icy prig, lacking compassion for human weaknesses. In Stewart's hands, she melts and becomes sympathetic.

Too drunk to remember the moonlight swim she took with Stewart or what happened afterwards, she is unable to soothe the anger of her fiancé. We know that Stewart is to be believed when he says that nothing occurred between them. "Why? Was I so unattractive, so distant, so forbidding?" demands Hepburn. "You were extremely attractive," replies Stewart, "And as for distant and forbidding quite the reverse, but you were also a little the worse, or better, for wine and there are rules about that." It's part of John Howard's failings as a fiancé that he can't be satisfied and calls off the wedding.

This gives Stewart the chance to propose to Hepburn that he should take Howard's place at the ceremony, which is about to start. It provides a moment of acute tension for Cary Grant and Ruth Hussey as onlookers. He wants his wife back, she loves Stewart, but both have to give him his chance while hoping Hepburn will turn him down—as she does in a most eloquent and touching fashion. "I am beholden to you," she says, handing him back to Ruth Hussey and allowing Grant to step in and remarry her.

It's obviously the right ending, as Grant is the more mature man, one with whom life will be adventurous and risky—far more suitable for Hepburn in the long run. However, Ruth Hussey is not going to be much compensation to Stewart for losing someone as exceptional as Hepburn and so he really ends up once again as the classic loser, the "other man" in Hollywood romantic comedy along with that other discard, John Howard. Grant had shrewdly chosen the role that came out ahead in the end.

It is instructive to compare the performances of Grant and Stewart. Grant plays his part in a very restrained manner, with a minimum of animation. He stands around, observing, mischievously stirring things up when he can, slyly biding his time. Stewart is, as the part requires, far more open and expressive: he talks more, moves more, does more. Grant expresses a rock-like strength and dependability against Stewart's racing enthusiasm and high ideals. (By contrast, John Howard is a handsome blank.)

Stewart won the Academy Award as Best Actor for 1940. It is easy to underestimate the sheer skill that a polished light comedy performance requires (and this one also had a number of scenes in which he had to play drunk) but it does seem odd that he should have been victorious at the expense of his good friend Henry Fonda whose great performance as Tom Joad in *The Grapes of Wrath* had earned him a nomination. The other contenders were Charles Chaplin for *The Great Dictator*, Raymond Massey for *Abe Lincoln in Illinois* and Laurence Olivier for *Rebecca*.

Many felt that the Academy voters were making amends for

[67]

not having given Stewart the Oscar the previous year for *Mr. Smith Goes to Washington*, which was certainly a more demanding part. Stewart himself is recorded as saying, "I never thought that much of my work in *The Philadelphia Story*" and commenting "It could be true" to suggestions that he had really been rewarded for the earlier performance. Stewart knew that, in any case, his showing in *The Philadelphia Story* owed much to his co-stars. "When you work with Grant and Hepburn, you *work!* You let up for a second and they'll steal the movie from under your nose! They're the best sort of competition an actor can have. Talent like that keeps you on your toes."

The Oscar statuette went on display in a window at the family hardware store at Indiana, Pennsylvania. Another Stewart won an Oscar for the film: Donald Ogden Stewart for his skillful adaptation of Philip Barry's play for the screen. But George Cukor, Katharine Hepburn and Ruth Hussey, who were also nominated, failed to win and the film itself lost out in the Best Picture category to *Rebecca*. Still, it was an enormous box-office success and restored Hepburn to favor in Hollywood.

Stewart made three more films in rapid succession after *The Philadelphia Story*. He had done two of them before it even opened and had completed all three long before his Oscar win. None of them did his career much good, although the trade felt they did better business following the publicity given to Stewart's enlistment as well as his Oscar victory.

Stewart stepped directly into *Come Live with Me* following his work on *The Philadelphia Story*. It was a romantic comedy that gave him billing ahead of co-star Hedy Lamarr. He was now becoming the established star who could help newer names like Hedy consolidate their appeal. Here he was, the starving writer from the sticks, Bill Smith, who is trying to make a success of himself in Greenwich Village. He agrees to marry Hedy's Austrian refugee, Johanna Janns (who calls herself Johnny Jones), to stop her being deported. She has become the mistress of publisher Barton Hendrick (Ian Hunter) and she only needs Stewart for the marriage certificate. In exchange, he gets a check every week to cover his living expenses until he can sell one of his novels.

He uses his situation as the basis for a book and sells it to Ian

Hunter. Hedy now wants to marry Hunter but Stewart is keen to hang on to her and drags her off for a weekend at his grandmother's farm in Pennsylvania, the right setting for her to discover she really loves her husband. It is slight stuff, insufficient even for its modest running time of eighty-six minutes. But it coasts by on Stewart's charm and the beguiling beauty of Hedy Lamarr.

Also in the romantic comedy line, Stewart was reunited with Carole Lombard for the radio version of *The Moon's Our Home* on "Lux Radio Theater." It was first broadcast on February 19, 1941. Margaret Sullavan and Henry Fonda had starred in the 1936 film version of Faith Baldwin's novel.

Stewart rushed straight from *Come Live with Me* onto the set of MGM's musical melodrama *Ziegfeld Girl*. It was a minor assignment, even though it gave him top billing over the real stars— Judy Garland, Lana Turner and Hedy Lamarr. He was very much in support of the Lana Turner character and also somewhat miscast as Gil Young, the Brooklyn truck driver boyfriend of Lana Turner's Sheila Regan whom he calls "Red." She is an elevator girl in a department store who becomes a Ziegfeld showgirl, renamed Sheila Hale, and drops Stewart for Ian Hunter's wealthy playboy.

Stewart has only two scenes independent of Turner and only one at his place of work, getting into a fight over a juicy gossip item on Turner that's appeared on the truck depot noticeboard. The other has him rather awkwardly getting drunk and succumbing to proposals that he drive bootleg liquor to earn enough money to impress his girl. When he is caught and jailed, we only find out through Turner going to visit him. (Ian Hunter fares no better as his abandoning of her is another offscreen event.)

The film is a star-building exercise for Lana Turner as the tragic heroine who loses everything. Stewart's perseverance with her serves to make the audience regard her more seriously. In his acting he tries to convey a sense of infatuation and sincere concern that almost makes us understand why he still bothers with her. There's his fervent attempt to awaken memories of their first meeting at Coney Island and his later effort to lift her spirits by painting a mental picture of them as a happy couple raising ducks, but more convincing is his bitterness when she

[69]

does belatedly seek a reconciliation. Still smarting from an earlier rejection, he kisses her, is tempted to give in, but recovers himself and walks off with the stinging words: "Don't you know when you've been turned down? *I* did!"

Yet the part never suits him. There is something forced about his smugness and peppy good humor in the first elevator scene with Turner. We never see him in a truck but he doesn't seem the truck-driving type. The role ideally needed someone more streetwise like Spencer Tracy or James Cagney. Stewart was never the type to play blue collar characters—he hadn't the manner or the accent for it.

It was Stewart's last film at MGM as a long-term contract artist. Apart from the basic servitude imposed by the long-term contracts with their one-way options, he had no complaints about working there: "A lot of people have written books describing Hollywood in the thirties and saying how awful it was. I never found it so. It was a lot of fun. And this stuff about no freedom! Nobody told Lubitsch what to do, or Frank Borzage, or John Stahl. And you could bargain about parts—you didn't have to take *everything* they offered—you could make deals."

It's hard to understand, then, why Stewart consented to be loaned out for *Pot o' Gold,* an independent feature that he joined immediately he had completed his work on *Ziegfeld Girl.*

Pot o' Gold was produced by President Roosevelt's son James in an attempt to cash in on the popularity of Horace Heidt and His Musical Knights with their radio show of the same name (in Britain the title was changed to *The Golden Hour*). Heidt's twice-weekly broadcasts were made from the RKO-Pathe lot while the film was in production there. Stewart was reunited with the director of *Destry Rides Again,* George Marshall, as well as with its cameraman Hal Mohr and character actor Charles Winninger. (Even his co-star Paulette Goddard had been considered for the role of Frenchie in *Destry* and had played it in a radio adaptation.) Alas, *Pot o' Gold* was a thin and contrived musical comedy that did no one's reputation any good.

Stewart played Jimmy Haskel, first seen as the broke but happy proprietor of a music shop. Later he joins up with an out-of-work band who live in a tenement and can produce music from the

[70]

knives, forks and spoons on the dinner table. The film develops a Capraesque notion that poverty equals happiness and that wealth equals unhappiness. Stewart's father died broke but had the biggest funeral the town had ever seen whereas his rich industrialist uncle (Charles Winninger) lives in a huge empty mansion with only a manservant for company and hates the sound of music. He is tormented by the noise of the band's rehearsals from the neighboring tenement where Stewart is living. (He even ends up in jail, like Edward Arnold in *You Can't Take It With You*, with a musical number going on around him.)

The slim problems created in the film are that Stewart dare not tell his father that he is associated with the musicians and dare not tell the landlady's daughter (Paulette Goddard) that he is related to the ogre who is trying to stop the band from practicing. Stewart conspires to move his uncle to Canada so that the band can appear on the radio program he sponsors; Goddard finds out the truth about Stewart and announces there will be a big prize in the next show, a strange form of revenge that brings the film to a clumsy and tedious climax. The uncle, who as played by Charles Winninger isn't really such an ogre, learns to live with music but the film omits to return Stewart to his music shop which would have provided the neat wrap-up it lacks.

Stewart was involved in two musical sequences. One is in the jail cell where he leads an impromptu song and dance routine, playing the harmonica and talking/singing "You're in the Army Now"; and the other is a bizarre fantasy sequence in which Paulette Goddard sees Stewart's face in the moon and this cues a short medieval episode in which he serenades her in song, climbing up to her balcony (his singing is dubbed here). Milady's father (Charles Winninger) appears and orders Stewart's arrest and death—at which point Goddard wakes up from her nightmare and seizes him in terror, leading to a clinch.

Having won his Oscar, Stewart ought to have been able to command better parts from MGM but the studio seemed set on treating him as indifferently as ever. Before his Oscar win he had been allocated a co-starring role with Jeanette MacDonald in the latest re-make of *Smilin' Through*, under Frank Borzage's direction. There was talk of putting him with Spencer Tracy and a big-name female star in a film version of Louis Bromfield's *Bombay Nights* since the company had had such success with three-star combinations in *Boom Town* and *The Philadelphia Story* despite the higher salary costs. And he was to be given a film to star in on his own called *Wings on His Back*. As it happened, less than a month after the Academy Award banquet Stewart succeeded in obtaining a more important outside role that he had been wanting for months and MGM had to make do without him.

8

A Star at War

WEIGHT WAS THE PROBLEM. STEWART had tipped the scales at 130 lbs. when he first came to Hollywood. He had tried to improve his bony physique working out in the gym at MGM and eating heartily but he remained as skinny as ever. His father had served in the Spanish-American War and had been one of the first people in his part of Pennsylvania to sign up for World War One; his grandfather had fought in the Civil War. Stewart wanted to carry on the tradition and he bought a yellow two-seater Stinson 105 plane to practice flying so that he had over 400 hours of civilian flying time behind him when he volunteered his services. He and Henry Fonda also did a double act as inept magicians, which they presented at training camps.

On his first attempt to enlist at an Air Corps recruiting office in November 1940, he got the thumbs down for being 10 lbs. too light for his height at 140 lbs. So he went to a slimming specialist and asked him to reverse his efforts for a change. Stewart fattened himself on a high-calorie diet of steaks and steam puddings and a few months later Uncle Sam was prepared to have him. He became a private in the Army Air Corps on March 22, 1941, accepted for a year of military training. This was more than eight months before the bombings of Pearl Harbor catapulted the United States into the war.

Stewart was one of the first screen stars to enter service. Eventually, one third of the American film industry's employees served in the armed forces. But the studio moguls were not happy to lose their big names. Metro was particularly badly hit: Robert

Montgomery quickly followed Stewart's example, as did Clark Gable in 1942 and Robert Taylor in 1943. Studio heads like Louis B. Mayer maintained that their stars did more for public morale by making movies (directors like W. S. Van Dyke, who returned to active duty in the Marine Corps in October 1940, were more easily replaced.) The moguls even wanted to use their influence to have draft boards defer calling up some of the bigger draws. When they were thwarted, they were then dismayed to find that the stars very often didn't want the studio publicity machines exploiting their sense of patriotism.

It was impossible for stars to avoid the attention of the media. The actor Burgess Meredith, who was then living in Stewart's Brentwood home, and the talent chief Billy Grady wanted to drive Stewart down to the induction center but he insisted on being transported in a trolley with the other enlistees. Meredith and Grady followed to make sure Stewart wasn't rejected at the last minute. Recalled Grady, "Suddenly a door flew open and a tall skinny guy in his shorts, carrying his clothes over his arm, ran past us, screaming like a banshee. "I'M IN—I'M IN—I'M IN!" He waved a goodbye and was off to Fort MacArthur." Cornered by the press, he was more restrained. "Uh . . . uh . . . it's a little early in the morning—but . . . uh . . . I know I'll get a lot out of Army," he said. His pay as a private was only a few dollars a week—something of a drop from his Hollywood salary, then many thousands a week.

Stewart was soon at Moffet Field, an Air Corps training base in northern California where he learned to eat fast to avoid spud-peeling duties for not finishing his meals and also learned to be an aircraft mechanic. With his flying experience, he was soon able to win corporal's stripes. He quickly found he had a problem being famous—officers expected him to attend their social gatherings and pose for photographs, even when it interfered with his training. He was offered a desk job but he turned it down.

Before long he was dispatched to Kirkland Field, New Mexico, to fly four-engine bombers. "When I was transferred to heavy bombers I had to work pretty hard at subjects I'd forgotten and was never any good at anyway. Math, for instance. Most of the fellows were quite ten years younger than I and they'd work out in a few minutes the navigational problems that I'd have to mull over for an hour or more," said Stewart. But in nine months he had risen to the rank of lieutenant.

He wasn't entirely lost from public view. In his lieutenant's uniform, he presented Gary Cooper with the Oscar for being Best Actor in *Sergeant York* on February 26, 1942, a year after his own victory. He did a radio version of *The Philadelphia Story* with Cary Grant, Katharine Hepburn and Ruth Hussey, billed as "Lieutenant James Stewart" and it was broadcast on July 20, 1942 as a Victory Show for the U.S. Government. He also narrated two 1942 shorts: *Winning Your Wings* about the Army Air Corps, and *Fellow Americans,* dramatizing the implications of the Japanese attack on Pearl Harbor.

Stewart served as an instructor of Flying Fortress pilots and was promoted to the rank of captain on July 4, 1943. In November of that year, he flew a B-24 Liberator from Florida to Brazil and there received orders to head for West Africa and then Europe. He landed at the Norfolk village of Tibenham on November 25. It became his home and that of the 445th Bombing Group. Once again, he insisted on being treated like any other serviceman and when reporters and photographers descended on the base he would often find a way of getting airborne to be out of reach.

Stewart skippered his B-24 Liberator in twenty combat missions, some of them in daylight. He took part in spectacular raids on Bremen in December 1943 and on Berlin during 1944, and was advanced to major. He won the Air Medal and Oak Leaf Cluster and for his leadership of the 703rd Squadron of bombers during the February 20, 1944 raid on aircraft factories at Brunswick, in Germany, he was awarded the Distinguished Flying Cross. Commanding a bomber wing, he was promoted to colonel before his release from active duty in the autumn of 1945 as chief of staff of the 2nd Combat Wing, Eighth Air Force.

Stewart has never talked in detail about his war-time experiences or how he won his many commendations and decorations during his total of 1,800 flying hours. "I had a lot of close calls . . . the whole war was a close call . . . but I was just doing my duty," is as far as he likes to go. But he did elaborate a little for Lesley Salisbury of *TV Times*. "There were, oh, lots and lots of times when I must have wondered whether I was going to get back after a mission but I didn't think of it at the time. There just wasn't the time. Afterwards, well, you thought for a few seconds, then before you knew it you were up there again." To another journalist, Herbert Kretzmer, he said, "When I was piloting bombers over here I was always afraid I'd make a mistake at the controls, make a wrong decision. A lot of guys depend on you when you're in charge of a Flying Fortress. Fear of a mistake was stronger than fear for my personal safety . . ."

He has recalled one particular night. "Our group had suffered heavy casualties during the day, and the next morning at dawn I would have to lead my squadron out again, deep into enemy territory. Imagination can become a soldier's worst enemy. Fear is an insidious and deadly thing; it can warp judgment, freeze reflexes, breed mistakes. Worse, it's contagious. I knew my own fear, if not checked, could infect my crew members, and I could feel it growing in me. I remembered talking to my father when I was a boy and asking him about his experiences in World War One and the Spanish-American War. I had asked him if he'd been afraid. He said, 'Every man is, son, but just remember you can't handle fear all by yourself. Give it to God. He'll carry it for you.' I re-read the 91st Psalm that my father had given me when I left and I felt comforted, felt that I had done all I could."

When the war ended, he tried to go home quietly to see his folks but he walked into a hero's welcome. The mayor had even arranged for *Life* magazine to cover his return in September 1945.

Later he returned to his eight-room house in Brentwood, and took stock. There had been eighteen months left on his MGM contract when he went into the service, but a court case brought during the war, Olivia de Havilland versus Warner Bros, had established that absences could not be used to extend contracts beyond the lengths of time originally specified. MGM would have been glad to have him back but Hollywood had changed. Most of his friends like Henry Fonda and Gary Cooper were freelancing. He wasn't even sure whether acting was a serious enough profession after all he had seen during the war. But he was sure that he wouldn't make any gung-ho war movies.

Fortunately it turned out that Frank Capra had a "little thing" in mind for him.

9

Freedom in Hollywood

*J*AMES STEWART RECALLS: "FRANK Capra called me one day and said
he had an idea for a picture. He seemed very embarrassed about
discussing it and it was obvious that he was not at all clear how he
was going to do it. He got the inspiration from a Christmas card
that somebody sent him. There was a verse on it saying, in effect,
that everybody was born for some purpose and that the world
would be a sadder place if they had not lived. 'It starts in Heaven,'
he said. I replied that if it started in Heaven and he wanted to
make it, then I would be glad to do it."

It was more of a short story, sent out at Christmas in 1939 by
Philip Van Doren Stern, about a man in a small town who
becomes so depressed at his apparent lack of achievement that he
wishes he had never been born. A guardian angel shows him how
much he has meant to the community and how much worse off it
would have been without him. The filmic potential had been
obvious and RKO had acquired it with Cary Grant in mind for
the principal role but hadn't been able to develop a suitable script.
Frank Capra took it over, had it rewritten, wrote parts of it
himself, and made it into what is technically and thematically his
most dazzling and complex work. It turned out to be his favorite
picture—and is Stewart's favorite, too, of all his films.

Stewart's George Bailey is a man who suffers twenty years of
frustrated ambition. Brought up in the small town of Bedford
Falls, he graduates from high school full of plans: "I'm shaking the
dust of this crummy little town off my feet and I'm gonna see the
world, Italy, Greece, the Parthenon, the Coliseum, and then I'm

coming back here and go to college and see what they know, and then I'm gonna build things. I'm gonna build airfields, skyscrapers a hundred stories high. I'm gonna build bridges a mile long . . ." (It could almost be the real Stewart speaking at the same age, since he had intended to be an architect.)

But things turn out differently. His father's stroke and subsequent death cause him to cancel his trip and stay behind to run the family building and loan business while his younger brother goes off to college and becomes a football star. His honeymoon with Donna Reed's Mary Hatch goes by the board when he has to put up all his spending money to see the business through a crisis. With his poor hearing (the result of a good deed in childhood), he is only able to serve as an air-raid warden during the war while his brother is decorated by the President for gallantry in combat. When a bank deposit goes astray, he is faced with bankruptcy and scandal. He decides to commit suicide. A bumbling, white-haired, second-class guardian angel, Clarence Oddbody (Henry Travers), intervenes to show Stewart what he has meant to the community which, unknown to him, has rallied around and replaced the missing money.

Capra's film is so richly detailed, so effectively constructed, so *busy*, that it has an irresistible immediate appeal and conviction even though points are pushed to extremes. The nightmare vision of the town as it would have been without Stewart is an exaggeration, like the Dickensian villainy of Lionel Barrymore's crippled (in body and spirit) banker. Would Donna Reed really have remained an old maid without Stewart to marry her? As in *Mr. Smith Goes to Washington*, the people are disturbingly impressionable and in need of leadership, panicking and almost busting the mortgage and loan with their withdrawals at one time but coming up with the money to rescue the business and save Stewart at the end.

And Stewart himself is a figure of extremes. Capra emphasizes his moments of disappointment with huge close-ups and has him articulate his obvious resentment and anger. There is something disconcerting about his jealousy over his brother's achievements, his overweening ambition—human enough, believable enough, but too openly registered. And Stewart becomes disturbingly unpleasant as he grills his absent-minded uncle (Thomas Mitchell) over the missing money—seizing him by the lapel, shaking him and shouting, "One of us is going to jail and it's not going to be me," even though we know that he would never let Mitchell take the blame and it's his own selflessness and sense of responsibility that annoys him so much. Equally distressing is Stewart's rough treatment of his wife and children when he gets home.

But this has to be balanced against Stewart's courage in humiliating himself before the wicked banker to try to save the day, and there is his warm, loving side in many scenes with Donna Reed such as their walk home, dripping wet from the high school dance (where they had plunged into the swimming pool under the floor), stopping to throw rocks at the old house that will become their home; the scene of the long distance phone call where he shares the receiver with her as she talks to her beau and, overcome by the smell of her hair, realizes that he loves her; and the joyous reunion at the end when he comes to realize that all that is wrong with his life, like the irritatingly loose knob on the bannister post, is what is *right* with his life, that it's a wonderful life after all.

Capra found Stewart "older, shyer, ill-at-ease" after the war but his portrayal of George Bailey shows no sign of hesitancy. He was fully up to the great range of emotions required and it is impossible to think of anyone who could have got as much out of the part and conveyed all the stubbornness, tenderness, the dreams and depressions that make up George Bailey. Stewart was rightly rewarded with an Oscar nomination for Best Actor, but he and Laurence Olivier *(Henry V)*, Larry Parks *(The Jolson Story)* and Gregory Peck *(The Yearling)* lost to Frederic March in *The Best Years of Our Lives*, the film which also beat *It's a Wonderful Life* in the Best Picture stakes.

Capra's film has gone down in the history books as a box-office flop but its failure was only relative. It had cost around two million dollars, an enormous sum at that time, and lost $525,000 on its first release. Still, it could have done better. Whimsical fantasy flourished in 1947, as in *The Bishop's Wife* and *Miracle on*

34th Street, which makes it unlikely that Henry Travers' angel put audiences off, so it seems more likely that Capra's love-thy-neighbor philosophy seemed too naive for the post-war world.

After the ultimately invigorating experience of working again with Capra, Stewart looked forward to an equally rewarding collaboration with Robert Riskin, who had written the screenplays for many Capra movies (*Meet John Doe, You Can't Take It With You, Lost Horizon, Mr. Deeds Goes to Town* and others). Riskin had become an independent writer/producer based at RKO and interested Stewart in starring in his first venture, *Magic Town*. Though he surrounded himself with many of Capra's associates, like assistant director Art Black, Riskin was determined to prove himself without Capra and declined his participation, engaging William Wellman to direct. Unfortunately, there was nothing magical about *Magic Town*.

For the second time Stewart played a character called Smith—here Lawrence "Rip" Smith. The basic idea was the reverse of that in *Mr. Deeds Goes to Town* and *Mr. Smith Goes to Washington*. In those, a country bumpkin went to the big city; here, a city wise guy invades a small town. But the threat was the same: false urban values almost destroy the simple beliefs out in the hinterland. Stewart was cast, ill-fittingly, in the role of the predator, the big businessman—in fact, the heavy. Perhaps it was time for him to play a more worldly type—but this wasn't it.

He is the opinion pollster, down on his luck, who is delighted to find a "magic town" that is absolutely average in its thinking about everything. (Incidentally, the set for the local hardware store was modeled on the one owned by Stewart's father.) Masquerading with his assistants as insurance salesmen, he can discreetly sample local opinion on any issue—by snooping, in fact—and provide a national viewpoint quickly and cheaply, confounding his rivals. It doesn't sound a very workable idea, it doesn't look easy, but the film insists it makes Stewart into a roaring success. His big ambition is to make a million bucks. "It may be a rat race but I'm out in front and I'm gonna grab mine," is his angry form of self-justification.

Jane Wyman played the local newspaperwoman who is campaigning to have the town change for the better with a new civic center. Stewart successfully opposes her in order to keep the town the way it is, the way he needs it, and begins a romance to further quell her suspicions of him. Of course, the difference between a real heavy and Stewart is that he has become thoroughly ashamed of himself even before she finds him out and exposes him in print. The town then becomes self-conscious, loses its averageness, and almost dies. It takes the combined efforts of Stewart, Wyman and the town's determined children to make the adults stop feeling sorry for themselves and get to work putting the place on its feet again.

The film never works. In the first place, there is little concern to be generated by the activities of an opinion poll organization. Secondly, Stewart is obviously not able to put right all the damage he's done and so never becomes a totally sympathetic figure. Thirdly, the fate of a community as a whole is not nearly as involving as the fate of an individual like Jefferson Smith with his Senate filibuster or Longfellow Deeds on trial for insanity. Fourthly, the film lacks the Capra energy and richness of detail. Audiences rumbled its failings and stayed away: it lost heavily. William Wellman summed the film up: "It stunk! If you think *Magic Town* has anything good about it at all, there's something wrong with you." Stewart blamed the film's failing on its being developed with him in mind (although clearly not tailored to his usual image). It made him declare, "I've no time for pictures written specially for me. This one was—it wasn't so hot."

An old friend, actor Burgess Meredith, approached Stewart and Henry Fonda to participate in his independent production, then called *A Miracle Can Happen*. Meredith was to appear in a framing story as a roving reporter who would ask various people "What great influence has a baby had on your life?" and the answers would form the various episodes of the film. Henry Fonda explained what happened next (in an interview with Roberta Ostroff): "Right after the war, Jimmy Stewart was living with me. We had been going to a lot of parties and we would go and listen to the music—we both loved jazz and we were always sitting around, drinking beer and listening to music and we would say how there was never a movie made, a real movie, about musicians . . . What we meant about musicians were the sidemen,

[83]

the guys that sit back there with the trumpets and the trombones. These are characters unlike any other characters in the world. They are a breed apart and we talked about this a lot." So Fonda and Stewart suggested a story about this breed of musicians. Meredith was enthusiastic and wondered if they had a writer in mind. They suggested John O'Hara, and the famous novelist was brought to Hollywood to write a script. He stretched the premise somewhat by having as his baby a six-foot tall, red-hot babe called Lola who blows a mean trumpet. The episode looked even more promising when John Huston agreed to direct it.

Stewart played a piano player called, appropriately, Slim and Henry Fonda was a cornetist named Hank. They began by shooting the scenes with Meredith where he comes to the nightclub where they are working and they begin telling him the story of their "baby." There wasn't time to shoot the actual story then because of other commitments and when Fonda and Stewart were both free again, John Huston was still busy and George Stevens came in to finish it. He shot them in the flashback as down-at-heel musicians who bring their band to a small town and rig up a music contest for the mayor's son to win. They haven't reckoned on the shapely Lola, played by Dorothy Ford, who enters the contest and wrecks their scheme with her expert trumpet playing and shapely bathing costume, and who takes their band away from them. It was a deliciously wry anecdote that opened the film and got it off to a terrific start. Stewart and Fonda gave relaxed performances that makes their work seem almost improvised and years ahead of its time. Unfortunately the other stories were weak, the idea of an episode film did not prove appealing, and the film was patchily exhibited.

A great deal of interest was created in 1947 when James Stewart made his return to Broadway, appearing in the hit play *Harvey* by Mary Chase from Monday July 1 for a seven-week engagement. *Harvey* had opened on November 1, 1944 and restored the fortunes of vaudevillian Frank Fay who starred in it as the eccentric dipsomaniac Elwood P. Dowd, whose best friend is a large and invisible white rabbit. Bert Wheeler had briefly substituted for Fay to give him a break in 1946; now Stewart was to take over

[84]

from the 141st week of the run at the 900-seat 48th Street Playhouse, while Fay took the play to Colorado. Universal had already bought the screen rights for a million dollars and it was widely thought that Stewart was demonstrating his suitability to star in the film version. The play had to be slightly revised for Stewart's benefit—Harvey, the invisible quadruped, was described as being 6 ft. 5½ ins. tall, an increase of four inches from when the much shorter Fay was playing opposite him, and a line was added in which Stewart warned Harvey to watch his head when going through doorways.

The theater critics interrupted their holidays to cover the first night. Stewart did not enjoy his debut. "I became a little belligerent about it—you know, over-determined to make a success of it, with the result that on the first night I was awful and received a real roasting from the critics. But I got better. And I must have done the job reasonably well because I was asked to do it again the following summer, which I did."

Whatever other critics thought, *Variety*'s observer was highly complimentary about his opening night. "The charm of Stewart imbues his acting. He may be somewhat gawky in gesturing, for he's six foot three, but Stewart has plenty on the ball . . . reappearance as a star is a triumph for him . . . Stewart was letter perfect in his first performance. The part, of course, is generally considered actor-proof. . . . During the second act Josephine Hull, back from vacation, scores on the laugh register as Elwood's sister Veta, but it is in that section of the play that Stewart wins the house. His scene with Dr. Chumley, the psychiatrist, who thinks he sees the big rabbit, too, after a session in a bar and grill, is highly amusing."

Stewart left *Harvey* to take on the somewhat self-effacing role of a reporter in *Call Northside 777* for 20th Century-Fox. It was one of Fox's documentary-style dramas like *The House on 92nd Street* (1945), *Boomerang* and *Kiss of Death* (both 1947). The screenplay was based on fact and filmed by a unit of seventy people where the original story took place, in Chicago. It was a new experience for Stewart, working almost entirely on location with the *Chicago Times* journalist that he was portraying, James P. McGuire, on hand as consultant and adviser.

[85]

Renamed McNeale of the *Times*, Stewart is the reporter who investigates a small ad placed in the paper by a Polish cleaning woman who has literally scrubbed floors to save $5000 as a reward for evidence that will prove the innocence of her son (Richard Conte), convicted of murder many years before.

Like the newspaperman he portrayed in *Next Time We Love*, Stewart's reporter is far removed from the Hollywood cliché of the hard-drinking wise-cracking newshound, even if he does keep his hat on in the office and stands up to the editor (Lee J. Cobb), exposing the little lies he tells to get his way (Stewart is happy to oblige but doesn't want his boss to think he's putting anything over on him). Stewart is at first skeptical about Conte's innocence, doubtful if new evidence can be found, but he slowly becomes convinced and turns his work into a crusade, attacking the police and a key witness in print to try and stir things up.

Eventually he has to go out on a limb. First he has to push his publisher into accepting the offer of a new parole board hearing (Stewart uses his commanding height and much brisk arm-waving to present his case standing in front of the publisher's desk)—even though a decision against Conte at this stage might harm his future chances of parole. Then there is the hearing itself with Stewart turning up late, promising conclusive evidence but stalling for time—shades of Jefferson Smith filibustering as he natters on about the sword of justice to the increasingly impatient board members.

The film makes much of technological progress—showing the use of a lie detector, miniature camera and the wire transmission of pictures—and the climax hinges on a new police photographic enlargement process: can a small area in an old photograph be blown up enough to show the date on a newspaper under someone's arm and will that date be the right one to discredit the testimony of the key witness? The scene is milked for suspense as the parole board are dragged to the dark room and we wait for the picture to form in the developing tank with Stewart's voice whipping up the excitement: "Remember this is the area I showed you—now watch the date—*watch the date!*" (Other actors might have remained silent but Stewart cultivated a busy image—the more words and gestures the better. It was the key difference between him and Gary Cooper, who was a more taciturn figure altogether.)

Of course, Conte gets his release from jail and the film ends with his being reunited with his family, Stewart standing watching at a distance, hands in pockets. Even though events have been simplified and rearranged (there were two reporters on the original story, not one, and it seems unlikely that there was such a close call with the parole board), the film is more absorbing than suspenseful as the voice-over narration indicates that the outcome has already been settled. But the documentary method used has its advantages: no studio set could rival the vast circular cell-block in the then brand-new Stateville Prison near Joliet, Illinois, which is the location for Stewart's visit to the other man sentenced with Conte. And Stewart is seen pursuing his investigation in the tough districts of Chicago which are far more convincing than confined, familiar studio streets.

This is a role that certainly wasn't tailored for Stewart. It simply required an actor with an interesting manner and a stubborn streak about him. But one suspects Stewart himself may have arranged the little bit of eccentric humor in his relationship with his adoring wife (Helen Walker) that has him saying softly to her, while toying with a jigsaw puzzle in their home, "Will you marry me? Oh, that's right—you did," without giving her the chance to answer. It's a warm, loving relationship economically conveyed by the two players.

After some hesitation, Stewart branched out even further from his set image by portraying Rupert Cadell, the teacher whose ideas are an inspiration for murder, in Alfred Hitchcock's *Rope*, based on the 1929 Patrick Hamilton play. As Hitchcock had demonstrated before with Gregory Peck in *Spellbound*, he preferred the security of a name star to casting a more suitable character actor of lesser box-office appeal. Stewart tried very hard to change his style with some success. His performance is technically impressive but he still seems miscast.

John Dall and Farley Granger starred as the two playboys—the arrogant Brandon and the weaker, more sensitive Philip—who strangle a college friend for the thrill of it and then invite those closest to the deceased—his fiancée (Joan Chandler), his romantic rival (Douglas Dick), his father (Cedric Hardwicke) and his aunt (Constance Collier)—to a cocktail party soon afterwards in their penthouse apartment, the food being laid out on an unlocked chest which contains the corpse. The star guest is Stewart, the publisher of philosophy books who, when he was the pair's housemaster at prep school, created their conceit that they are "superior men" entitled to live above the law. His party talk shows his mordant sense of humor about murder being a permissible act and we sense a strong contempt for ordinary people. The non-appearance of the dead man is a topic of conversation and from the panicky behavior of Farley Granger and the cocky manner of John Dall, Stewart realizes something is wrong and slowly during the evening comes to suspect what has happened.

Stewart is the last guest to arrive—found by the slowly panning camera standing in the doorway, having been admitted by the housekeeper. It's a star entrance, the kind that would produce a round of applause in the theater. Stewart speaks his opening lines in a clipped, brisk manner quite different from his usual delivery, his voice seeming deeper than usual. He smokes, for almost the only time on screen—partly so that he can use a missing cigarette case as an excuse to return after the other guests have gone, partly so that he can draw on a cigarette for dramatic pauses in his final, fearful discussion with the two men.

Alone with them, Stewart cannot bring himself to voice his suspicions until—led on by John Dall to theorize about how they might have killed the missing guest—he does so and then produces the rope they used, provoking Granger's virtual admission of guilt. The biggest close-up in the picture comes in a pan upwards as Stewart opens the chest lid and we see his anguished face as he gasps "Oh, no—no . . . !" at the sight of the body. At first Stewart seems to accept part of the blame for the crime as he collapses into a chair ("You've given my words a meaning that I never dreamed of—and you've tried to twist them into a cold, logical excuse for your ugly murder") but then he stands up and walks around John Dall, denouncing him for having something deep inside him, something uniquely rotten, that would make him do something that Stewart could never have done. Stewart tells them that they are both going to die for their crimes and that he'll help to see it happens. One feels that Stewart might more logically be too crushed by his share of the guilt to condemn them so vigorously—and that his preaching is really to deliver the film's message, to ensure that no one in the audience can glory in the killers' views or what they've done.

The actor recalled the experience of working with Hitchcock for journalist George Perry and the London *Sunday Times Magazine* in 1983: "Hitchcock didn't explain what he wanted of the role in *Rope*. . . . He expected us to have worked out the characters and how they should be played, and he went along with it. If he didn't like it he would come up afterwards and suggest trying it another way for comparison. But he didn't say my way's right and yours is wrong."

Apart from being almost impossible to see for many years (until very recently) and being Hitchcock's first film in color, *Rope* is also noted for the director's method of filming it in ten-minute takes with "invisible" cuts to create the impression that the whole drama is happening continuously. There was nothing original about the very long take *per se* and it is doubtful if audiences did notice the absence of cutting. Done on a single set, the technique creates the impression of watching a stage play in close-up but the camera is forced into some awkward maneuvers at times, especially crossing actors' backs for a momentary blacking out of the image to make an invisible reel change. Stewart explained another drawback in his interview with George Perry: "After the film was finished, Hitchcock himself felt that, although it was an interesting idea to try to tell a story without cuts, he was giving up an essential element in pictures. So much of film acting is reacting. And this is done very effectively by the cut. It can be much more effective on film than on the stage. You can have the instant reaction to a line or situation. Well, the very fact that the camera had to move off the person saying the line to the person reacting did something to the tempo and the effectiveness of the reaction."

The actors had to learn their parts perfectly and ten days of rehearsals with the camera, the performers, and the lighting were necessary before any shooting could be attempted. One can imagine the nervous tension of the players, afraid of fluffing a line and ruining these elaborate takes, and James Stewart has said the technical problems made the acting suffer—although the cast seem to have been so well chosen that no weakness is really evident. However, the experimental technique was rather pointless and Stewart was expressing reservations about the film in 1950: "It wasn't altogether a success. The audience wanted to be —just audiences. They didn't really want to become the eyes of a mobile camera. Nevertheless, the film was cheaply made, for a Technicolor production, and it made a very fair profit. This was just as well, as some of us had profit-sharing arrangements for the film." It was also Stewart's first Technicolor picture (except for the color sequence in *The Ice Follies of 1939*).

On finishing *Rope*, Stewart headed for Broadway and did four more weeks of *Harvey* while Frank Fay played with another company in Philadelphia. Stewart opened on March 29, 1948 (the 178th week of the run) and finished on April 24. Jack Buchanan, James Dunn and Joe E. Brown then took over before Fay's return. Universal had still made no announcement about casting the film version.

Burgess Meredith wasn't the only performer turned producer who wanted to use James Stewart. Joan Fontaine had formed Rampart Productions with her husband William Dozier and they recruited him for their comedy *You Gotta Stay Happy* to play a part for which he was ideally qualified—that of a pilot who had served in the Army Air Force. He even took second billing to Fontaine.

Unfortunately, the film was as forced as its title. It was a throwback to the runaway heiress cycle of the thirties (based on *It Happened One Night*) with Joan Fontaine as Dee Dee Dillwood, a scatterbrain who has jilted at least seven suitors and flees her stuffy bridegroom (Willard Parker) on their wedding night. Stewart is Marvin Payne, staying in the same hotel, trying to catch some badly needed sleep. He takes in Fontaine in her pyjamas, thinking she's a poor girl escaping rape, and gallantly gives her his bedroom. She gets aboard his flight to California along with a smoking chimpanzee, six sickly lobsters, a corpse in a coffin, an embezzler and two ardent honeymooners. For added complications, the plane has to make an emergency landing en route. Later on, Fontaine thoughtlessly uses her money to buy

[90]

Stewart a whole fleet of planes for his air freight business whereas he's the kind of fellow who likes his independence and feels she's buying him as well.

The script should have been grounded (Fontaine had wanted to call it off—but only because she had become pregnant). Despite H. C. Potter's proficient direction, it didn't have enough originality to make a big impression at the box-office and it proved that Fontaine was no comedienne. Stewart enjoyed making it and was surprised it wasn't more successful.

The Stewart career began taking a turn for the better towards the end of 1948 when he returned to his old studio, MGM, for *The Stratton Story*. He wasn't first choice to play Monty Stratton, the real-life baseball pitcher who lost his right leg in a hunting accident at the height of his career. Van Johnson and Gregory Peck had both been lined up for it, but he was undoubtedly more effective than they would have been. He was reunited with director Sam Wood whose *Navy Blue and Gold* had shown him to such good advantage in the thirties and who had already made one hugely successful film about a stricken baseball star, *The Pride of the Yankees* (1942) with Gary Cooper.

June Allyson was an improbable co-star if only because of the discrepancy in height between her at 5 ft. 1 in. and Stewart at 6 ft. 3 ins. But they proved so effective as a team they did three films together, the later two for director Anthony Mann who would disguise the difference in height wherever possible by having Stewart lean over her or sit or kneel next to her. In *The Stratton Story*, she was the ideal foil as a sensible, practical girl to his naive country boy, marrying him, bearing a son and helping him recover from his setback. Apart from a slight misunderstanding (his mysterious absences for "press interviews" are not another woman—he's taking badly needed dancing lessons), his rise to the top is straightforward. Even his Ma (Agnes Moorehead on this occasion) has no objection to him leaving the farm to play baseball.

There is a spell after the accident when Stewart loses all interest in life and refuses to read the letters of sympathy or use an artificial leg, but the sight of his young son struggling to walk inspires him to do the same and soon he is pitching in the back yard and June Allyson is doing the catching. The film ends with his successful return to a professional game. As had happened with *Call Northside 777*, the man Stewart was portraying was on hand as an adviser and also coach for Stewart's pitching scenes.

The picture was ranked sixth by *Variety* in the top-grossing films of 1949 for North America, after *Jolson Sings Again, Pinky, I Was a Male War Bride, The Snake Pit* and *Joan of Arc*, whereas Stewart's other release of the year, *You Gotta Stay Happy*, was very much an also-ran in 53rd place. Though the film's baseball background limited its appeal abroad, *The Stratton Story* demonstrated that Stewart could still revive his pre-war image of the callow country kid to advantage.

Stewart stayed at MGM for another picture that wasn't so hot. *Malaya* was a pet project that production head Dore Schary had retrieved from his tenure at RKO. Spencer Tracy had already been assigned the main role but Stewart agreed to co-star for the opportunity to work again with the star of his very first picture, *The Murder Man*. Stewart played the war-time foreign correspondent John Royer who devises a scheme to remove badly needed rubber from Malaya under the noses of the Japanese occupying forces. He is given the help of Tracy's cynical adventurer Carnahan, who is specially released from jail and promised his freedom and gold in exchange for using his knowledge of Malaya. The two men are complete contrasts: Tracy simply in it for all he can get and wanting to give up when the going gets tough, and Stewart as a man driven to avenge his brother's death at the hands of the Japs. Stewart's own death in action prompts Tracy to complete the mission.

Based on fact, the film might have had some morale-boosting justification if made during the war. Ponderously dialogued, anonymously directed (by Richard Thorpe), it makes the Japanese into incredibly stupid figures and is really the kind of war-glorifying exercise Stewart had wanted to avoid (although he was not playing in uniform). Even with a powerhouse supporting cast (Sydney Greenstreet, Lionel Barrymore and Gilbert Roland included), It had poor box-office prospects, and it certainly didn't do Stewart's reputation much good to be killed off before the climax of a picture. MGM was more concerned with Tracy's

[92]

standing as he was under long-term contract and so the film was held up and slipped out in the wake of an obvious crowd-pleaser *Adam's Rib*, which Tracy made after *Malaya*. The damage to his career was minimized but Stewart as a freelancer had no such protection. *Malaya* was retitled *East of the Rising Sun* for British release.

10

Westerns and Wedlock

*T*HE *STRATTON STORY* WAS NOT the kind of success Stewart could easily repeat and *Malaya* was the kind of film he couldn't afford to keep making. "After the war audiences had changed and I was fishing around for parts, just trying to get through to people who didn't seem to know their own minds anymore," he commended. "As a star, I felt I was getting nowhere. I had several pictures that didn't go very well, and I just realized I was going to have to try something else."

He had done one western before, the highly successful *Destry Rides Again*, and when he was offered the lead in *Broken Arrow*, to be filmed in Technicolor by 20th Century-Fox, it provided a fairly safe step as westerns invariably had an audience. He had another advantage: "I'd always known how to ride—my father'd always had a horse around and he insisted I learn how to ride as a kid and this stood me in good stead." And so he went off to Arizona to shoot the movie in the summer of 1949.

Broken Arrow was the most influential of a small group of westerns that presented the Indian in a favorable light. Stewart played Tom Jeffords, the former army scout (and Indian fighter) who has turned prospector. He nurses a wounded Apache boy back to health and decides to learn the Apache language and see if he can bring about a peaceful end to the ten-year war in the territory. He wins the trust of Cochise, the Indian chief played with statesmanlike dignity by Jeff Chandler. He also embarks on an unlikely romance with the Indian princess Sonseeahray— unlikely because the girl is already promised to a brave. But he feels so stubborn about it that he threatens to take her away when he thinks he has been refused permission to marry her, putting his happiness ahead of establishing harmonious relations in the area. However, Stewart and Debra Paget play the developing relationship so sincerely that even the gap in their ages is smoothed over and the years seem to fall away from him (she was sixteen, he was forty-one). When, after their successful marriage, they are lying on the ground by a river and he tells her, "I'm afraid if I open my mouth my happiness will rush out in a funny noise like—yahoo!', he recalls the restaurant scene in *You Can't Take It With You* in 1938 and another trapped yell. There it was a joke, here it's a way of putting his feelings into a simple form for the Indian girl, but both times it reflects a boyish humor.

Stewart is always clean-shaven and neatly dressed in this film (we even see him shaving in a mirror fixed to a tree). There is a certain hardening of his image—in the way he flares up when provoked by the Indian-hating Ben Slade (Will Geer), for instance—and his greatest display of emotion is reserved for his discovery of his wife's dead body. He weeps and shudders as he holds her body close, demands a knife to kill a captive survivor from the band who shot her, and denounces the peace he's brought about as a lie, only to be calmed by Jeff Chandler's Cochise.

The romance was invented for the film to broaden its appeal and was not part of the novel on which it was based. It has been argued that racial attitudes at the time made it inconceivable that the marriage could work out happily, that the Stewart character had to be punished for transgressing racial barriers. Yet the film does need some event to test the strength of the peace and Debra Paget's death balances that of the Indian chief's brother which started the ten-year war, this time putting "a seal on the peace" as it shocks the decent whites as well.

The film's treatment of the Apache way of life now seems simplistic, ignoring those features that audiences might find hard to stomach and suggesting a potentially idyllic existence; but on its own terms the picture is still very appealing. Fox makes use yet again of voice-over narration—spoken by Stewart himself—partly to set the scene and partly to place events firmly in the past so that the hurt of Debra Paget's death fades and the more up-beat notion of her spirit riding everywhere with Stewart ends the film. In this way, the studio may well have avoided the box-office failure of MGM's *Devil's Doorway* in which Robert Taylor's proud Shoshone Indian came to an uncompromisingly stark end.

Soon after finishing *Broken Arrow,* Stewart confounded the fan magazines and gossip columnists by getting married for the first time. Over the years, the press had continually hounded him about the subject. He had been Hollywood's most eligible bachelor for a dozen years. In 1947, for instance, his name was being romantically linked with Rita Hayworth, former child star Mitzi Green and (inevitably) the co-star of his then-current picture, *Call Northside 777.* A typical reply he gave at that time was: "Oh, you just look and look and look and you get older and older and older. However, one never gets too old to stop looking."

June Allyson, happily married to Dick Powell, knew the bachelor Stewart. "The poor dear weighed only 154 lbs. before he was married and he was all of six feet two or three inches tall," she recalls in her autobiography. "Jimmy hated being photographed when he was out with a girl and he seldom took his dates to nightclubs. Instead, he fed them steak that he grilled himself in his own backyard. If they didn't like that and wanted the limelight, they were not for him. Jimmy's humor frequently featured his housekeeper [the gray-haired Daisy Dooley] whom he swore handed his dates their stoles or other wraps at midnight, letting them know in this *subtle* way that it was time to go."

The marriage took place on Tuesday, August 9, 1949 at Brentwood Presbyterian Church and the bride was Gloria Hatrick McLean, the ex-model daughter of the Hearst newspaper group executive Ed Hatrick. Stewart had first met Gloria two years previously, reputedly when she was seated opposite him at a dinner party given by Gary Cooper. She was ten years younger than he and had two sons by her earlier marriage to Edwin McLean, the son of Evalyn Walsh McLean of Hope Diamond fame—Ronald was born on June 19, 1944, and Michael on February 5, 1946. The Stewarts honeymooned in Honolulu.

"Writers kept asking me why I was getting married at forty-one. They seemed to resent it," he complained. And he reflected: "My bachelor years, let me tell you, were just wonderful . . . just wonderful. Boy, did I have some good times! But when you're forty-one, life means more than just a bookful of phone numbers. I needed the security of a permanent relationship with a woman I loved. I needed a family and I needed to put down roots. I can say all the usual things about meeting the right girl and falling in love. But it was also the right time."

June Allyson adds, "Gloria was the perfect choice for him. They were so suited to each other—both tall and slim and dignified and both with the same wry sense of humor."

"I didn't set out with the idea of remaining married to the same woman all my life because you know what Hollywood is. But it worked out fine," commented Stewart twenty-four years later.

Gloria was not the type to hang around the set while her husband was working; besides, she had young children to bring up. But she worried about the future of her marriage, as she confessed in 1977 to interviewer Clive Hirschhorn. "It gave me a lot of cause for anxiety, because, during this period Jimmy was working with some of the most glamorous women in the world—women such as Kim Novak, Joan Fontaine, Marlene Dietrich, and Grace Kelly. And, of course, my constant fear was that he would find them more attractive than me and have an affair with one of them. A lot of men in Hollywood constantly became involved with their leading ladies—and as Jimmy was a red-blooded American male, naturally I thought it could happen to him too. I was convinced, initially, that it would only be a matter of time before the phone would ring and it would be James telling me he had to work late at the studio, or that he would be out playing poker with the boys. Well, no such phone call ever came. And I can honestly say that, in all the years we've been married, Jimmy never once gave me cause for anxiety or jealousy. The more glamorous the leading lady he was starring opposite, the more attentive he'd be to me. He knew the insecurities I was going through, and made quite sure that they were totally unfounded. His consideration was incredible and one of the reasons why our marriage has lasted so long and is still so good."

Now that he had acquired a wife and family to support, Stewart went to work with a vengeance and made no less than four films in 1950, going straight into a fifth one in 1951.

Universal was finally ready to shoot *Harvey* and discussed it with a more-than-eager James Stewart, who found they had not just one film in mind: "When I made *Harvey* into a movie, another script that had been around town for years that nobody would have, called *Winchester '73*, was put into that as a sort of package deal; they wanted to get rid of the script." The deal that Stewart's agent, Lew Wasserman of MCA, negotiated with Universal has become a Hollywood legend as the first time that an actor participated in the profits instead of being paid a regular salary or flat fee. According to one source, Stewart received fifty per cent of the profits after the deduction of production and distribution expenses. Of course, the rub was that there might not be any profits.

Universal favored such a deal because it was not a wealthy studio and was helped by saving a star's salary, whereas other studios like MGM resisted the idea of losing some of their authority over players by such a partnership arrangement. In fact there were many precedents for stars sharing profits in place of salaries (as at hard-up RKO in the early thirties) and it later emerged that Universal's then biggest moneymakers, Abbott and Costello, had struck a similar deal long beforehand. (Incidentally, the story of Universal's 1947 Abbott and Costello comedy *The Wistful Widow of Wagon Gap* had been written with James Stewart in mind to play the part of a gunman who cares for the widow and seven kids of a man he shot. Lou Costello took it over.)

It seems the Universal producer Aaron Rosenberg first had the idea of starring Stewart in *Winchester '73*. The heads of production believed that Stewart would seem too weak and irresolute to carry off the role of a tough western hero, but they were persuaded by the thought of his war record that he could do it. Stewart proposed Anthony Mann to direct the film, having been impressed by Mann's work on *Devil's Doorway*, and Mann brought in Borden Chase to rewrite the existing script by Robert L. Richards.

Stewart took his role very seriously and impressed Mann with his preparation, especially for firing a Winchester rifle. "He studied hard at it, you know? He worked so hard his knuckles were raw with practicing, so that he could be *right*. And we had an expert from the Winchester Arms Company who taught him how to use the gun really *uniquely*." Stewart found a worn costume for the part, to look more authentic. He wore his battered, sweat-stained hat in subsequent westerns until it wore out and then kept the remains on the set for good luck—"to cancel out the curse."

The weakness of the film is that it is split between following the coveted Winchester '73 rifle—a perfect weapon, "one of a thousand"—as it passes from hand to hand, and the bitter feud between James Stewart's Lin McAdam and Stephen McNally's Dutch Henry Brown, eventually revealed to be Stewart's brother Matthew who shot their father in the back. The two storylines are merged at the start. Stewart rides into Dodge City with his friend High-Spade (Millard Mitchell) to participate in the Centennial Rifle Shoot, knowing that the event will attract McNally. He outshoots his brother and wins the Winchester, only to have it taken from him by force when McNally waylays him in his hotel room. Stewart's hatred of his brother is so intense that the theft of the Winchester hardly makes any difference.

"He'll be there," says Stewart firmly at the very beginning and his desire to kill his brother is all-consuming. "We've been chasing him since I can't remember," says Mitchell at one point. Stewart refuses to rest up while the trail is warm; he has given little thought to the future after his task is accomplished. He may even be enjoying his obsession, as Mitchell suggests. There's a marvelous moment when the brothers catch sight of each other unexpectedly as Stewart enters a saloon in Dodge City: his eyes open wide, he crouches and his hand reaches for the holster, only to find it empty, while McNally leaps up from his card game, crashing back against the wall, clawing for his missing guns. Both have had to surrender their weapons to the town marshal, Will Geer's Wyatt Earp, in an ingenious piece of scripting that stokes the enmity while enforcing restraint as the two men shoot at the targets under the watchful eye of Earp and his deputies. The script is also extremely clever in staggering the release of details of what has caused Stewart's hatred, so that we only know the full story just before the final shootout. However, we can become a little impatient at some of the sub-plots that get in the way of the feud's resolution.

The Stewart character has his relaxed moments. He's polite, charming and thoughtful, especially where a woman traveler (Shelley Winters) is concerned. But the actor's performance is stripped of all the old mannerisms—he speaks to the point, without vacillating, his actions are equally firm. Here he is laconic and it is his pal who likes to jaw and gets his words tangled, with Stewart advising him to spit to unravel his tongue in a rare moment of humor.

There had been occasional moments of intense passion in earlier films but nothing like the way Stewart's anger erupts here. Hate pours out of his eyes as he wrestles with McNally on the floor of the hotel room and momentarily gets the upper hand, pressing down the barrel of the Winchester on the man's chest, the two of them panting and grunting with the physical effort. Later he manages to restrain himself when questioning Dan Duryea's Waco Johnny as to his brother's whereabouts but when Duryea breezily replies, "Supposing I don't tell you?" Stewart's patience snaps and he grabs him, grips him around the throat and forces his face down to pin one outstretched arm on the surface of the bar while he bends the other behind the man's back, threatening to break it, his face contorted, his voice quivering with anger as he repeats the question. We understand why the tough Duryea immediately gives in.

The shootout finally takes place between the two men high up in a rocky outcrop. McNally is above Stewart and armed with the Winchester. The setting enables the duel to be prolonged as each man takes cover and tries to out-maneuver the other and use all his skill and cunning. The way bullets explode and ricochet on the hard rock surfaces brings home their lethalness. McNally's long fall past a sheer rock face when he is finally shot is a suitably emphatic end.

What makes *Winchester '73* so effective besides the inventiveness of the script and its flavorsome dialogue is the brilliant way that Mann and his cinematographer William Daniels shoot the film. The camera is always in the most effective place. It is set at floor level in the hotel room to intensify the fight scene between the brothers; it is placed low behind Stewart during the shooting match as he fires upwards at the target; it is placed in the final shootout so that we always know where the two actors are in relation to each other among the rocks.

And then there are the performances—and especially Stewart's. Riding, shooting, brawling, he is totally convincing as a seasoned man of action. He really throws himself into the part, as in the way he crouches down and winces as his brother's sharp-shooting in the final shootout pins him down in a crevice or the way he returns to town, battered, exhausted, empty, to be embraced by Shelley Winters at the end.

The film's screenwriter, Borden Chase, recalled, "The most frightening experience I ever had was *Winchester '73* when we previewed it and the minute Jimmy Stewart's name came on the screen, everybody laughed." Fox had held back *Broken Arrow* from release—perhaps to let *Winchester '73* take the risk of introducing Stewart as a western hero, or perhaps because the subject matter was touchy and it preferred to let the similarly themed *Devil's Doorway* appear earlier and soften up audiences. So it was *Winchester '73* that came out first and proved to be a huge hit, re-casting the Stewart image and paving the way for the most successful decade of his career. "It was a desperation move, a life-saver," Stewart has said repeatedly of making *Winchester '73*. There were, in fact, some precedents that might have encouraged Stewart. Joel McCrea, another actor with a "light" image, had kept his career going by taking up westerns. Even more strikingly, Dick Powell had shed his old crooner image for good when he played Philip Marlowe in the 1944 *Murder, My Sweet*. But Stewart's good fortune in teaming up with Anthony Mann had most to do with it.

11

The Turning Point

W HILE WAITING TO SEE HOW THE two westerns panned out, Stewart went back to light comedy roles. First, there was his long-awaited opportunity to film *Harvey*, which had been contractually delayed until the play's run ended. Under the direction of Henry Koster, he was simply splendid as the forty-two-year-old bibulous dreamer Elwood P. Dowd whose best friend is a "pooka," the invisible white rabbit called Harvey (whose height is set at 6 ft. 3½ ins. on this occasion). like Stewart himself, Dowd is a Taurean, which could possibly explain why Stewart identified with the part so closely. For the film, Stewart made himself look a little untidy with a crumpled jacket and baggy trousers and his hair on the long side. He adopted a beatific smile and an infinitely gentle, dreamy tone of voice as the good-natured Dowd who has become a social embarrassment to his elder sister Veta Louise (Josephine Hull) since the day he left a bar and first met the long-eared creature: "I started to walk down the street when I heard a voice saying 'Good evening, Mr. Dowd.' I turned, and there was this great big white rabbit leaning against a lamp-post. Well, I thought nothing of that because when you've lived in a town as long as I've lived in this one, you get used to the fact that everybody knows your name."

The rabbit is the character's way of getting through life as pleasantly as possible. "I wrestled with reality for over thirty-five years and I'm happy to say I finally won out over it," he declares, and recalls his mother's advice: "In this world, Elwood, you must be oh so smart or oh so pleasant," adding: "For years I was oh so smart but now I recommend pleasant." He spends his time with Harvey frequenting bars and getting to know people. "Harvey and I warm ourselves on these golden moments. We come as strangers—soon we have friends." The others reveal their hopes and frustrations. "Then I introduce them to Harvey and he's bigger and grander than anything they can offer me. When they leave, they leave impressed. The same people seldom come back."

Stewart's Elwood is an affecting, poignant figure—forever inviting people for a drink downtown or to dinner at his house but not having them accept. He has invented Harvey for companionship. Labelled a comedy, the film really isn't funny as a whole, only at moments when it's sad as well. Stewart felt he was too young to play the part but the fact that his Elwood is middle-aged rather than elderly increases the poignancy since he has given in to the delusion that much earlier in life. He is really the Capratype hero who didn't make a success out of life, who doesn't matter to the community, who let his eccentric frame of mind take over his life entirely.

"Loonies are happy until they are cured," says a taxi driver—and fortunately Stewart is never cured. Indeed, his condition appears to be contagious as his sister occasionally sees Harvey too—much to her disgust. (Fine as she is, Josephine Hull doesn't seem right to be his sister—the dumpy actress ought to be an aunt, or possibly mother.) The film makes mistakes, I think, in suggesting that Harvey does exist by having doors open as he allegedly passes through and by showing him in a portrait painting rather than leaving him to the imagination. The audience wants to believe in him—and it enhances Stewart if Harvey does exist, by making him sane—but we should have been teased far more delicately with the possibility. Another weakness of the film is that it hasn't really been opened out and re-thought to take advantage of the change of medium—it's dully shot and too obviously "the film of the play" with minimal changes to avoid the risk of disappointing those familiar with it on stage.

Harvey did well at the box-office but not as well as it had to in order to recoup its production costs and the high price paid for the rights to Mary Chase's play. Quite possibly Stewart's fans didn't want to see him in such an unconventional role. His profit participation didn't do him much good but he was nominated for the Best Actor Academy Award along with Louis Calhern (for *The Magnificent Yankee*), Jose Ferrer (*Cyrano de Bergerac*), William Holden (*Sunset Boulevard*) and Spencer Tracy (*Father of the Bride*). Ferrer and his big nose job won. Josephine Hull was also nominated—and did win for *Harvey*.

From *Harvey* at Universal, Stewart moved straight over to *The Jackpot* at Fox. It was a then-topical, now-dated comedy suggested by the case of a prizewinner in a radio quiz show who found he couldn't afford to pay the income tax on his winnings. The same fate befalls Indiana department store executive Bill Lawrence, played by Stewart. He gets a tip from a newspaper buddy (James Gleason) about the likely identity of a mystery figure on a radio program and wins the jackpot. Soon he and his wife Amy (Barbara Hale) are up to their ears in prizes, including the services of a fashionable interior decorator (Alan Mowbray) to brighten their home and an attractive portrait painter (Patricia Medina) to paint the winner. Stewart starts selling some of the prizes to raise money and on a business trip to Chicago is arrested trying to peddle a wristwatch in a betting parlor. Barbara Hale is none too amused by the arty alterations to the house or the interest the glamorous artist is showing in Stewart. It is an agreeably complicated, run-of-the-mill affair. It was rushed into release ahead of *Harvey* which was kept as a 1950 Christmas attraction. By this time, Stewart was in Britain with director Henry Koster finishing *No Highway* for Fox. He had arrived in August with his wife and stepchildren (both of whom were sent to school in Kensington) and started work in September. It was Stewart's last venture into full-scale eccentric comedy characterizations for very many years since the actor now knew that he had hit the jackpot himself with the two westerns, *Winchester '73* and *Broken Arrow*, which had come out in the summer of 1950 and put him in the Top Ten box-office stars for the first time in his career.

The story of *No Highway* was a dramatic one about a scientist's belief that the Reindeer, a new type of British aircraft already in commercial service, will crack up from metal fatigue after a certain number of hours in flight. While the scientist is conducting an experiment to prove his case, one of the Reindeers crashes in Labrador. He goes off to investigate and finds himself flying in another of the planes which he calculates is about to crack up. The flight is completed without mishap but Stewart wrecks the undercarriage to prevent it taking off again. Eventually, his test vindicates him and there is much jubilation (no mention of the setback to the British aircraft industry). *No Highway* proved to be sadly prophetic as metal fatigue downed two British Comet jets in the Mediterranean in 1954, killing fifty-six people and prompting commentators to recall the film and the Nevil Shute novel on which it was based.

The scientist has a comical name, Theodore Honey, and an absent-minded manner that makes it harder to believe his case. In Stewart's hands, he becomes an untidy widower with a teenage daughter (Janette Scott) who confuses his house with the one next door on the estate even after eleven years and who sets out for home after a conversation with his boss (Jack Hawkins) only to find that he's already there ("That's very easy to do, you know," mumbles Stewart). At the airport when he's flying off to Labrador, he reaches for a handkerchief to stem his daughter's tears but walks off using it to wipe his nose instead.

As a scientist, Stewart has professed not to be concerned with people but it's different when he finds his own life in danger. He tries to explain the situation to a passenger, the film star Monica Teasdale (Marlene Dietrich), whose work his late wife particularly enjoyed, and to the friendly stewardess Marjorie (Glynis Johns). His earnest suggestion that Dietrich would be safer in the men's lavatory does not help his argument.

The film then sets Stewart up as a kind of latter-day Longfellow Deeds whose sanity is in doubt and who loses the will to fight until his spirit is revived by a woman. Jean Arthur put the fight back in Gary Cooper in *Mr. Deeds Goes to Town*; here Glynis Johns does it for James Stewart, even if the context is nowhere near as rich as in Capra's classic. (Another Gary Cooper role, that of the architect in *The Fountainhead* [1949] who blows up a new building because it is an *artistic* failure is faintly similar.) Part of Stewart's problem is that scientists are discredited as a group in the film (Stewart's colleague at the plant has peculiar habits as well). "A boffin has to be a bit barmy to be a boffin," concludes the head of the plane manufacturers. "The line between being a genius and

[106]

just plain crackers is so thin you never know which side they're on—nor when they've crossed it either." The public relations men try to paint Stewart as being mad to counter the bad publicity he's given them in sabotaging the plane and suggest that he be tested as well as the aircraft. He sees three psychiatrists who apparently agree he is insane. "They showed me a page of ink blobs and asked if it reminded me of elephants or tigers—it didn't remind me of elephants or tigers, it was just ink blobs," complains Stewart to Glynis Johns. But when the test plane doesn't break up at the time Stewart had predicted, he begins to doubt himself and declares that he'll sit at the board's inquiry and not say a word in his defense, just like Deeds at the hearing on his sanity. But Glynis Johns is insistent: "If you believe something is right, you have to do it if you want to live with yourself . . ."

When it comes to the vital board meeting, Stewart decides to have his say after all and defends his actions, echoing her words, "When you believe in something, that's what you've got to do, isn't it!" He resigns and walks out, threatening to wreck more Reindeers, offering a parting "That's all!" as he disappears through the door. There is a quieter, more appealing moment of wondrous jubilation just after he has wrecked the Reindeer. "It just folded right up and sat down—there'll really be a delay for everyone now, won't there? I don't know what they're going to do," he prattles on, relishing the way he has surpassed himself.

Certainly Stewart's performance is more entertaining than the film as a whole and it's a pity that his reunion with Marlene Dietrich doesn't amount to much. Her part seems artificially expanded as it is—it's hard to believe both she and the stewardess would take the trouble to visit his home to help him.

During production, after twenty-one days on the plane interior set, Stewart went down with appendicitis. He had his appendix removed on November 15, returning to the set ten days later to complete the last day's shooting on that sequence. The delay meant that the film wasn't finished until after Christmas, by which time he was urgently needed by Cecil DeMille for his next film. While in England, he learned that his wife was pregnant and Gloria went back to the States early to see her doctor, phoning him to say that he could expect twins.

The DeMille picture was the circus extravaganza, *The Greatest*

Show on Earth, in which he took the role of Buttons the Clown, who is really a fugitive on the run, hotly pursued by Henry Wilcoxon's suspicious detective. He is a former doctor wanted for the mercy killing of his wife. Being a circus clown is apparently the perfect disguise since it enables him to stay fully made up with putty nose, unrecognizable, all the time (since even on train journeys between towns he is never seen without it). Stewart was coached for his part by the celebrated clown Emmett Kelly. There is a spectacular train wreck for the climax of the picture, just as the cops are about to nab Stewart. This poses the question: will he escape or will he stay and give medical aid to the badly wounded circus boss (Charlton Heston)?

DeMille's shameless concoction of clichés still draws admiration for the gusto with which it is slammed over, although 153 minutes of comic strip narrative is a bit wearying. Still, it was a good picture to be in from a career viewpoint even if the role Stewart played was more of a glorified cameo than a starring one. The film industry was reeling from the effects of dwindling attendances and *The Greatest Show on Earth* served up color and spectacle that audiences couldn't get at home and brought them back into the theaters. A grateful Hollywood gave it the Academy Award for the year's Best Picture, snubbing *High Noon* and *The Quiet Man* as well as (more understandably) *Moulin Rouge* and *Ivanhoe*.

The Stewarts' twin daughters, Judy and Kelly, were born on May 7, 1951. Gloria tells a story to suggest that Jimmy's absent-minded professor of *No Highway in the Sky* was for real. He came to collect her from the hospital, put her in a wheelchair, took her down in the elevator, and went off to get his car. He then forgot all about her and drove home. Gloria took it in good humor: "I just said: 'Take me back upstairs—he'll phone.' We went back—sure enough, the phone rang."

"I'm a dreamer," Stewart used to say. "I'm very guilty of day-dreaming. Just can't seem to keep my mind on one idea . . . That's why I don't read much—just film scripts. My wife won't let me take the children in the car when I'm driving. I'm a terrible driver . . . I don't seem able to concentrate. I have this terror that I will drive into something one day. Lots of times I have felt grateful to drive into my garage . . ."

It was time for Stewart to follow up his new-found success as a western star. According to Borden Chase, the actor himself came up with the idea of filming a novel called *Bend of the Snake* and bought the rights without reading more than the jacket after it was recommended by a friend. Chase claimed he threw the book away and wrote an original screenplay. Whatever its origins, the resulting film, *Bend of the River,* reunited the star, writer, director and producer of *Winchester '73* for an even more satisfying western, this time in Technicolor. In Britain, it was retitled *Where the River Bends.*

Stewart played Glyn McLyntock, a former border raider who is trying to start a new life guiding a band of pilgrims into the upper Snake river country to establish a farming community of which he hopes to be part. Once again, he's dressed convincingly, in a grubby, worn costume with chaps and stained hat. He keeps his past secret from the leader, Jay C. Flippen's Jeremy Baile, who doesn't believe a man can reform. "When an apple's rotten, there's nothing you can do except throw it away or it'll spoil the whole barrel," says Flippen. Stewart is determined to prove that there's a difference between apples and men. It's Arthur Kennedy's Emerson Cole, another ex-raider rescued by Stewart from a near-lynching, who prompts Flippen's remark.

Stewart and Kennedy work well together at first, disposing of a small band of Indians near the wagon train's night camp and liberating vital supplies that have become inflated in price during a gold rush boom and are needed to survive the winter. Kennedy is grateful to Stewart for saving his life and helps him out in what needs to be done. Kennedy has no faith that they can live down their pasts and thinks they should divert the supplies to miners who will pay handsomely for them rather than deliver them to farmers who won't be grateful. Kennedy's attitude is a practical one while Stewart is the idealist.

Rock Hudson plays a young gambler, Trey Wilson, who is at risk of becoming a rotten apple. He helps the other two claim their supplies by force and joins them in ambushing the owner who brings a bunch of riders after them. When the men turn back under a withering hail of bullets, Stewart stops shooting and tells the other two, "Let them go." "Why?" asks Hudson. The grinning Kennedy keeps on firing. At least Hudson is willing to learn. It is a succinct expression of the differing mentality of the three men. Even Stewart, though, is not beyond reverting to savagery in the heat of the moment. When the hired packers injure Jay C. Flippen in an attempt to take over the supplies, Stewart goes for the leader (Jack Lambert) and is about to finish him off with a knife before a scream from Flippen's daughter (Julia Adams) makes him stop and stare at the gleaming knife in his hand as if he didn't know how it got there and had been startled out of a trance.

Kennedy is ultimately unable to resist hijacking the supplies high up in the mountains but he stops the packers from killing Stewart and gives him enough food to get to safety on foot. There is an unforgettable shot as the badly beaten Stewart rises unsteadily on his feet, heroically outlined against the blue sky and distant peaks, telling Kennedy that he should have killed him. "You'll be seeing me," warns Stewart. "Every time you look back in the darkness and you bed down for the night, you'll wonder if I'm there. One night I will be. You'll be seeing me!" It's the same dogged spirit that Stewart expressed as Jefferson Smith in the senate, refusing to accept defeat, and it's a measure of Kennedy's intelligence as a villain that he takes the threat seriously. Also, their enmity is increased because, as Julian Petley has observed, "the charming villain functions as a reflection of the hero, as his more or less unbalanced *alter ego*." As in some other Mann westerns, this is what gives the confrontation of hero and villain such epic power.

Kennedy's brutal treatment of Flippen when the latter releases a horse for Stewart puts him beyond salvation (even if his fury is motivated by fear of Stewart) while Hudson atones for siding with Kennedy by trying to stop the beating. When Stewart overtakes the supply train, it isn't long before he and Kennedy are fighting it out in a cascading river with Kennedy being knocked unconscious and swept away, a decisive cleansing of the environment. Stewart is accepted by Flippen and the other farmers, and never has a western hero done so much to redeem himself. There is a real sense of hard-earned achievement to this happy ending.

In its unpretentious way, *Bend of the River* is a great western. It combines well-developed characterizations with a superb use of the landscape. There is a minimum of studio work and Anthony Mann really makes the actors sweat in the rugged terrain to impart a sense of real effort and exertion.

Stewart finished 1951 back at MGM for the first of two pictures. In *Winchester '73*, he'd shown he could handle a weapon convincingly, so now they let him portray the inventor of one in *Carbine Williams*. The real Williams was on hand to advise Stewart, who recalled: "He actually invented the carbine rifle while he was in prison for murder. He came to me and told me the way he wanted himself portrayed. In a way I listened, you know—the fella *had* shot a couple of people."

The part didn't suit Stewart at all. The character is shown as a rugged individualist who, rather than work on his father's cotton farm in North Carolina, operates a string of illegal corn whisky stills during the Prohibition era. He boastfully shoots a couple of quail while kissing his wife and childhood sweetheart (Jean Hagen). In a gun battle with the cops, a man is shot and killed and Williams gets a thirty-year sentence for manslaughter. Stewart has to play him as an irritable, sullen, boorish, argumentative figure who for three years refuses all help and cuts himself off from his wife, child and relatives, earning spells on the chain gang and in solitary confinement for his rebellious attitudes. It just doesn't fit Stewart's image or personality at all. He became more at home conveying the character in the grip of his obsession to put together the automatic carbine rifle he has thought up, working at first from bits of scrap metal with a handfile and hacksaw in the prison blacksmith shop. Eventually a sympathetic warden (Wendell Corey) even gains permission for Stewart to fire test rounds in the jail. His reward for inventing a more efficient weapon of destruction is a pardon. He is shown with greying temples being reconciled with his fourteen-year-old son. It is interesting to compare the film with *Birdman of Alcatraz* (1962) in which Burt Lancaster played a convicted murderer who became an expert on bird life and then penology while in prison but *didn't* get his freedom.

Carbine Williams has proved to be Stewart's most negligible film of the fifties—the only serious career mistake he made amid a stream of remarkably fine pictures. On a lesser level, Stewart erred in undertaking a western series for radio (following in the footsteps of Joel McCrea's *Tales of the Texas Rangers*). The series was called *The Six-Shooter* (again the emphasis on weaponry). "Unfortunately it came out at a time when drama on the radio at home went out of the window, so it wasn't a successful series," reported Stewart. The stories were re-used for a television series called *The Restless Gun* with John Payne but Stewart held back the rights to a few of the scripts (mostly by a writer he regarded highly, Frank Burt) and re-did them himself over the years in occasional television appearances.

12

The Golden Years

Over the six years from 1952 to 1957, Stewart made eleven feature films, working with only four directors. He made six films with Anthony Mann, three with Alfred Hitchcock, one with Billy Wilder—and one with James Neilson that was only because Anthony Mann dropped out of a picture at the last minute. Stewart went back in to the annual Top Ten box-office stars for 1952 on the strength of *Bend of the River* and *The Greatest Show on Earth* and stayed there until the end of the decade. In 1955 he was regarded as *the* top draw at American movie theaters. He was certainly a top favorite in British cinemas as well. It was an astonishing turnaround for Stewart after his post-war decline. Though the best pictures weren't always the biggest hits, he maintained a level of artistic achievement probably unparalleled in any other major star's career.

It began with another Anthony Mann western, *The Naked Spur*, the first of four pictures Stewart made with Mann in direct succession. It was a first screenplay by two radio and television writers, Sam Rolfe and Harold Jack Bloom. Apart from a group of non-speaking Indians, the film has only five characters, all of them fully developed. Stewart played Howie Kemp, the bounty hunter; Millard Mitchell was the old prospector who helps him hunt down Benn Vandergroat, the outlaw with a $5000 reward on his head, played by Robert Ryan; Janet Leigh was the daughter of a deceased badman who accompanies the wanted man; and Ralph Meeker portrayed the dishonorably discharged ex-army lieutenant Roy Anderson who aids Stewart in capturing his quarry.

It's a brilliant cast who perform most of their scenes on location high in the Colorado Rockies. Once again it pays off with a much heightened sense of reality (you never feel the caterers are waiting just off screen with the box lunches). Mann's camera often shows you actors doing exactly what the characters do without benefit of cutaways to save them effort: it's visibly James Stewart ducking out of the way of a rock slide within the same shot, not a double with his head turned away from the rocks. Mann and his players come up with the little points that make the action more vivid. In Stewart's case there's the way his eyes flare with alarm when he loses his grip on a rope while hauling himself up a rock face and the way he rubs his scorched hands after sliding to the ground. He makes you feel the impact when he's knocked off his horse and his back thuds into a tree, arresting his slide; and his big fight with Ralph Meeker is highly physical as they really seem to be attempting to break limbs and strangle each other. Of course, the camera angles and the sound effects help but Stewart in particular seems to throw more of himself into his western roles than any other star of the genre.

This is another in which he suffers, being shot in the leg but riding on until he collapses, even then refusing to be left behind to recuperate. He is once again a man with an obsession, but unlike *Winchester '73*, he is on his own here, completely friendless. He is after the reward money for bringing in the outlaw, dead or alive, so that he can buy back land that once belonged to him—until he went off to war and entrusted it to a fiancée who sold it and ran away. Only then can he forgive himself for his stupidity. He is unwillingly forced into a partnership with the prospector and the ex-soldier after they help him capture Ryan.

He reveals a softer side talking to Janet Leigh, his voice warmly evoking the rewards of running a ranch, the pleasures of music and dancing; and in his troubled sleep he reverts to being the loving suitor, voicing his sweet talk to the woman he once loved. He even hints of marriage to Janet Leigh, only to find she has betrayed him (for his own safety) by distracting him from Ryan's escape attempt.

He is angered by any attempt to make him face up to the inhumane figure he has become. When Ralph Meeker says of their prisoner, "He's not a man, he's a sack of money—that's why we're all here, especially you," it makes Stewart tremble with rage and provokes their brawl. At the end, Stewart hauls Ryan's body out of a raging torrent onto a flat slab of rock like a fisherman landing a prize catch, and he insists to Janet Leigh that he is going to hand over the body for cash. By now Leigh has given up protesting and she merely asks if she can stay with the bounty hunter. In a wonderfully conceived and played scene, Stewart carries on arguing. "Tell me why, why?" he cries, asking for a better reason to give up the corpse. "I'm taking him back, I swear it!" He is really arguing with the submerged better half of himself, and losing the argument; and there's an appropriately huge close-up of him weeping as he realizes that he cannot go through with his plan. We leave him a cleansed man, starting to dig with his shovel and agreeing to take Janet Leigh to California, where she was headed with the now dead outlaw.

Only Stewart survives. The other men destroy themselves— the prospector fooled by his greed for non-existent gold invented by the wily outlaw; the ex-soldier drowned in his eagerness to recover the outlaw's body; and the black-hearted outlaw himself, who doesn't reckon on Janet Leigh upsetting his ambush plans. It's a psychological drama in a western setting, a familiar story of discord over treasure, only here a living man rather than a pile of gold is the disputed object. The bounty hunter was a new figure in the western and Stewart's performance became the model for many actors in similar roles that followed. If *The Naked Spur* has a drawback, it's the lack of humor and the variety of mood that Borden Chase brought to his scripts for Stewart and Mann. It's a very grim western.

Even though it was several months before the star and director were at work on *Thunder Bay*, Mann was quick to admit in later years that it was one of their poorest collaborations. He told Chris Wicking: "*Thunder Bay* was made in the Florida bayous and the Gulf of Mexico. Its story was weak and we never were really able to lick it. I think it was a little too commercial and it fell down on its basic plot. Some of the things we showed were effective and beautiful . . . but I don't think it was a very good script. Borden worked on it, John Michael Hayes worked on it who was a good writer and has developed into a very good one. There were too many writers, and it became too fabricated. They wanted a picture with Jimmy Stewart and we concocted one." Stewart himself took the project seriously: "I spent more than month in advance of shooting with the oil-riggers and fishermen in the Gulf of Mexico, learning their trade."

One of the film's problems is that it is hard to identify with the James Stewart character's dream of bringing up oil off the Louisiana coast in 1946, especially when it means disrupting the shrimp fishing industry and the peaceful lives of the local inhabitants. Even if, as Stewart argues, the fishing and oil industries can co-exist, it is difficult and troublesome as the film demonstrates. It's more a case of "You can't stop progress—nobody can," as Stewart insists at the end, his argument being clinched by black oil promptly showering down on him as he cackles gleefully and rubs his hands together. It's a *positive* quest (compared to those in Mann westerns like *Winchester '73* and *The Naked Spur*) but it is nowhere near as much of an achievement as being accepted as a member of the farming community in *Bend of the River*.

Also, the film lacks real villains. To some extent, this is turned to advantage as Stewart's partner is played by Dan Duryea in his usual crass, crude manner and, because of his association with villainy, we expect him to cause trouble when he takes up with a young and innocent local girl, Francesca (Marcia Henderson), promising her a penthouse and mink furs. Duryea confounds us and Stewart by marrying the girl.

The opposition to the oil drilling scheme is led by Francesca's sister Stella (Joanna Dru), a graduate from the school of hard knocks who can't help falling for Stewart and visits him on his oil rig ostensibly to help her sister escape Duryea's clutches but actually to succumb to Stewart's advances. Right then, an attempt is made to dynamite the platform by one of the fishermen and Stewart burns with anger, thinking she has been a decoy (the same way he felt about Janet Leigh in *The Naked Spur*, only here Joanne Dru didn't know about the attempted sabotage). Stewart's fight with the fisherman as a storm lashes the platform, followed by his attempt to save the latter from drowning, provides the most exciting sequence in the picture.

[116]

When money runs out, Stewart implores his crew to work on for nothing but they turn him down. (In westerns like *Bend of the River*, the drama was stronger as men could be forced to finish a task which, in the case of food supplies, was more vital than the possible discovery of oil.) When Duryea turns up, having just got married, Stewart fights him, allegedly because he wasn't there to tackle a blow-out but really to vent his fury at the other men's withdrawal. Here again Duryea surprises us by winning the fight and pinning Stewart down on the floor of the rig to tell him, quite reasonably, "With me this is no holy crusade, it's only a job. You've been crowding the men, you've been crowding the rig, but you don't crowd me!"

Stewart responds by ordering everyone off the rig: he'll carry on by himself, he'll do the job alone. Here again we glimpse the determined streak that characterizes the Stewart hero, that sets him apart from ordinary men. Once more Duryea surprises us by rallying the men behind Stewart who is still so tense that he knocks Duryea to the ground at the mention of his bride's name, not taking in what he has said, and only then asking disbelievingly if he really did marry her. Stewart is visibly grateful for Duryea's intervention but he can't bring himself to say anything.

It seems as though the modern setting eliminates the case for extreme figures like Stewart's western heroes and for extreme forms of action. Reason wins the argument but it is less dramatic than force. *Thunder Bay* is thoroughly entertaining but it hasn't the ingredients to measure up to the westerns.

There was no basis for intense conflict in the next Mann/Stewart collaboration, *The Glenn Miller Story*, but there were many compensations, not least the Miller music. The film still gave Stewart a quest, an obsession to find a particular *sound*, but Mann drew on the actor's comic persona and revived the idea of the strong woman pushing him to achieve his goal. June Allyson told Tom Vallance how she came to be reunited with her co-star of *The Stratton Story*: ". . . Jimmy called me and said, 'Hey, I've got two films that I want to do and I won't do them without you.' I said, 'Marvelous, what are they?' and he told me *The Glen Miller Story* and *Strategic Air Command*. He said 'I'll send the scripts over,' but I said, 'Don't bother, I'll do them, I don't have to read the scripts.'

[117]

Working with Jimmy, you don't—you know that he's pretty sharp! . . . It was the best thing I could have done, but I didn't do it because I was wise, I did it because Jimmy asked me."

June Allyson played the girlfriend that Stewart's Glenn Miller had at college. Humor is based on Stewart's shyness being masked by a ridiculous degree of self-assurance: he rings her up, not having spoken to her for two years while he's been traveling around as a trombonist, and expects her to recognize his voice instantly as though she's been waiting all that time for his call, and when he turns up at three o'clock in the morning to pick her up for a date "after work" he knows she'll forgive him, just as he knows (or hopes) that she'll come straight to New York to marry him when he calls her up long distance after another two-year interval and tells her to do it. The screenplay (by Valentine Davies and Oscar Brodney) amusingly turns the tables on Stewart by making him wait on their wedding night, first when the couple are given a surprise party and then when she enjoys herself so much at a nightclub she doesn't want to leave.

Stewart is prepared to forget his musical dream in order to earn a living as a trombone player and it is June Allyson who revives it, by telling him that what made him exciting was that he had a goal. She uses her savings to set him up with his own band so that he can play his special arrangements *his* way. Eight years later she is still urging him on to find that elusive sound, which he finally does discover by chance.

Stewart's stubborn streak is not entirely absent, but June Allyson proves to be one jump ahead of him. When he stutters and stumbles about telling her that he has gone ahead and enlisted in the armed forces during the Second World War, she already knows and she knew what he would do before even he did. There is no outsmarting her. Stewart does have an assertive moment on his own in the services when he has the band play in a livelier tempo as men are marching past in a review.

Mann realized the project was "fraught with sentimentality" and there are occasional lapses into it, especially when Stewart is given a newly adopted baby to feed. It is also remarkably free from friction and bad temper—everyone is warm-hearted and understanding. Yet such is the skill with which it is handled that

the film always remains agreeable and entertaining with opportunities to hear the most famous Glenn Miller numbers. The
bandleader's death, when his plane disappears between London
and Paris, gives a bite to the end of the film but the writers
ingeniously contrive to reach an up-beat conclusion by demonstrating that the music—his sound—will live on, giving him a
kind of immortality, and by introducing his posthumous gift, the
arrangement of "Little Brown Jug," earlier described by Stewart
as a "tin-ear tune," that is cheerful and bouncy and not in the least
lachrymose.

Did Stewart play the trombone? "No," he answers. "I was
determined to look like a trombone player and fortunately it
wasn't too difficult to learn the positions. The tremolo, that was a
little hard to get. I was assigned a coach, a fellow by the name of
Joe Yukl, a very fine trombone player, and he said it's very easy.
After five days he said to me, 'I'm gonna have to quit because the
noises that you are making as you're trying to play the trombone
are affecting me mentally and I used terrible language to my wife
last night when I came home, I kicked my dog, which I've never
done'... But I talked him into staying and we solved the problem.
I plugged up the mouthpiece so that it was impossible for me to
make a sound but I learned the breathing and the positioning of
the trombone. It was certainly cheating but it was the only way."
Joe Yukl dubbed Stewart in the film.

The Glenn Miller Story was a huge hit, far more popular than any
of his westerns or indeed any of his starring vehicles. With Rear
Window not far behind it, the cozy musical biography gave Stewart two 1954 releases high in the American box-office Top Ten.

Hardly had the Glenn Miller team had a chance to catch their
breath than they were off to Canada to film a new Borden Chase
script, The Far Country, set in the Yukon gold rush era. Besides
Mann and Stewart, the new western also retained the services of
producer Aaron Rosenberg, cameraman William Daniels, unit art
director Alexander Golitzen, assistant director John Sherwood
and editor Russell Schoengarth. The cast line-up in support of
Stewart was very different, however, with only Henry "Harry"
Morgan appearing in both films.

The Far Country doesn't have quite the striking visual impact of

[119]

the other four Mann/Stewart westerns, despite the promise of its setting, but it's still a great western, of particular interest as a completely original screenplay by Borden Chase that provides the clearest expression of the recurrent theme at the heart of the writer's work: the need for a man to work for others, for the good of the community instead of being obstinately independent and self-centered. There is no revenge *motif* to cloud the issue as in *Winchester '73*. Here Stewart's Jeff Webster takes almost the entire picture to be persuaded that he wants to be part of a community (instead of having taken that decision already, as in *Bend of the River*). Until the turning point, when he becomes the force that single-handedly revives the idea of setting up a proper town, he has been ostinately, obsessively opposed to helping anyone else— except, at a pinch, his loyal traveling companion, Walter Brennan's Ben Tatem.

As in *Winchester '73*, the old-timer does the talking. He is useful for telling us things about Stewart because Stewart himself is particularly terse and unforthcoming. We learn that two absent drovers who were helping to bring in his cattle "tried to turn back" and only when brought to mock-trial for their murder by the crooked town boss, John McIntire's Gannon, does he elaborate: "I figured they shouldn't have turned back and taken my cattle with them."

"I take care of me. When you're older, you'll find that's the only way," Stewart tells the freckle-faced French youngster played by Corinne Calvet. He minds his own business to the extent of taking his cattle the long valley route to the mining town of Dawson City instead of across the snow-covered high mountain pass because he once saw similar weather conditions lead to an avalanche—but he doesn't warn the people using the other route of the possible risk and they are buried by a huge snow slide. He refuses to turn back and help dig out survivors until he is subjected to the combined urging of his old friend, the French girl, and another companion. "Why? I didn't kill them," Stewart argues. "If you don't know why . . ." replies Corinne Calvet. Stewart is like Rock Hudson when told to hold his fire in *Bend of the River*: both have to learn why. ("If you don't know why, I can't tell you," Stewart told Hudson in the earlier film.) And when Walter Brennan tells Stewart, "You're wrong" and that he has to help, it echoes the way the same actor told another bullheaded character, John Wayne's Tom Dunson in *Red River* (largely scripted by Borden Chase), that he was wrong there.

Stewart finds himself in agreement with the resourceful saloon keeper played by Ruth Roman who doesn't trust people either. "I trusted a man once," she recollects. "That's quite a coincidence," responds Stewart. "I trusted a woman . . ." Although she elaborates on her amorous betrayal, we never hear any more details of Stewart's unhappy experience. In a way, Ruth Roman's self-centered attitude is proved right for when she puts herself out to save Stewart's life she stops a bullet and dies. "You crazy fool!" says Stewart. "Why didn't you take care of you?"

He turns down Brennan's suggestion that he should become marshal of Dawson, even though Brennan presses him to accept and to make Dawson their home. "Law and order costs lives," replies Stewart. "It means someone has to stand up and get himself shot at. Well, that's not why I came to Dawson. We've got ours and we're getting out. At least, *I'm* getting out." Only when Brennan is murdered, and Stewart himself barely survives a bushwhacking by McIntire's men seeking the gold they've prospected, does Stewart see the light and become the strongest advocate of establishing law and order, beginning with the disposal of McIntire and his gang.

In at least fifteen riding parts, Stewart rode the same horse, Pie. The horse is called by that name in *The Far Country* and has his most prominent role in this film. Here is what James Stewart has had to say about the performer who did more films with him than anyone else:

"A most amazing horse! I rode him for twenty-two years. I never was able to buy him because he was owned by a little girl by the name of Stevie Myers who was the daughter of an old wrangler that used to wrangle horses for Tom Mix and W. S. Hart. And he retired and he gave the horse to her. And he was sort of a maverick, he hurt a couple of people. Audie Murphy had ridden him a couple of times, he damn near killed Glenn Ford—

ran right into a tree. I saw him when I started making westerns and I liked this darn little horse—he was a little bit small. There was a little quarterhorse—Arabian—in him.

"I got to know him like a friend. I actually believe that he understood about making pictures. I've run at a full gallop straight towards the camera and pulled him up and then done a lot of dialogue and he's sat absolutely still and never moved. He was smart as a whip. He knew when the camera would start rolling—when they did the slates. He knew that, because his ears came up and I could feel him under me get ready and he always moved . . . and the other horses didn't know what was going on, so he'd stand out.

"I remember in *The Far Country* the bad guys were in the saloon and I had a little bell on the saddle that was sort of an identifying thing and the heavies knew when I came into town by the bell. And the camera started panning on Pie's feet as I got near the saloon and the guys got ready to kill me. And then the camera goes up and there's nobody on Pie. Of course, I'm back behind and I kill the whole crowd of 'em.

"Somebody came up before we did this and said, 'How are you ever gonna get the horse to do this?' I said, 'Well, let me talk to him.' And there was a fellow that worked with the horse with me a lot, name of Jack Sanders. And I just talked to Pie, 'Now just start here and you go to the other end and stop,' and Jack Sanders was at the other end. And they said, 'How long is this gonna take?' And I said 'Do it right now.' And Pie did it."

Although *The Far Country* was finished in 1953, for some reason Universal did not release it until early in 1955 and it was preceded into the theaters by the next film Stewart made, Alfred Hitchcock's *Rear Window*, shot at Paramount.

Working for Hitch was in total contrast to working for Anthony Mann. Whereas Mann filmed on location as much as possible, Hitch made *Rear Window* entirely on one soundstage and not only confined Stewart to one room but also put him in a wheelchair. He played L. B. Jeffries, an ace news photographer with his left leg in a plaster cast. Stewart was the ideal actor to extract humor from the situation—prodding with a stick inside the cast at an itch near the top end or scratching his big toe with the stick where it protrudes at the other end.

His co-star was Grace Kelly, playing the fashion designer Lisa Fremont who is determined to marry him. There's also the redoubtable Thelma Ritter as the insurance company nurse who nags him about marrying the eminently desirable Kelly. Stewart resists her because he views their lifestyles as incompatible and because she is so domineering. Hitchcock amusingly suggests her as a threat and a menace visually as he lies helpless and asleep by having her shadow fall across his face before she leans down to kiss him. She relishes the opportunity to look after him and has dinner delivered by a restaurant. "Lisa, it's perfect—as usual," he comments in both praise and criticism.

His career has been based on going into dangerous spots—he broke his leg photographing a car race from the track. It's not a suitable world for a woman. "Those high heels—they'll be great in the jungle," he observes. Her idea is that he should take up fashion and portrait photography instead—she can find him plenty of work (again, a threat to his independence). Her bossy manner shows further in the way she exchanges his cigarette case, a souvenir of a job in Shanghai, for a "more suitable" silver one.

However, she also makes an extremely erotic figure with her plans to stay overnight and the flimsy transparent nightdress she produces from her handbag. Even sexually, she is the aggressive one but she finds that Stewart is far more interested in a possible murder across the way. He has been passing the time observing his neighbors through binoculars in apartments across the back yard and suspects that a man has murdered his wife. The thought so absorbs him that he pays no attention to Kelly's attempts to kiss him and she has to give up and consider with him the possibilities of murder having been committed. She and the nurse then both become interested and it provides her with the chance to prove her willingness to live dangerously and takes risks like Stewart does by entering the murderer's flat in his absence. There she finds the wife's loose wedding ring, confirming their suspicions, and she slips it on to her finger when the man unex-

[123]

pectedly returns, both to hide it and to nudge Stewart into putting a wedding ring on her finger himself. She can't resist pointing it out to him as he watches and tips off the murderer as to his existence before she is taken away for questioning by police that Stewart has hastily summoned to rescue her.

Until now, Stewart has been in a God-like position, peering at his neighbors in safe detachment. He has been merely amusing himself, even when he sends the killer an anonymous note to test his reaction. But his position of superiority vanishes when the man knows he is there. He is now particularly vulnerable. With the nurse gone to put up bail for Grace Kelly, he is alone and his front door has been left unlocked since he can't get to it easily. The outside world that was so remote, that he had spied on so smugly, is about to come barging into his flat, claiming revenge for his hubris. We see Stewart's face in close-up as he swallows anxiously, his eyes dart around: there's a splendid high-angle shot of his slow turn in the wheelchair away from the window to face the door, and then his backing away from it. It's characteristic of Hitchcock's tight sense of construction that Stewart should use his profession to help him out of the tight spot, picking up his camera and firing off flashbulbs to blind the killer temporarily when he appears in the doorway (although the attempt to convey subjectively the effect on the murderer's vision is overdone). In the ensuing fight, Stewart is physically ejected from his formerly cozy haven, and even if his life is saved, there is a price to be paid for his prying curiosity—another broken leg.

Rear Window has one major weakness. The vignettes of life in the other apartments—a lonely spinster, two newlyweds, etc.— all illustrate aspects of male/female relationships and thus reflect back on the Stewart/Kelly relationship but they are so crudely presented, like mime theater, that it's impossible to take them seriously. But otherwise the film is a triumph and here Hitchcock's idea of restricting himself to the view from Stewart's apartment (with just one or two brief exceptions) instead of leaving it (to accompany Grace Kelly on her visit to the killer's apartment, for instance) is most effective.

The Stewart/Kelly relationship is a cleverly balanced one. Stewart is clearly not a young man and ought to settle down (his narrow escape on the racetrack was a warning) but Kelly's determination to turn him into the kind of man she wants, and her advantage over him while he's an invalid, make us feel sympathy for him. Even now she has shared his adventurous way of life, we leave her still determined to make him settle in her sophisticated world. Grace Kelly is obviously a highly desirable woman but disconcertingly forceful for a heroine in this kind of film relationship.

As an actress, she won Stewart's total admiration. He said recently to George Perry: "I think Grace Kelly did an amazing job as my girlfriend who has to do my dirty work. It was wonderful casting on Hitch's part. I always liked the moment when she's over in the killer's apartment looking for evidence, when he comes back, and I realize that her life is in danger—that it's my responsibility because I can't go myself, and she's there for me."

The two stars clicked so well together there were plans to re-team them at MGM and it was Stewart's great regret that it never happened. "I was supposed to do *Designing Woman*—kind of a funny picture—with Grace Kelly, and we were all set to go—we had the costumes all ready, the final touches were being put on the script and the sets were built—and Grace came in one day and said, 'I'm going to get married.' And they said, well, now, you do it with somebody else, but somehow I wanted to do it with Grace because she was right for it and I'd done *Rear Window* with her, and I wish I'd done that picture. Greg Peck made it with Betty Bacall— did a very good job."

For some time Anthony Mann had been working on a project to improve the image of the Strategic Air Command and the Air Force generally at a time when SAC was making itself unpopular by calling up airmen on reserve and damaging their careers (and possibly their marriages as well) by putting them on twenty-one months of active duty at very poor pay. Mann and his writers (Valentine Davies from *The Glenn Miller Story* and aerial specialist Beirne Lay Jr.) were fully briefed by General Curtis LeMay and his staff on the activities of SAC. As an officer in the Air Force Reserve, Stewart was the obvious choice of star, quite apart from his previous associations with Mann.

Mann later recalled: "The co-operation of the Air Force was

[125]

vital, and we were held within the bounds of what they wanted. The story itself was restricted and the whole concept of its shooting was confined to what they would let me show, which is perfectly all right. I went into it purely as a service to the Air Force and as Jimmy Stewart was one of the Force we accepted this handicap and just tried to make an exciting film, not out of the characters which were papier-machê, but out of the B36 and B47—we tried to dramatize them as our two great characters." Of course, these aircraft are no longer the novelty they were then and the passage of time has made *Strategic Air Command* even duller than it was in 1955. Still, North American audiences flocked to see it and it was almost as successful as *The Glenn Miller Story* and a bigger draw than any of Stewart's Hitchcock movies.

Stewart played Robert B. "Dutch" Holland, the third base player for the St. Louis Cardinals baseball team. As an old B29 commander, he smiles when Air Force planes fly over but is aggrieved to be called back to serve in SAC when he still has a few good years of sport left in him, has only been married five months, and is about to settle in a new home. But the fine judgment and co-ordination he displays on the baseball field are what commend him to SAC, and so he goes off to learn to fly jets.

June Allyson is the long-suffering wife who does break with him after he's signed up to stay in SAC instead of returning to baseball and hasn't even consulted her. But he flies off to Japan and she immediately regrets her decision and is the one who apologizes when he comes back. He finally leaves SAC not because of her but because of a bad shoulder. The warmth of their scenes when they are together don't really compensate for his treatment of her.

The film lacks real drama. "This is a new kind of war," says Frank Lovejoy's commanding officer. "We've got to stay ready to fight without fighting." The best the writers can manage is a fuel fire on a test mission and a crash landing in Greenland, but the footage of the aerial plane-to-plane refueling is a classic piece of erotic symbolism. Although the film recognizes the problems that recall into SAC create (the Alex Nicol character loses his business), the men all come around in the end and Stewart never misses baseball once he's settled in. Only at the end does he look

[126]

for a team manager's job when he can no longer fly. There's a touch of the old stubbornness when he takes off with the troublesome shoulder, knowing that he should have reported to the doctors, and a touch of the old euphoria when he learns by telegram that his wife has given birth and tells each onlooker in turn that it's a baby girl.

Late in 1953, the former production head of Universal, William Goetz, set up as an independent producer releasing through Columbia. Mindful of the success he had had with films like *Winchester '73* and *Bend of the River*, he flew to Canada while James Stewart and Anthony Mann were shooting *The Far Country* to try and involve them in making a western for him. He got Stewart interested in filming a James O'Mara novel, *Ambush at Ghost Creek*, which had been serialized in the *Saturday Evening Post* and would be retitled *Dawn in the Sky* as a movie; but, in the event, Goetz's first independent venture was based on another *Post* story by Thomas T. Flynn, *The Man from Laramie* with Mann directing and Stewart starring. Borden Chase wasn't used in the writing but Stewart brought in Frank Burt, whose work on *The Six-Shooter* he had admired, to collaborate on the screenplay with Philip Yordan. The result was another superb western.

Stewart played the laconic but likeable westerner Will Lockhart. He gives away a minimum of information about himself. He is vague about his background when he arrives in Coronado ("I can't rightly say any place is my home" is as far as he'll go) but we slowly gather that he is an army captain at Fort Laramie who has taken leave to track down the gun runners whose weapons in Indian hands killed his kid brother. He has been traveling with Wallace Ford's half-Indian old-timer who volunteers to help, giving as his reason, "I'm a lonely man, Mr. Lockhart. So are you. I don't suppose we spoke ten words coming down here but I feel that I know you and I like what I know." Those last remarks eloquently sum up the feeling audiences had about Stewart.

"Lockhart" is an appropriate name, for the Stewart character locks away his feelings about his brother's death (only we see the agitation in his eyes as he stands on the spot where his brother died, his back to the others with him). He is equally reticent about his feelings for the beautiful Barbara Waggoman (Cathy O'Don-

[127]

nell), complimenting her on her beauty but not kissing her ("Goodnight *again*, Mr. Lockhart," she says with schoolma'am firmness when he prolongs a conversation). At the end of the film, instead of proposing to her, he rides off, merely suggesting she come to Laramie later on and ask for him.

Trouble visits Stewart rather than the other way around. He and his men are peacefully loading salt onto freight wagons when the hotheaded Dave Waggoman (Alex Nicol) rides up with a bunch of cowboys (a wonderfully composed set of images) and accuses Stewart of stealing, ropes him, and drags him along the ground and through a fire before burning his wagons.

There's a remarkable sequence later in which Stewart spots Nicol in town and strides purposefully over to him, dragging him off his horse and laying into him. As he walks towards Nicol, the camera retreats in front of him, then pulls hastily away to one side as he reaches his enemy. The way the scene is shot, together with the mounting score by George Duning, displays Stewart in a particularly forceful and tough light.

Later Stewart is quietly combing out strays from a herd for an independent rancher (Aline MacMahon) when Nicol and his men come along and start shooting. Stewart takes cover and fires back, wounding Nicol in the hand. Nicol's men capture Stewart and he is accused of rustling. Nicol has two of his gang hold Stewart and then he deliberately puts a bullet through Stewart's right palm. The camera observes Stewart's face.

Earlier, when roped and dragged by Nicol, Stewart reacted with a frantic, seething combination of fear and anger. Here again his reaction is just as intense and the way he gasps the words "Why, you *scum!*" as he is shot in the hand still carries the force of a much stronger outburst that censorship wouldn't permit in 1955. Anthony Mann explained his astute choice of location for the scene: "It could have been done in many places but in the middle of this plain it was frightening because there was this beautiful expanse of country with all this evil going on in it." There is no dwelling on the gory details but nevertheless it represented a new high in sadistic violence at that time.

Nicol is the wayward son of the area's wealthiest landowner (Donald Crisp) and it transpires that he and his foster brother

(Arthur Kennedy) sold the guns to the Indians in retaliation for the old man's repressive treatment of them. When Kennedy kills Nicol in an argument over a further cache of weapons, Crisp believes Stewart is responsible. In another memorable sequence, the half-blind figure charges on horseback, wildly shooting his pistol, as Stewart stands facing him and fires his rifle with his unwounded left hand to make Crisp's horse rear and throw him. Mann moves the camera behind each of the men in turn, reinforcing the sense of imminent impact, while one jerky traveling shot behind Crisp seems to crystallize the man's crazed determination.

When Stewart discovers that Kennedy is the man he's after, there are some magnificent images of him riding across the CinemaScope screen silhouetted against a night sky. The two men finally face each other at the remaining wagonload of rifles on the side of a hill. Confronting the unarmed Kennedy, Stewart savors the long-awaited moment of revenge. "I came a thousand miles to kill you. I'm not going to rush it—I've waited a long time for this." But before he can shoot, the approach of a bunch of Indians to collect the weapons means that he needs Kennedy to push the wagon over the edge of the hill to keep the redskins from obtaining them. Even though Kennedy does most of the work shifting the wagon, it is Stewart who is breathing the hardest afterwards with his intense hatred. He seems all the more angry—with himself—when he finds that he can't kill Kennedy and gasps, "Get away from me!"

As at the end of *The Naked Spur*, the Stewart character has overcome the demons in his soul. Even though he could hardly kill an unarmed man under the censorship of that time and retain his status as a hero, it is entirely appropriate that he should refrain because Kennedy did not directly kill his kid brother and isn't basically an evil man, just a flawed one (Kennedy was an especially skilled actor at suggesting ingrained weakness of character). In fact, the real villain and real sufferer could be said to be the stern Donald Crisp—but even he has his reasons and a woman (Aline MacMahon) to forgive him.

The Man from Laramie proved to be the last collaboration between Mann and Stewart and a wholly fitting conclusion if there had to be one. Mann saw it in many respects as a summing up of their past work. "I wanted to recapitulate, somehow, my five years of collaboration with Jimmy Stewart: that piece distilled our relationship. I reprised themes and situations by pushing them to their paroxysms. So the band of cowboys surround Jimmy and rope him as they did before in *Bend of the River* . . . but here I shot him through the hand! There are some scenes that I thought very successful: the sequence on the salt flats, the one in the market place, the one where Arthur Kennedy returns with Alex Nicol's body . . . I benefited from CinemaScope and from a perfectly harmonious crew: the shooting was easy and the film went very well. Do you know that Jimmy wound up back in first place in the Top Ten?" It's a great pity there are few opportunities to see *The Man from Laramie* in its original CinemaScope because Mann's skill in composing for its proportions is exhilarating and the entire film is visually the finest of their collaborations (by a short lead) as well as being as dramatically satisfying as any of them.

Stewart's next project, *Jewel of Bengal* at 20th Century-Fox, fell through. The Indian spectacular would have co-starred him with Jane Russell. It was quite a few months before he was back before the cameras for Hitchcock's *The Man Who Knew Too Much* but he did fill in time by making his television acting debut in a half-hour production for the *G. E. Theater* slot called *The Windmill*, shown in April 1955 and based on one of the old *Six Shooter* scripts for radio. He played a poverty-stricken rancher called Joe Newman who needs money to build a windmill to provide water for his spread. When he is refused a bank loan, he is forced to reveal the well-kept secret of his true identity . . . Stewart was reunited with his co-star of *The Jackpot*, Barbara Hale, and with John McIntire from *Winchester '73* and *The Far Country*.

Stewart stepped into the role that Leslie Banks had played in the original *The Man Who Knew Too Much*. He was ideal casting for Hitchcock. He made the most of some slight humorous angles early on as doctor Ben McKenna, on holiday with his wife Jo (Doris Day) in Morocco, visiting a local restaurant and trying to work out what to do with his legs when seated on a low cushion, leaning back to find there is no back, then having trouble tearing the bread and cackhandedly trying to eat a strip of meat using

[130]

only two fingers in the local manner before giving up and chewing on it in a more comfortable way.

He was also especially good in conveying the emotional anguish of being the father of a kidnapped child. He is established as a volatile figure when he becomes fairly irate on seeing Bernard (Daniel Gélin) in the restaurant after the Frenchman has canceled his invitation for them to dine with him. Following the trail to London, to a taxidermist's premises in Camden Town, he goes off the handle trying to obtain news of his son when in fact it is a false lead and nobody knows anything.

There is a slight suggestion of the kind of career conflict that occurred in *Rear Window* but here it has been resolved in Stewart's favor. Doris Day has given up her career as a musical comedy star so that he can practice medicine in Indianapolis. But the film gives her two chances to sing—the Academy Award winning, chart-topping "Que Sera, Sera" as a lullaby to her son and a song at a reception in a foreign embassy so that Stewart can sneak away to search the building for the missing boy.

The lad was taken to prevent Stewart revealing what he knows about an assassination plot. He arrives at the Albert Hall in an attempt to prevent the murder taking place and is seen arguing with the various tiers of authority—a constable, then a sergeant, etc. "I had one helluva speech which more or less explained the plot," recalled Stewart. "Well, suddenly Hitch told me to cut all the talk and act with my hands and face because, he said, the words were drowning out the playing of the London Symphony Orchestra. And the orchestra, he said, was more pleasant to listen to than my voice!" In fact, the emphasis on the music serves to remind us of the approaching passage with the cymbals which is the moment for the assassination attempt. Stewart may have his dialogue cut but he does get a chance to grapple with the gunman in his box after Doris Day's scream has disturbed his aim and to knock villain Bernard Miles down the stairs at the embassy.

The whole film, while pleasant enough, is too simple and straightforward to register as major Hitchcock or even important Stewart. The casting of Doris Day and the introduction of songs suggests an attempt to bolster the box-office appeal of a weak

[131]

project, one to which Hitch had given his most imaginative effort twenty years before (with a tense rooftop finale that is omitted the second time around). Compared to his arduous location work for Mann, Stewart again has it easy with Hitchcock, who readily used doubles and back projection, although the actor did some filming in London and Morocco before the picture was finished in Hollywood.

Stewart was not put out by Hitch's total lack of instructions, but Doris Day was. Stewart tried to reassure her that she *was* pleasing the director and explained to Doris's biographer A. E. Hotchner, "He didn't believe in rehearsals. He preferred to let the actor figure things out for himself. He refers to this method as planned spontaneity.' Of course, this is confusing to an actor who is accustomed to a director who 'participates' in a scene. In the beginning, it certainly threw Doris for a loop. Hitchcock believes that if you sit down with an actor and analyze a scene you run the danger that the actor will act that scene with his head rather than his heart, or guts."

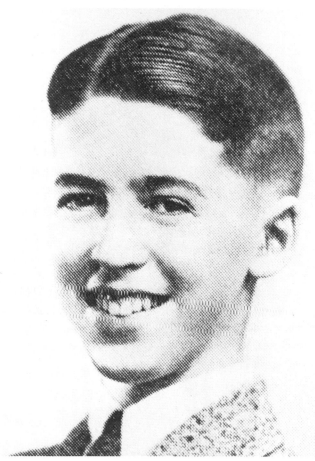

Soft and sensitive with Margaret Sullavan in the film she obtained for
him, *Next Time We Love* (1936)

Earnestly hers – with Ginger Rogers in his comedy break, *Vivacious Lady* (1938)

As the honest senator accusing a corrupt colleague (Claude Rains)
in *Mr Smith Goes to Washington* (1939)

At the climax of
Destry Rides Again
(1939) as the
mortally wounded
Marlene Dietrich
collapses against
him

With Genevieve Tobin and Charles Ruggles in *No Time for Comedy* (1940)

The fiancé (John Howard) is not amused but the ex-husband (Cary Grant)
doesn't seem too put out as Jimmy Stewart turns up with a blissfully
inebriated Katharine Hepburn in *The Philadelphia Story* (1940)

The romantic scene everyone remembers from *It's a Wonderful Life* (1947) –
with Donna Reed outside the old Granville place

Fearful he may be an intellectual accomplice in murder, Stewart starts to
raise the lid of the chest in *Rope* (1948) watched by the two anxious thrill
killers (Farley Granger and John Dall)

A pause in backyard baseball practice for Jimmy Stewart and June Allyson in *The Stratton Story* (1949)

With Debra Paget as his Indian bride in *Broken Arrow* (1950)

The new deadly serious look as a western star in the early 1950s

Immediately after the wedding ceremony – Gloria and James Stewart on 9 August 1949

Mr and Mrs Stewart with the seven-month-old twins, Kelly (left) and Judy, around Christmas 1951

The closing shot in *Winchester '73* (1950): the battered, exhausted James
Stewart returns from killing his brother to the arms of Shelley Winters

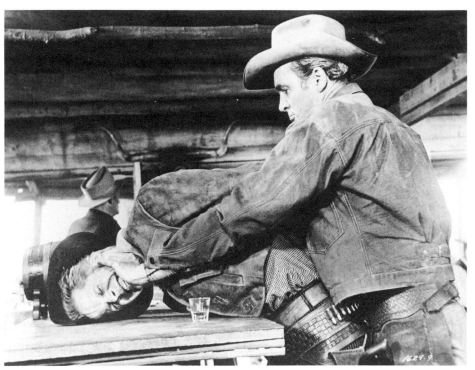

James Stewart impatiently extracts information from Dan Duryea in *Winchester '73* (1950)

James Stewart is on about his invisible rabbit again in *Harvey* (1950), much
to the dismay of his sister played by Josephine Hull

As Carbine Williams in the 1952 film of that name, with the man he was portraying at left, his father Alexander Stewart behind his pointing finger, his mother, and his wife Gloria

The band leader is reluctantly lured onto the dance floor by his wife (June Allyson) at a surprise party in their home in *The Glenn Miller Story* (1953)

As the complacent photographer of *Rear Window* (1954) with Grace Kelly as his perfect fiancée

Discussing a point with director Anthony Mann on location for *The Man from Laramie* (1955)

And conferring with Alfred Hitchcock on the set of *The Man Who Knew Too Much* (1956)

In *Vertigo* (1958) with Kim Novak as the woman he has rescued from drowning and brought to his apartment

The torn panties from *Anatomy of a Murder* (1959). In the witness box is Kathryn Grant

Jimmy Stewart and Gary Cooper as lookalikes on the set of *The FBI Story* (1959) with director Mervyn LeRoy

The famous long take on the riverbank with Stewart and Richard Widmark
in *Two Rode Together* (1961)

As Wyatt Earp, about to operate on Ken Curtis's foot in *Cheyenne Autumn*
(1964) with Chuck Roberson holding his legs and Elizabeth Allen's Miss
Plantagenet watching in the background

John Wayne argues that the only effective law is that of the gun to James
Stewart's tenderfoot lawyer in *The Man Who Shot Liberty Valance* (1962)

With Glynis Johns as his wife in *Dear Brigitte* (1965)

Resting between
scenes on *Firecreek*
(1968) with Henry Fonda

Doing his best in the final shootout in *Firecreek* (1968)

As the former jailbird with the glass eye in *Fools' Parade* (1971)

With John Wayne in *The Shootist* (1976)

As General Sternwood in the hothouse in *The Big Sleep* (1978)

A studio portrait from the late seventies

13

A Hitch and Two Mishaps

With eight box-office hits in a row behind him, it seemed unlikely that Stewart would give Warner Bros. what Jack L. Warner a few years later called "the most disastrous failure we ever had." It showed that audiences shouldn't be taken for granted. They still wanted to see Jimmy Stewart but they didn't want to see him play Charles A. Lindbergh in *The Spirit of St. Louis* or perhaps they never realized what the film was about. Its writer Wendell Mayes commented: "I think they should have called it *The Lindbergh Story* or something like that because when they put it out as *The Spirit of St. Louis* everyone seemed to think it was an old musical and they didn't know what the Spirit of St. Louis was."

Lindbergh had been a great hero of Stewart's ever since he made his 3,600-mile, 33½-hour non-stop flight in his one-engined monoplane from New York to Paris in May 1927, and Stewart chased after the part even though he was forty-seven years old and the film showed Lindy at age twenty-five and younger. He was helped because the producer was Leland Hayward, his agent in the thirties, former husband of Margaret Sullavan, and a good friend; and because Hollywood was desperately short of young leading men who could carry a picture. Co-writer and director Billy Wilder did search for a younger actor but those he considered suitable like John Kerr (of *Tea and Sympathy*) turned him down.

When Stewart pressed his claim, "They came up with the objection that I was too fat. Now I've been called many things in my time, but never too fat. Anyway, I was determined to play

Lindbergh ... so I went on a really tough diet. And it paid off! After two or three weeks they told me I had got the part, but at the same time to please stop dieting, because I was beginning to look terribly ill; my face was really gaunt and I had black rings under my eyes."

Stewart met Lindbergh just once for dinner before making the movie. "And I suddenly realized I had no questions to ask him," said the actor. He studied old newsreels and read what Lindbergh had written. "It didn't give me any help," reported Stewart. The film was an expensive one ($6 million), in part because Wilder took his cameras along the route of the historic flight and filmed the views of Newfoundland, Ireland, Britain and France that the aviator would have had. With variable weather conditions, costs mounted. There were no other stars besides Stewart; all the other parts were completely subsidiary.

The great problem was how to maintain interest in the very lengthy passages of Stewart flying alone in the aircraft. Part of the answer was to introduce flashbacks, largely comic in tone. We see the young flyer in camp with a special extension to his bunk to accommodate his long legs, and buying his first plane and barnstorming through middle America. Another partial answer was to introduce a fly with whom Stewart can converse during part of the flight.

Stewart puts on a convincing display of youthful enthusiasm telling his backers why he knows he'll succeed in the flight: "When I was a kid and the smallest in my class, I made up my mind to be six foot three—and I made it with a half inch to spare!" He is exuberant greeting people down below during his flight, yelling "Hey!" to a motorcyclist as he crosses Nova Scotia, calling out "Which way to Ireland?" to a fisherman in the ocean, and greeting an Irishman at Dingle Bay. He enlivens the film in such moments to a degree that a more reserved, stolid actor like John Kerr could not have managed.

There were opportunities for Stewart to do some flying himself before the cameras but he was upset when insurance officials vetoed his making the landing at the climax of the film at the reconstructed Le Bourget airport, set up just outside Paris in the Cheyreuse valley. A Warner Bros. spokesman bluntly explained:

"This is a tricky airstrip, a tricky plane to fly, and Stewart is a valuable piece of property." Stunt pilot Stan Reaver brought the plane down and Stewart took over for cockpit close-ups when it had landed.

Charles Lindbergh was reserved in his praise of Stewart's performance, complimenting him only on one moment—when he taps a couple of instrument panels to make sure the needles haven't stuck. This was a touch added by Stewart from his own experience of flying. In fact, Stewart's playing is really extremely skillful, maintaining audience interest and sympathy virtually on his own. He is more human here than in the westerns, prey to fatigue and boredom, pushing himself to the limits of endurance, while retaining that old determination to succeed in a quest. The lively, humorous flashbacks contrast with the solitary monotony of the flight. It was a difficult subject and the result far more to the credit of Stewart and Billy Wilder than the box-office figures would indicate.

Ever since *The Man from Laramie*, Aaron Rosenberg and the new heads of Universal had been after Stewart and Anthony Mann to make another western there. They offered a new Borden Chase script, *Night Passage*, which Stewart accepted and Mann provisionally agreed to direct. But Mann had begun to tire of Chase: "Borden had been an ideal screenwriter for a long time, but he always worked too much in the same way. The story was one of such incoherence that I said: 'The audience isn't going to understand any of it!' . . . But Jimmy was very set on that film. He had to play the accordion and do a bunch of stunts that actors adore. He didn't care about the script at all and I abandoned the production. The film was a nearly total failure and Jimmy has always held it against me . . ."

It seems Mann may have directed a few scenes before departing to undertake another western, *The Tin Star*, at Paramount with Stewart's old chum Henry Fonda starring. In any case, a new director had to be found quickly and it was decided to take a chance on James Neilson. "He was a television director, nice fellow," recalled Chase. "Jimmy Stewart wanted him . . . But he wasn't strong enough. It was very difficult." Stewart must have wished he'd stayed with *Designing Woman*, even without Grace

Kelly, as that had just gone into production and turned out to be quite a good comedy that would have suited Stewart far more than it did Gregory Peck.

Night Passage isn't a total write-off. It was photographed in Technicolor's new "horizon-spanning" wide screen process Technirama and some of the vistas (particularly the shots taken on a train snaking its way around the side of a mountain) are breathtaking on a theater screen. And it does have a great final shootout at an old mill, the only scene with real vigor and excitement in the entire film.

Stewart threw himself into the action scenes with all the energy and alertness he had given Anthony Mann. In this climax, he did far more than any other western actor would have done to make you really feel he was in a dangerous spot, reacting to bullets flying around him, moving fast when he changed position, and taking great care with the aiming of each shot instead of haphazardly blazing away. Earlier, there's a fight with Robert Wilke's Concho that has an intensity reminiscent of the scraps in the Mann films.

And Stewart shows great emotion at the demise of his kid brother, the outlaw Utica Kid (Audie Murphy), at the end of the film, after he is shot by Dan Duryea's dastardly Whitey. Stewart cradles the body and, as others arrive, looks up proudly because Murphy died saving his life. "I'll take care of my brother," says Stewart, finally admitting that the notorious bandit is his blood and kin.

Unfortunately, Audie Murphy is too sweet an actor to hold up his end in what ought to be a lively relationship between the brothers, and the key event when Stewart as a railroad troubleshooter caught Murphy attempting a hold-up, lectured him and gave him a horse to make a getaway, happened well in the past. The part called for a more obstreperous performer to make it work, someone like Alex Nicol who animated the conflict in *The Man from Laramie* so well.

The film opens with Stewart still hanging around the railroad five years after he lost his job and the respect of his girl (Elaine Stewart). For the first time, Stewart is noticeably white-haired, an old man eking out a living playing the accordion, his hat laid out to receive tips as rail gangs dance with the painted ladies or their plain wives, or simply accompanying himself singing "Follow the River" to the boy (Brandon de Wilde) as they sit on a flat car and the train wends its way upwards. (The accordion comes in useful much later in the film to dislodge a lantern so that Stewart can escape from a tight spot—but it seems wrong that it should simply be left to burn.)

After three payrolls are lost to a band of train robbers led by Duryea and including Audie Murphy, Stewart gets a crack at safeguarding the next consignment of money. He manages to hide it in Brandon de Wilde's lunchbox when another hold-up happens but the boy rides off with the gang and Stewart has to follow them (even though the gang are hungry, they seemingly never spot the lunchbox and so don't discover the money). Dan Duryea proves to be a somewhat comical gang boss—the actor's performance is as much out of control as his leadership of the outlaws—and Robert Wilke becomes the principal menace. By then the entire drama is falling apart until the end gun battle wraps everything up.

Perhaps Mann was right to drop the picture and no amount of re-working could have tightened the script. *Night Passage* is watchable enough but a far cry from the splendid set of films that Stewart and Mann had done together. For the director's part, he still hoped to work with Stewart. "I'd love to use him again," he said in 1965, "but I haven't had a script. I couldn't use him in *El Cid*; I couldn't use him in *God's Little Acre, [The Fall of the] Roman Empire*; I couldn't have used him in lots of films. It has nothing to do with him; it's just the films are entirely out of his element. With the westerns, he had a great quality." But Mann died in 1967 before anything suitable came up.

In the autumn of 1956, as Stewart began filming *Night Passage*, he signed with Hitchcock to star in *From Among the Dead*, later retitled *Vertigo*. It was not shot until a year later, because of script problems. Stewart filled in the gap with two more television productions for the half-hour *G. E. Theater* slot hosted by Ronald Reagan. They were stories that he had retained from *The Six-Shooter* radio series.

In *The Town with a Past*, Stewart was the curious stranger who helps an eccentric old woman hold on to an apparently worked-out silver mine against pressure from the townsfolk who want her to sell out to the railroad. More interesting was the western version of Charles Dickens' *A Christmas Carol,* because for the first and only time Stewart turned director. Richard Eyer played the small boy disillusioned by Christmas who runs away from home and meets a character called Bart, portrayed by Stewart, who tells him the Dickens story but sets it in the old West. John McIntire appeared as Ebenezer Scrooge. In providing an off-screen narration, Stewart didn't have to act in the main story and could concentrate on directing the players. Fifteen years later he recalled, "I liked directing that very well . . . I would welcome that type of directorial chore if it comes along." But it wasn't to happen.

The Hitchcock film was also delayed by leading lady complications when Vera Miles had to withdraw owing to pregnancy and Columbia's rising star Kim Novak was chosen instead. Studio boss Harry Cohn used the opportunity to strike a deal whereby Columbia obtained Stewart's services for two pictures in exchange for what was stated to be his usual salary at the time, ten per cent of the gross. The actor was not altogether enthusiastic about his change of co-star. "I was alarmed when I saw her first—this great big busty blonde, twice the weight I was," Stewart recalled. "But it worked. It was there. We had 'the chemistry.'"

Vertigo provided the most emotionally complex and demanding role Stewart ever had. The result was one of his most satisfying performances, a totally convincing portrait of an ageing detective in the grip of a romantic obsession. The story is told in such a way that we can identify with Stewart's developing fascination with the woman he is hired to follow.

His Scottie Ferguson is a loner—"Some people prefer it that way." He was once engaged at college to a woman (Barbara Bel Geddes) who still adores him. He has to leave the San Francisco police force after developing a fear of heights during a rooftop chase—and his wearing of a corset from a back injury results in more itches and comic suffering as in *Rear Window* but the mood is never as light as in that earlier film. He is engaged by an old college friend (Tom Helmore) to follow the latter's wife (Kim

Novak) who seems to be possessed by a spirit out of the past. Stewart trails her to the tombstone of a Spanish woman Carlotta Valdes who died a hundred years before, to an art gallery where she sits absorbed in the same woman's portrait, to a faded apartment house where she rents a room. He learns the tragic history of the real Carlotta who committed suicide aged twenty-six. Consequently, he is not surprised when Novak tries to kill herself by jumping into San Francisco Bay beneath the Golden Gate Bridge.

Stewart dives in to rescue her and brings her back to his apartment where he undresses her and puts her to bed. Of course, we aren't allowed to see Stewart disrobing her but this is made evident when she comes around and emerges from the bedroom into his living room wearing only his dressing gown. The fact that he has brought her all this way to recover and to his place rather than her husband's clearly indicates his urge to possess her. Now that he can openly talk to her, he becomes more and more hooked. The next day he joins her on her wanderings instead of following her and when they reach a redwood forest on the coast tries to justify his ever-increasing attachment to her: "I'm responsible for you now. You know, the Chinese say that once you've saved a person's life, you're responsible for it forever. So I'm committed." She tells him about her premonitions of death, and shudders, clinging to him for protection; he comforts and kisses her as waves crash behind them. His passion for her is now fully declared. She is his "darling."

Recognizing the old Spanish mission of her dreams, he takes her there to try and free her. She breaks away from him, rushes up the bell-tower and apparently throws herself off. Stewart is affected by his vertigo and can't follow quickly enough to save her. He sees a body plunge past before he can reach the top of the stairs. Harshly criticized by the coroner for his hesitancy, he has a nervous breakdown and spends three months in a sanatorium, withdrawn into himself, suffering from acute melancholia.

On his release, he takes to wandering the streets and keeps imagining he sees his lost love. Then a year later he does spot an ordinary shop assistant, also played by Novak, who resembles the dead woman closely. Stewart bullies her into making herself over

[139]

to look like the woman he loved. Hitchcock pinpointed part of the macabre appeal of this: "That scene in *Vertigo* where James Stewart forces Miss Kim Novak to alter her whole personality by altering her lipstick, hairstyle, even hair-tint—for me it has the compulsion of a striptease in reverse. The woman is made insecure by being forced to make up, not take off." "Please, Judy," Stewart implores her softly to put her specially dyed hair up to complete the transformation. His awful desperation persuades her, plus the fact that she does love him—for, as Hitchcock reveals to us but not to Stewart, at this most unexpected moment in the film—she *was* the woman Stewart had come to love previously, employed by the husband to masquerade as his wife so that the real wife could be pushed off the bell-tower with Stewart unable to save her because of his known fear of heights.

As Hitchcock has explained, he threw away a surprise twist for the greater suspense of having the audience know the truth and wonder when Stewart will cotton on and what he will do about it. There's also the advantage that it distracts attention from the absurdity of the murder plot (suppose Stewart had examined the body on the ground? How could his time of arrival at the tower be accurately predicted?) and concentrates on Stewart and his unstable state of mind. We can also share Novak's worry, because she has come to care for Stewart and regrets deceiving him, and her distress because he has no interest in her as herself, only in the woman she had pretended to be.

When the transformation is complete, Stewart gratefully and passionately embraces her. But later when she inadvertently gives away her secret, he brutally compels her to go through the bell-tower episode again so that he can be "free of the past" and have a "second chance." He conquers his vertigo in his anger at being deceived and forces the details of the murder plot from her at the top of the bell-tower, his face in darkness as she stands in the harsh light being interrogated. Even as she confesses, Hitchcock keeps us from being too involved in the details of the plot by having us wonder whether Stewart will forgive her and accept her. Though he does seize her and kiss her feverishly, his reconstruction of the crime goes one stage further beyond his control and this time she does fall to her death. There is a final, unforgettable image of Stewart standing, arms stretched out after her, looking down where she has just fallen. At the start of the film, he clung onto some guttering for dear life with an abyss stretching out below him; now he confronts another abyss and may well jump after her, since he has nothing left to live for.

To be deprived twice of the woman he loves is undoubtedly the harshest fate to befall a Stewart character on screen. (There is no way that he could ever accept the ordinary, bespectacled Barbara Bel Geddes with her sensible, practical outlook.) Once again, Stewart is most convincing as a man obsessed. He looks his age now (forty-nine) and so there is the added sense of a man grasping at a last chance of happiness with a woman half his years. Yet he doesn't lose the audience's respect. The vivid depiction of his near-fall to death at the start enables us to identify with his acrophobia; his gradual involvement with Novak is sympathetically handled; and his gentle and caring manner causes her to fall in love with him even while she deceives him. (Novak's performance is marvelous: she combines allure with a sense of timidity that makes her seem to be in need of protection.) Stewart can't be blamed for falling in love with a client's wife but there is something of the voyeur of *Rear Window* in his spying on her and a real sickness in his obsession with recreating her through another woman. As Hitchcock put it succinctly: "The man wants to go to bed with a woman who's dead; he is indulging in a form of necrophilia." Once again, Stewart's image of niceness smooths over the more disturbing aspects of a character.

In his recent book on Hitchcock's life, Donald Spoto records that Stewart kept after the director to appear in his next project. But Hitch knew that *North by Northwest* was more suited to Cary Grant (the role being that of a suave figure suddenly deprived of the crutches of civilized metropolitan life). Truffaut discussed the two actors in his book-length interview with Hitchcock, suggesting to the director: "It might seem as if Cary Grant and James Stewart were interchangeable in your work, but you actually use each one in a different way. With Cary Grant the picture is more humorous, and with James Stewart the emphasis is on emotion." Hitchcock agreed, and as *North by Northwest* was a comedy thriller, Grant was the obvious choice. There were discussions between the director and Stewart about another film in the early seventies but they came to nothing. *Vertigo* was the fourth and last film they did together.

14

Finishing the Fifties

Without Hitchcock and Mann, Stewart's career seemed to be floundering a little in 1958 and 1959 as he tried a varied set of roles.

Sophisticated comedy had never been his forte and he was out of place in *Bell, Book and Candle*, Columbia's film version of John Van Druten's 1950 stage hit. He played New York book publisher Shepherd Henderson who falls among witches and warlocks in modern Greenwich Village. As *Time* magazine's critic aptly put it, "James Stewart stumbles around most of the time with a vaguely blissful expression—rather like a comic-strip character who has just been socked by Popeye." He was teamed again with Kim Novak who was credible but monotonous as the witch who decides she wants Stewart when he's about to be married to an old college rival of hers played by Janice Rule. Novak puts a spell on Stewart so that he is bewitched by her and calls off the marriage (Janice Rule is a cold specimen with some nasty habits, so Novak is doing him a favor.) Even when Novak confesses, Stewart doesn't believe what has happened to him until she demonstrates her powers. He seeks the advice of other witches and drinks a special brew to free himself to pursue Janice Rule again, only to find she is unforgiving. Meanwhile, Novak finds that she has lost her powers and has become normal because she is in love.

The trouble with this kind of comedy is that anything can happen according to the complicated rules of witchcraft and there is no freedom of action for Stewart. In the urbane hands of Rex

Harrison who starred in the original stage production (as well as in the similarly fantastic *Blithe Spirit*) the part could be milked for a certain bemused delight in being taken over and manipulated, but in Stewart's hands the character seemed merely confused by it all.

Even with crisp Technicolor and a powerful supporting cast (Jack Lemmon as a warlock, Hermione Gingold and Elsa Lanchester as two witches, Ernie Kovacs as a witchcraft expert), the film fizzled rather than sparkled.

Stewart may have felt he owed Warner Bros a solid box-office winner after the debacle of *The Spirit of St. Louis*. He certainly gave them one by starring in *The FBI Story*, as Chip Hardesty, a veteran member of the Federal Bureau of Investigation who lectures recruits on his experiences, cueing flashbacks to episodes of Bureau activity fighting racists, gangsters, Nazi agents and Commies. He is even seen twenty-five years before as one of the earliest agents with only token make-up adjustments, and appears to have been a key participant in almost all the Bureau's most notable cases.

Stewart's co-star was Vera Miles. ("Nice girl, but her teeth were too shiny—reflected in my eyes," joked Stewart years later.) Seeing her with Stewart made it impossible to believe she could ever have been very effective in *Vertigo*; here they impart a mild warmth to the domestic scenes as they play out some half-heartedly written career-versus-marriage conflicts. She leaves Stewart for a year but then decides to accept the constant moves and dangers.

Terribly dated by its obsequious attitude towards the FBI, shown never putting a foot wrong (but operating clandestinely in South America during World War Two), it is highly unreal in ripe Technicolor, and vastly overlong at two-and-a-half hours' running time. It could have done with the more incisive handling that Anthony Mann brought to the equally reverential *Strategic Air Command* instead of the anonymity of Mervyn LeRoy's direction. There is one good joke at Stewart's expense: "A fella as thin as you are—nobody'd know where to find you," says an insurance salesman when he declines a policy in case he is murdered.

It was a wise career decision on Stewart's part to make *Anatomy of a Murder*, Otto Preminger's film of a bestseller about a murder trial, in which he played the small-town defense lawyer Paul Biegler. It was a large and demanding role, written by Wendell Mayes without Stewart in mind and not adapted for him in any way. Stewart had to go to Upper Michigan in the spring of 1959 as it was shot entirely on location there and he had a huge amount of dialogue to learn as he was involved in almost every scene of the 160-minute film, getting only one free afternoon during the eight weeks of intensive shooting.

It was a dangerous part as far as his reputation was concerned since an allegation of rape was discussed in clinical detail, using words that had never been previously heard in American movies, and he handled a pair of torn panties, a primary piece of evidence (it produces a snigger from the court until quashed by the judge who reminds everyone—the theater audience included—that it is a serious matter under discussion). This frankness and explicit detail undoubtedly made the film into a considerable box-office (and critical) success but Preminger could never be accused of crudely exploiting the subject. Still it was all a bit of a shock for some of Stewart's long-time fans to find him in such an adult role and they wrote letters of protest. Against that, Stewart was named Best Actor of the Year by the New York film critics and won an Academy Award nomination, along with Laurence Harvey (for *Room at the Top*), Jack Lemmon (for *Some Like It Hot*), Paul Muni (for *The Last Angry Man*) and Charlton Heston, the winner for *Ben-Hur*.

Looking back now, Stewart should undoubtedly have won on merit. He brilliantly inhabits the part, vividly conveying the private side of the character as well as the somewhat different image he chooses to present in court. We see him first as a resigned bachelor, returning late at night to his untidy apartment from a fishing expedition with a catch of trout and downing a few shots of whisky with his old crony, Arthur O'Connell's Parnell McCarthy, and relaxing as jazz blares out of the radio.

When the lawyer is invited to defend Ben Gazzara's Lt. Manion (on a charge of murdering the bartender he alleges raped his wife), Stewart doesn't rate the chances of acquittal highly. Furthermore, Gazzara is cocky and disagreeable, banking on "the unwritten law" to get him off and choosing "an irresistible

[145]

impulse" and "temporary insanity" as lines of defense from those suggested to him by Stewart. "You don't have to love him—just defend him!" says his secretary, played with acerbic humor by Eve Arden, pointing out that Stewart hasn't had enough money to pay her for weeks.

Stewart is wily enough to use his "honest" appearance to impress a jury. "I'm just a simple country lawyer," he says, hoping to gain their sympathy when George C. Scott's high-powered prosecutor is brought in from the big city to mow him down. Stewart dresses the sexy wife (Lee Remick) (who enjoys flirting with him) in a prim outfit for her court appearance to disguise from the jury her normally provocative manner. (This role was originally assigned to Lana Turner, but Stewart's reunion with his co-star of *Ziegfeld Girl* was terminated when she refused to wear the costumes Preminger wanted.) And Stewart tricks a police witness (coached, but not well enough, by the prosecution) into admitting the vital issue of rape into the trial.

What makes *Anatomy of a Murder* so interesting is that the issues are not clear-cut. "People aren't just good or bad—they're many things," says Stewart. In a conventional film, like *Call Northside 777*, the hero would ensure the freedom of somebody who proves to be innocent. Here we are tempted to think Gazzara is guilty (because we don't like him for one thing, and because Stewart thinks he is) but neither Stewart nor we know the truth of the matter. There is no convenient flashback to the events described. Even the psychiatrists judging Gazzara's state of mind reach diametrically opposing viewpoints. We see more than the jurors but we still have to make up our own minds.

Rather, the point is that Gazzara is entitled to be defended even if he is guilty and it is Stewart's job to present his client in the most favorable light. Stewart does a fine professional job of getting Gazzara the benefit of the doubt. That proves to be his sole satisfaction, except for the good done his reputation, as an irresistible impulse grips Gazzara to run off with the wife he apparently detests and leave his bill unpaid.

Stewart was used to having competent performers around him but *Anatomy of a Murder* was a case where his work was sharpened by exceptionally keen competition for the acting honors. The novice actor, sixty-eight-year-old Joseph C. Welch, who played the kindly, witty judge, was far from left behind (but then he had been acting in a way all through his career as a celebrated lawyer). Sordid as the subject may be, *Anatomy of a Murder* provides the exhilaration of seeing great ensemble acting rather than one or two outstanding performances.

The second film Stewart made in 1959 tried far too hard to make a significant statement. Working again for William Goetz's company at Columbia, Stewart starred in *The Mountain Road*, the kind of thoughtful war film in which he could appear without qualms. It did nothing to glorify conflict—quite the reverse—and Stewart played a jittery officer hard put to cope with the stress of commanding an eight-man demolition team in south-east China in 1944. His Major Baldwin makes an honorable decision not to fly out as the Japanese advance brings them within forty miles of his position: instead, he stays behind with his team to blow up the airfield and retreat by truck, destroying the bridges, roads and arms dumps useful to the enemy along a 230-mile stretch between Liuchow and Kweiyan.

But Stewart finds that the never-ending stream of refugees who hamper his work are more of a trial than the enemy. The English-speaking widow of a Chinese general tries to explain their point of view: how they need the roads he is wrecking to live, how they need the bridges he is blowing to escape themselves. His irritation turns to hot anger when one of his men is killed in a riot while distributing food to the starving people and his fury knows no bounds when two more of his men are killed by Chinese army deserters. Despite the anguished plea of the widow, he destroys an entire village, killing men, women and children, to halt the advancing enemy. But he comes to realize that he has misused his power.

The main problem is that the film makes its case too explicit. Despite some spectacular explosions (filmed, though, in black-and-white) and a tentative love scene between Stewart and the Chinese woman while sheltering from a series of blasts under a truck, the picture was too downbeat and remote in its concerns to attract huge English-speaking audiences. It is a well-meant, honorable failure.

Also in 1959, Stewart made another foray into television. This time it was *Cinderella*'s turn to be westernized into *Cindy's Fella* as a Christmas attraction and actor Gower Champion directed the comedy. Stewart played a Yankee peddler, Azel Dorsey, who is given a helping hand in a saloon brawl by George Gobel's wandering troubadour known as The Drifter. The latter, plucking his guitar, lures Stewart to the farm of a Widow Parks and her three daughters but Stewart proves to be no Prince Charming to George Gobel's fairy godmother.

15

Enter John Ford

JAMES STEWART WAS THE LAST big star to become one of the John Ford regulars. He and Richard Widmark had already been signed to appear in the western *Two Rode Together* at Columbia before Ford agreed to direct it, on condition that he could rewrite the script with one of his favorite writers, Frank Nugent. The result was a film extraordinarily similar in content to his 1956 masterpiece *The Searchers* but a complete contrast in mood and attitude. Both films concern the rescue of long-held white captives from the Comanches but whereas John Wayne's drawn-out quest to recover lost kin was a personal obsession in the earlier film, here Stewart's cynical Guthrie McCabe carries out his mission reluctantly and then only for financial gain.

Ford begins the film by showing Stewart, the indolent marshal of Tascosa, leaning back in his chair with his feet up on a porch rail. The image is one that Ford used for Henry Fonda's Wyatt Earp in the 1946 *My Darling Clementine.* Both are considerable lawmen. Stewart has only to mention his name to two pushy gamblers for them to clear out of town. But whereas Fonda was a man of complete integrity, Stewart operates as marshal by taking ten per cent of all the business done in Tascosa and is waited on hand and foot on the porch. He is, though, less than a match for saloon owner Belle Aragon, who wants to marry him for his wealth (this is a wonderfully spirited performance by Annelle Hayes, the ex-actress wife of Mark Stevens who was lured out of domesticity for the part). Honesty and idealism reside in the poorly-paid army officer played by Widmark, but they are accompanied by a naivete that helps weaken the character.

Dan Ford, John Ford's grandson, has reported that Ford directed the film with as little effort as possible, having lost interest before shooting began. Though it lacks visual splendor (and the color is grating), Ford still had too innate a sense of cinema for the film not to hold together. There is the famous 3¾-minute single take in which James Stewart discusses his relationship with Belle and reveals his high income to the envious Widmark as they sit on a river bank. Stewart recalled: "It was early in the morning and he was sort of grouchy and he walked out and for some reason put the camera in the river. He didn't have to put the camera in the river, but I think he did it because that meant that all the crew had to walk out up to their waists in the river. He's like that, and it was terribly cold. Widmark and I did this—it was a long, long scene—we did it and left." It's a comic scene and the two actors seem relaxed as they skillfully and playfully needle each other with the dialogue seeming almost improvised and spontaneous in the pauses and uneven rhythms of the conversation. It's a wonderful stretch of film to which the admiring François Truffaut paid tribute by copying it in *Jules and Jim*.

This is the first time that Stewart has played an unapologetically corrupt figure and he brings to it his flair for comedy to make his cynical attitude palatable, to turn Guthrie McCabe into an amusing opportunist. Refusing the Army's request that he should visit the Comanches and trade for their white captives in exchange for regular army pay, he is asked by the commander (John McIntire) if more money would influence his position. "Ye-es!" he responds with a comic vocal exaggeration that suggests it should never have been doubted, recovering to add more calmly "It might" as an invitation to further negotiations. This was one of the earliest westerns to present corruption in such a matter-of-fact, uncritical manner.

However, Stewart does show that he has some scruples. Even after he agrees to take on the job on a fee-per-head basis for the anxious kin clustered at the fort, he knows it's a fool's errand and advises one parent (John Qualen) to give up his quest since his now-sixteen-year-old daughter will have been fully integrated into Indian life and passed beyond rehabilitation (he still takes down the details when the man insists). He is disgusted by the request of Willis Bouchey's Henry Wringle who offers him a thousand dollars to bring back any white kid to make his wife happy. "You're like me—you make your own luck," says Bouchey. But Stewart is disgusted with himself for being like Bouchey and for accepting the offer. He gets drunk and is hilarious pretending to be more woozy than he actually is, mock saluting Widmark. Still under the influence, though, he is forced to look at a picture of a five-year-old who's been in Comanche hands for twelve years and he paints an unsparingly accurate portrait of the young buck he will have become. Here Stewart is not cruel to be kind but severely lacking in compassion.

He is compelled to take Widmark along with him into Indian territory, and contact is easily made. Stewart's attempt at deceiving the half-breed Comanche leader Quanah Parker over Widmark's identity makes sense but again is not the kind of honorable behavior seen in *Broken Arrow* or John Wayne's visit to an Indian chief in Ford's *She Wore a Yellow Ribbon*. Even the Comanche chief is devious, happy to stir up trouble for his rival Stone Calf by letting the latter's Spanish-American wife (Linda Cristal) go with Stewart. Stone Calf's attempt to reclaim his woman, armed only with a knife, is predictable and doomed since Stewart ruthlessly shoots him down. The Indians in this film are not viewed with any sympathy at all and their way of life is depicted as harsh and primitive, quite without the idyllic possibilities presented in *Broken Arrow*.

Stewart returns empty-handed except for a young buck he has taken against his will to get the thousand dollars from Bouchey, and the Spanish-Mexican woman. His attitudes begin to look less reprehensible when compared to what happens at the camp: Bouchey refuses to take the captive boy, disgusted by his animal behavior, and so becomes contemptible by not honoring his agreement; and the group of searchers then lynch the boy after a deranged woman amongst them sets him free and he kills her. Stewart sees a grace and elegance in the formerly aristocratic Linda Cristal and becomes disgusted by the hostile attitude taken towards her at the army post—the men refusing to partner her at a dance, the women sidling over to pry into her past, then scurrying away. Stewart denounces the group for their racism and declares that she was better treated by the Comanche. She decides to leave by the next stage.

Back in Tascosa, Stewart finds his deputy has assumed his position and style as marshal but he is merely amused and joins Cristal on the stage—having, as Widmark remarks, "found something he wants more than ten per cent of." So the Stewart character is reformed by love. Yet one doubts if his compassion would have been aroused had Stone Calf's woman been less attractive—he would have simply left her to fend for herself.

Ford makes no attempt to point any moral and the film does lack any real sense of urgency or purpose. There are such lapses as Stewart's drawing a gun on Widmark and threatening to really shoot him that seem absurdly out of character. Yet *Two Rode Together* is undeniably fascinating and, at times, richly amusing.

It is infinitely more engaging than Stewart's episode in the sprawling epic *How the West Was Won*, the first fictional film in Cinerama. He was billed tenth in the alphabetical listing of the $14.5 million film's major stars and was the first actor seen, in a montage accompanying Spencer Tracy's opening narration—as a mountain man on horseback in the 1830s, descending a rocky slope, leading a second horse loaded with pelts, then canoeing across a mountain lake and receiving a welcome at an Indian camp. These opening vistas are wonderful but the film is so ponderously written that only its spectacle in later sequences and its intimate John Ford Civil War vignette give it any impact.

Stewart's character, Linus Rawlings, is written as a rip-roaring bear of a man who claims to be "deep dark sinful" and anxious to whore, fight and drink when he comes down from the mountain. This is not James Stewart. Kirk Douglas or Ernest Borgnine or Lee Marvin, yes, but not the pleasant, agreeable Stewart. But to Carroll Baker's Eve Prescott, traveling with her family on the Ohio river to seek new farmland, he is an intriguing figure and she makes no bones about wanting him. "Ain't you being just a little bit forward?" he asks as he obliges her by telling her how pretty she is and embraces her. When she wants more, he says in a line typically cumbersome, "You make me feel like a man standing on a narrow ledge face to face with a grizzly bear—there just

[152]

ain't no ignoring the situation." The next morning, with Stewart gone, Baker has trouble convincing her incensed father (Karl Malden) that she didn't go too far.

Down river, Stewart falls into a den of thieves who relieve him of his furs and almost his life. When Carroll Baker's group are held up by the gang, Stewart starts a fight and saves them. But he insists to Baker that he's not cut out to be a husband and once again leaves. Then he hears that they've taken the wrong fork of the river and comes back to see if they've survived the dangerous rapids. She has, but her parents haven't. Stewart wants her to go to Pittsburgh but she insists on starting a farm right there in the wilderness. He agrees to settle down, and so the roaming trapper is tamed by an Eastern girl half his age. If Stewart looks exceedingly uncomfortable throughout, he is not alone—Gregory Peck is equally awkward attempting to play an expansive con man in the next episode. Fortunately, the use of Cinerama and skillful promotion ensured that, as in the case of *The Greatest Show on Earth*, the mass audience came and Stewart's career was unharmed.

The star was also making more appearances on television, not just in occasional drama but guesting as himself on comedy shows. With his wife Gloria he became an annual visitor to *The Jack Benny Show*, recording his 1961 contribution on August 14. That year he also provided the narration for a minor feature *X-15*, evidently attracted by its subject matter of test pilots' work at a California air base.

He and John Wayne had been in separate episodes of *How the West Was Won*. Now John Ford put them together in *The Man Who Shot Liberty Valance*. The film was curiously old-fashioned—Ford's first western in black-and-white for twelve years, and stripped of background life, theatrically lit. And both its stars were too old—ridiculously old, one would have thought, in the eyes of the mass audience—to take on roles as young men of ambition out West, but at least Stewart had also to be aged to play his character as a pipe-puffing, white-haired, stiff old man. Stewart would have been best suited to play Ransom Stoddard as a tenderfoot lawyer at about the time he played in *Mr. Smith Goes to Washington* since the part calls for the same youthful idealism, the same sense of optimism and decency that he embodied there.

[153]

At the start, his Stoddard is ruthlessly beaten up by Lee Marvin's Liberty Valance, leader of a band of robbers, when he tries to protect a lady during a stage hold-up. Marvin sniggers at his law books and tears them up before practicing his own law on Stewart with a whip. He is found by Wayne's Tom Doniphon and brought into the nearby town of Shinbone to be nursed by Wayne's girlfriend Hallie (Vera Miles) and the Swedish couple who run a restaurant (John Qualen and Jeanette Nolan). Wayne is amused at Stewart's determination to bring the outlaw to justice, knowing that the tubby town marshal (Andy Devine) is too scared to go near him.

Since there is no effective law, there is no need for Stewart's services as a lawyer and he has to become a dishwasher and waiter. But he finds a way to introduce progress by teaching Vera Miles and others to read and write, making some of them give up valuable time for the sake of a vague better future. Stewart's enthusiasm for liberty is contagious in the classroom—real liberty, not the selfish type represented by Lee Marvin's first name. Stewart continues to wear drab, Eastern-style suits—a measure of his insistence that the West must adjust to his ways. Wayne is just as dogged in resisting change. Stewart rejects his suggestion that the only way to deal with Lee Marvin is to kill him. "I don't want to kill him—I want to put him in jail," cries Stewart, who won't even pack a gun.

But a humiliating encounter with Marvin in the restaurant makes Stewart start to practice secretly with a revolver. Vera Miles is so worried she asks Wayne to help him. Wayne is annoyed at his girl's interest in Stewart and makes a fool out of him in a shooting lesson.

Stewart starts to organize the people to use their votes in favor of statehood, which upsets the big cattle interests who are afraid of losing their power. Marvin is hired to deal with Stewart. The inevitable confrontation occurs when Stewart refuses to slip out of town, picks up a gun and faces up to Marvin in a darkened street. Marvin dies in the shootout and Stewart becomes a hero, winning the love of Vera Miles for his courage and marksmanship. He goes on to become a distinguished senator in Washington. As he had predicted, the wilderness becomes a peaceful garden of plenty.

Stewart is so scrupulous he can't bring himself to capitalize on his fame as a killer until Wayne reveals that it was he who picked off Marvin from the shadows. However, Stewart can live with the pretense if not the reality, for the sake of achieving progress, even though he is always remembered as "the man who shot Liberty Valance."

In the framing story, Stewart has returned to Shinbone with his wife Vera Miles for the funeral of John Wayne who has died in obscurity, a bachelor, an unhappy man. To judge by Vera Miles' manner, her marriage has been overcast by the lie they've accepted. She is the more upset by Wayne's death and closer to his old friends than her husband. Stewart is glad to tell newspapermen the truth at last but they refuse to print it and insist on preserving the legend.

Stewart has represented progress and adaptability—his career is built on a lie, but a useful one. The Wayne character is a far more poignant figure: he did all the right things but he was too stubborn to move with the times and embrace progress. He and Lee Marvin are two sides of a coin, equals in virile energy and individualism (they face each other in the restaurant while Stewart lies helpless on the floor). Wayne needs Marvin to bring out his own strength. They both impede progress and it is only when they are out of the way that Stewart can rise up and take over. No film has more eloquently depicted the taming of the Wild West, the repression of individual liberty for the sake of the community and the nation, and the cost in human terms.

16

Fordian and Family Humor

Sтеwart моved straight from *The Man Who Shot Liberty Valance* to conclude a busy 1961 at 20th Century-Fox making the first of what proved to be a trio of family comedies, all written by Nunnally Johnson and directed by Henry Koster. Stewart claimed he was adopting a faster way of speaking: "A slow drawl would have made me seem to be padding my lines, and that's not a good thing. I like to think that my style from here on should be more precise, not so much hemming and hawing as before."

In *Mr. Hobbs Takes a Vacation*, Stewart was playing his own age as banker Roger Hobbs but looking much more spruce than he had for some time. He was felicitously teamed with the redoubtable Maureen O'Hara, playing his wife, Peggy, who mounts a family reunion at a holiday cottage instead of the quiet vacation he'd been hoping for. The film turns into a comic horror story. The cottage is a ruin; the cook quits; their young son won't shift from the television set; their teenage daughter won't venture out because of the braces on her teeth; their older daughter arrives with her unruly kids, fresh from a marital squabble; another daughter brings her husband who is eyed by a voluptuous beach blonde; and an aging yacht-club Romeo wooes O'Hara. With much exertion and embarrassment, Stewart solves everyone's problems so well that his wife books a return visit the following year. He extracts all the fun possible (and a bit more) from being locked in the bathroom with Marie Wilson as the wife of his unemployed son-in-law's prospective employer (John McGiver) and other farcical situations. Helped by the presence of teenagers' favorite, Fabian, the film had surprisingly wide appeal.

In 1962 Stewart could be seen in *Liberty Valance* and *Mr. Hobbs Takes a Vacation* while *How the West Was Won* premiered at the end of the year. However, he did no feature film work at all that year, the first time this had happened. He should have done another family comedy at Fox called *Take Her, She's Mine* but this was the year of the *Cleopatra* catastrophe and the studio had virtually closed down while the company sorted itself out. There were also plans for a film called *Eighth Air Force*, which didn't pan out at Warner Bros.

Stewart did continue his association with John Ford by starring in a television drama, *Flashing Spikes*, as an old baseball player whose career was ruined by a bribery scandal; he still likes to hang around the training grounds and he strikes up a friendship with a young first baseman (Patrick Wayne), who helps him clear his name.

In August, Darryl Zanuck, who had returned to take charge of Fox, reviewed Nunnally Johnson's script for *Take Her, She's Mine*—in which James Stewart was to play the father of a girl going to an American college—and demanded that some of the action be shifted to Europe to widen the film's appeal. Johnson obliged, reluctantly, and the film became the first complete production to roll on the Fox lot for almost a year. Production chief Richard D. Zanuck hosted a small press reception at 9 A.M. on Tuesday, April 23, 1963 to celebrate the start of shooting.

This time Stewart was an ultra-respectable lawyer, Frank Michaelson, with Audrey Meadows as his wife Anne. Sandra Dee was the daughter who goes east to college and meets boys, beatnik folk singers and Ban the Bomb demonstrators. A worried Stewart dashes to her rescue and finds her demonstrating against book censorship—he gets arrested and jailed after telling the police the students have a right to be heard. When Dee goes to a Paris art school and is painted with five breasts by a French artist, her letters bring an alarmed Stewart rushing over to save her. (By now, less than four years after *Anatomy of a Murder*, words like "breasts" and "virgin" were permissible parlance in family comedies.)

The French episode has some *très* clumsy material with Stewart in language difficulties and being arrested by mistake in a vice

[158]

raid. However, there is quite a funny sequence in which he attends a fancy dress ball as Daniel Boone in what might be his outfit from *How the West Was Won*, which slowly falls off him. (Most of the girls come as Cleopatra, left-over costumes no doubt from *that* epic.)

The film uses a running gag (suggested by Zanuck) that the Stewart character, Frank Michaelson, resembles the movie star Jimmy Stewart. (Actually, the idea was used in a much more subtle, throwaway form at the beginning of *Thunder Bay* when Stewart and Dan Duryea arrive penniless at a Fourth of July celebration. "Can you juggle or something?" asks Duryea. Replies Stewart: "I can imitate a movie star.") Here the lawyer finds it simplest to give in to kids' demands and sign their autograph books, adding, "And remember me to all my other fans in your age group." Minus the rest of his costume and pestered by the French press, he dives into the Seine in his underwear and hits the headlines again. The final payoff is that Stewart can expect to go through all the same problems with another daughter, just as he had another ghastly vacation ahead of him as Mr. Hobbs.

At the end of 1963 Stewart worked for the last time with John Ford on the comic interlude to *Cheyenne Autumn*, the director's well-intentioned but leaden drama about the long flight of the Cheyenne tribe back to their ancestral lands in the Dakotas. Lasting about a quarter of an hour, the sequence was a tired rehash of earlier Fordian material, especially from *Two Rode Together*, delighting in cowardice, corruption and drunkenness.

Stewart was again a marshal, dressed very much as in the town sequences of *Two Rode Together*, once more on the take (receiving ten percent of gambling revenues) and indifferent to his duties, but this time he was presented as being Wyatt Earp in Dodge City. Playing poker in the saloon, Stewart mugs it up from the start, pretending he can't see the cards and mumbling, "Is that an ace? Blind as a bat . . ." but detecting that the Major (John Carradine) has removed one card from the deck by feeling its weight and flicking it past his ear. Challenged to draw his gun by Ken Curtis's cowboy, he tries to ignore the threat but shoots the man in the foot with his pocket Derringer when he goes for his gun. Even though Arthur Kennedy is on hand as Doc Holliday (and in *My Darling Clementine*, the same character, played by Victor Mature, carried out a surgical operation), here Stewart is left to extract the bullet from the wounded cowboy's foot with his pocket knife.

Stewart finally contemplates the threat apparently posed to the town by the advancing Cheyenne and decides on a "plan of campaign" which is to run in the opposite direction. The sighting of a solitary Indian causes wholesale panic. Stewart recalled: "John Ford rarely told you what he had in mind and kept you guessing. Ford does it by all sorts of means—terrible means sometimes! I remember Arthur Kennedy and I coming out of the saloon. There were 200 people in the square and Arthur Kennedy and I were supposed to get in a wagon with two horses and drive out of the square. Well, he told us to go in one direction but he had all his assistants tell the crowd that we were going in a different direction so that when we charged into the crowd they didn't know and there was a great confusion and people got pushed by the horses and screamed and yelled and ran and it was just a wonderful scene!"

The Belle Aragon figure of *Two Rode Together* is replaced here by Elizabeth Allen's equally spirited Miss Plantagenet. Stewart isn't sure if he knew her in the past, but when he sees her reduced to her frilly underwear in the flight from town, he declares, "By golly, I did know her in Wichita!"—echoing the intimate knowledge he had of Belle's stiletto strapped to her inner thigh in the earlier film.

The third mining of the trials and tribulations of parenthood at Fox was called *Dear Brigitte*. Though Nunnally Johnson wrote the script, he removed his name when Hal Kanter made some revisions. This time Stewart's spouse was played by Glynis Johns, an amiable and suitable reunion with his co-star of *No Highway* since once again he was playing an absent-minded professor, ordering a group of scientists to leave but then discovering he is standing in their laboratory, or coming home in a cab having forgotten he has a car.

As famous poet and English professor Paul Leaf, Stewart is desperate to find some artistic aptitude in his tone-deaf and color-blind eight-year-old (Billy Mumy). The kid does prove to be a mathematical genius, able to calculate figures twice as fast as a computer, and what little plot there is has to do with John Williams' trickster Upjohn exploiting the gift for monetary gain.

Stewart was impressed by Mumy. "The only kid actor I knew worth a damn was a boy name of Billy Mumy," he reminisced to Bill Davidson. "And the only reason he was any good was because he didn't want to be an actor at all. He wanted to be a ball-player. So I'd play catch with him all day and I never had to study my part. The kid had a photographic memory, and he'd be so anxious to get back to playing ball that whenever we went to work before the camera, he'd just feed me my lines. A fine boy, that Billy Mumy."

Once again, there was a French connection through the far-fetched device of giving the boy a passion for Brigitte Bardot, to whom he writes fan letters every day, hoping to marry her when he grows up. This alarms Stewart not at all and the film's approximation of a climax is a visit to Paris by father and son to see BB who is on her best behavior, a flower blocking her cleavage as she bends forward to talk to the mesmerized kid.

Stewart had fun playing the accordion again on screen but he is clearly trying too hard to overcome the basic thinness of the material, as in his emphatic reference to "racetrack toots" when he means touts, as though it were really funny. It was time to end this particular run of comedies.

17

A New Team

STEWART'S NEXT FILM WAS HIS biggest hit of the decade, *Shenandoah*. He was working for the first time with the writer James Lee Barrett and the director Andrew V. McLaglen. The combination of star, writer and director seemed so effective that they did most of their work with each other for the next six years. McLaglen directed Stewart in four films, three written by Barrett who also wrote another Stewart movie directed by someone else. Stewart made only two films that didn't involve one or both of them. He had now largely forsaken comedy and returned to being a dramatic actor in westerns and other period dramas.

Shenandoah was a strong Civil War drama, told from the point of view of the bystanders. James Stewart is Charlie Anderson, the prosperous Virginia farmer who in 1863 adopts an isolationist approach to the conflict—"This war is not mine and I take no note of it," he tells the Confederate officer who wants his six sons to enlist. Stewart says that he has never asked anything of the State but that his sons can enlist if they want to. All prefer to keep on with their work on the 500-acre farm.

But the war won't stay away. Cannon fire disturbs the chickens and cows, reducing the output of eggs and milk. A Confederate officer (Doug McClure) wants to marry Stewart's daughter (Rosemary Forsyth). And his youngest son, the one most precious because his beloved wife died giving birth to him, is seized by Union soldiers: "*Now* it concerns us," he says in a giant close-up. "I don't know how these people dare take a son of mine—when I catch up with them it's going to be a horrible thing to behold!"

[163]

Stewart's cigar-chewing patriarch dominates the film. None of his sons registers strongly. The concept is Fordian and Andrew McLaglen (the son of a favorite Ford actor, Victor McLaglen) does his best to invest it with some of the master's style. Here Stewart talks to his wife Martha at her grave, sixteen years after her death, much as John Wayne's Nathan Brittles reported on events to his dead wife, also called Martha, in *She Wore a Yellow Ribbon*. "I don't even know what to say to you, Martha," Stewart declares gently. "There's nothing much I can tell you about this war. It's . . . it's like all wars, I suppose—the undertakers are winning it. Politicians talk a lot about the glory of it. Soldiers, they just want to go home."

Stewart has a place left at the table for Martha. He has raised all his sons as Christians, going to church each Sunday to fulfill his wife's last request. But this is a proud, stubborn, dictatorial man. He thanks the Lord for the harvest but he doesn't mean what he says since he knows his labors have been most responsible. He almost seems to invite the tragedies that overtake his family because there are no half-measures, no compromise, about him. He leaves only one son to look after the farm and takes all the others to search for the abducted boy. Confederate looters call and kill the son (Patrick Wayne), then rape and kill his wife.

And Stewart doesn't find the missing lad. He evokes compassion as he struggles to explain why he made such an effort, knowing he was unlikely to succeed. "Somehow I just had to try," he tells his sons. "If we don't try, we don't do." He clasps his gloved hands together in emphasis. "And if we don't do, why are we here on this Earth? I hope you all understand." Only when this man has come to terms with the outside world is it appropriate for his missing son to return of his own accord to provide a happy ending.

Shenandoah scores in its evocation of the upset and horror of war, its feeling of events running out of control, of war spreading like a dark stain into tranquil backwaters. Yet it rests too much on Stewart's central performance and on the impact of particular moments like the sudden bayonetting of Patrick Wayne or Stewart witnessing the equally unexpected, accidental shooting of another son by a startled sentry. Stewart shakes with rage as he

[164]

grabs the soldier, finds out that he is merely a sixteen-year-old kid and then lets him go, almost stroking his face with his hands, to collapse in tears over the mistake he has made. The more peaceful episodes of family life have a slightly stilted air about them. It needed John Ford to bring them to life.

Stewart's next film (the first of two he shot in 1965) was also with Andrew McLaglen, the western *The Rare Breed*. It co-starred him again with Maureen O'Hara in an original screenplay by Ric Hardman which has a powerful basic storyline dissipated by lumbering direction and undistinguished dialogue. Initially, O'Hara has the stronger part as Martha Evans, the widow determined to carry out her late husband's plan to bring a prize Hereford bull called Vindicator to the Texas range to sire a new breed of sturdier cattle. James Stewart, as Bulldog Sam Burnett, is the cowboy she hires to take the bull from St. Louis to Texas to the cattleman who has bought Vindicator to try out her plan. He is bribed to turn over the bull to another cattleman en route but decides to stay honest when he finds that Maureen O'Hara and her daughter, played by Juliet Mills, will be coming along with him. He is discredited in O'Hara's eyes when she discovers the double-cross he had intended.

In fact, cattlemen merely pretend to be interested in her hopes for Vindicator: they are more interested in O'Hara herself. Only Stewart shares her belief in her dream and it is his faith, that goes beyond all reason, which provides the dramatic interest in the second half of the film and makes the part become so suitable for him. When Vindicator is put out on the range for what turns into the worst winter in memory, Stewart goes off looking for the bull and needs to be rescued himself before he has had any luck. When the search party locates him in the snow, he eagerly drinks some Scotch to revive himself and trembles as he declares intensely, "That Hereford bull's out here somewhere and I'm going to find him."

But here Stewart is not as physically all-powerful as he was in the Mann westerns. He has the passion but not the strength and has to abandon the search. "You planted an idea in me, Mrs. Evans," he tells O'Hara, "And the roots went deep . . ." Everyone gives up Vindicator for dead—but not Stewart. He vents his disgust at their lack of faith and is told by the cattleman (Brian Keith, giving a surprisingly dreadful performance as a Scotsman) that he can have any crossbred calves that he can find in the spring.

With splendid faith, Stewart builds himself a cabin and cattle pens in readiness. Even when he finds the dead body of Vindicator after the snow melts he still clings to his hopes, telling Juliet Mills, "I have this place and this idea . . ." and nothing will budge him. Eventually he is rewarded: he finds a white faced crossbreed and takes it in to show O'Hara. He gets into a fight with Brian Keith which he rather surprisingly loses (although it is consistent with his earlier lack of stamina). It is still his moment of triumph as he staggers back onto his feet to clutch Maureen O'Hara and tell her that the new breed will be all over the range as the camera tracks in on them to pick up their exultation. An interesting picture, *The Rare Breed* falls annoyingly short of its potential but at least it gives Stewart some most effective moments.

The Flight of the Phoenix is the odd film out from this period. Apparently, Gloria Stewart made her husband read the Elleston Trevor novel, insisting it would make a good movie. Stewart's enthusiasm for flying must have won him over but the part he played is a curious one for him, a character role of a veteran pilot, Frank Towns, whose cargo and passenger plane crashes in the North African desert. Said Stewart: "My character's sort of a sad man in a way. I felt he was a man who had been passed by, by the modern jet airplane and the computerized systems and automation. He doesn't want it that way. He wants to run the machine, he doesn't want the machine to run him."

Although the film is long (147 minutes), Stewart's prominence is reduced by the attention given to other survivors played by Richard Attenborough (drunken navigator), Peter Finch (Army officer), Ronald Fraser (Army sergeant), Ernest Borgnine, Ian Bannen, Christian Marquand, Hardy Kruger, Dan Duryea, and others.

Stewart takes the blame for what has happened, recording "Pilot error" after "Cause of crash" in the flight log because he flew into a sandstorm after the radio went dead, relying on the forecast of good weather instead of taking a different route as a precaution. Grizzled and unshaven, he sits and broods as the group faces death in the desert with little food or water. He then over-reacts to some of the misfortunes that attend the group. He blames himself when the mentally distraught Borgnine wanders off into the desert, saying (unreasonably) that he should have noticed, and he frenziedly shoots a lame camel to end its misery after Finch and Marquand are killed by nomads.

The key conflict in the film occurs between Stewart's practical, defeatist figure and the young aircraft designer of Hardy Kruger whom Stewart brands "a miserable Kraut" for his ruthless out-look. Stewart has to swallow his pride and submit to Kruger's authority when the German persuades them to build a new plane from the wreckage of the old. Stewart does come into his own after the plane is built, defying Kruger's advice to make the engine start and ordering him to start pulling it into position for take-off. The arrogant German is proved right, however, when the plane carries them to safety (although, in reality, it crashed, taking the life of veteran stunt flyer Paul Mantz).

Stewart's Towns is not particularly admirable, forceful or heroic—rather a figure of no more than ordinary competence whose career has hardly been a big success. There are no alterna-tive heroes in the film (the Kruger character could have been but for his unpleasant traits). The film loses by not having a figure to identify with, although it can be argued it gains in realism. Robert Aldrich's primitive style of direction and the crude color system are further handicaps but *Flight of the Phoenix* has enough novelty in its narrative details to hold the interest.

It was then more than a year before Stewart was back before the cameras, at the end of 1966. In 1959 he had been announced to co-star with Burt Lancaster and Kirk Douglas in the film version of A. B. Guthrie's novel *The Way West*. It finally went into production during 1966 with Andrew V. McLaglen directing and Kirk Douglas co-starring with Robert Mitchum and Richard Widmark. The result was a big disappointment and Stewart can't have felt sorry to have missed being in it.

But his own choice of a smaller-scale western, *Firecreek*, was little better. It had a certain value from casting Henry Fonda as a villain (well before Sergio Leone developed the same idea for *Once*

Upon a Time in the West) but it was long-winded, flatly directed (by Vincent McEveety) and forgettable.

Stewart was cast as the farmer Johnny Cobb, who also doubles as the sheriff of the quiet little town of Firecreek, a normally undemanding job that pays a token two dollars a month. Henry Fonda portrayed Larkin, leader of a bunch of desperadoes. Wounded in a range war, Fonda decides to recuperate in Firecreek, seeing it as a town of tired old men who pose no threat. His band make a thorough nuisance of themselves but Stewart only tries to reason with them, being preoccupied by the fact that his wife (Jacqueline Scott) is due to have a baby at any moment. When a stable-boy kills one of the gang to save an Indian girl from rape, Stewart puts him in jail for his own safety. However, the rest of the gang seize him and string him up, forcing Stewart at last to try and act. He unpacks his gun and manages to dispose of all the gang except Fonda.

Their shootout has some tension as Fonda shoots Stewart's gun from his hand and wounds him in the leg. Having partly reformed under the influence of a good woman (Inger Stevens), Fonda wants to let it go at that but Stewart drags himself towards his fallen gun and Inger Stevens has to shoot Fonda to save Stewart.

It was a western broadly in the *High Noon* tradition although the final gunfight recalls that of *The Man Who Shot Liberty Valance* in the way that Stewart is no match for his adversary, is wounded in the leg, refuses to back down, and someone else has to step in and save him by killing the badman.

Stewart's career took a turn for the better when he teamed up again with Andrew McLaglen and James Lee Barrett for a big-budget western at Fox, *Bandolero!* which was a hit at the box-office but mostly a miss artistically, due once again to uncertain scripting and weak staging.

Oddly (but entertainingly), Stewart mixes his broad comedy image and windbag ways with being a man of action. He plays Mace Bishop who masquerades as a hangman in stove-pipe hat and ill-fitting costume with faded carnation in order to free his brother Dee Bishop (Dean Martin) and the latter's gang from the gallows, relishing the chance to tease the gang before they know

[168]

who he is with grisly details of their apparent fate. Dean Martin is shown as both a ruthless killer and in a more sympathetic light as a man prepared to reform and settle down with a good woman (Raquel Welch). Stewart lectures him and advises him as if he were a kid brother, too wild to have known better, making Dean Martin far too mature for the role. As in *Night Passage,* the good brother/bad brother relationship isn't satisfactorily cast.

Stewart himself even robs a bank on impulse in order to buy a spread in Montana and settle down peacefully with his brother, but his hold-up does not involve the bloodshed and murder of Martin's earlier attempt. After both have been arrested, Martin is astonished to discover that his righteous brother has also held up the bank. It gives Stewart a rich opportunity to deliver one of those highly imitable roundabout replies, "Well, Dee, the bank was there . . . and . . . I was there . . . and there wasn't very much of anybody else there . . . and it just seemed like the thing to do. You know, it's not like something you've never heard of . . . a lot of people rob banks for all sorts of different reasons . . ." Pure waffle, but the sight of Stewart stalling and struggling in the hope of coming up with a convincing explanation is richly comic. Stewart makes a habit of repeating himself to try and lend substance to his subsequent answers to his brother's questions ("Yeah, that's about the way it was . . . as well as I can remember, yeah" and "Well, just don't say anything, Dee, just don't say a word" and "Just a thought, Dee, just a thought") before the sickening revelation of Stewart's brotherly devotion is terminated by George Kennedy's sheriff who can't take any more of it. The trouble is that it's not only Stewart's speeches which are repetitive but almost everybody else's as well.

It's odd that both Martin and Stewart are killed fighting bandoleros, the Mexican bandits who behave like bloodthirsty Indians. Morally, Martin would seem doomed by his earlier killings, but Stewart's tutoring him in romancing Raquel Welch and his willingness to turn a new leaf suggest he may have a future. Martin is mortally wounded while grappling with the bandit leader by a sudden, shocking sword thrust like the bayonet death of Patrick Wayne in *Shenandoah.* Stewart is shot in the chest trying to avenge his brother but at first seems not badly hurt, walking on, tears welling in his eyes as he looks down on his dying brother—then he suddenly falls to the ground. George Kennedy is on hand to shoot the bandit leader to death but the result is that Raquel Welch's sympathetic widow is deprived of Dean Martin, the man she loves, and left with George Kennedy whose embarrassing adoration leaves her cold. Though Stewart is never a contender for her affections, there's no reason why he couldn't have survived and escorted her away since he has already returned the money he stole. If the film was aiming at a bitterly tragic outcome, it's never pointed up by the direction nor properly arrived at by the script.

1968 was a blank year as far as film-making was concerned although both *Firecreek* and *Bandolero!* went into release. Stewart kept up the television appearances and made a specialty of performing corny old songs like "Ragtime Cowboy Joe" (from *Destry Rides Again*) on *The Dean Martin Show*. And he toured Air Force bases to address the men. But, having reached sixty, Stewart was retired, at the rank of brigadier general, from the Air Force Reserve. "It was the first time that I became aware of growing old," he said later. "I moped around for a while and then I went out to Burbank Airport and got myself a little Super-Cub plane. I keep it spotless, shined like a silver dollar, and I go out and fly it every chance I get—usually on Saturday afternoons, for three, four hours after golf."

Stewart also went on a handshake tour of Vietnam, walking around, signing autographs, visiting hospitals, talking to the men. He had earlier been on a B52 mission from Guam to a target ten miles east of the Cambodian border, near Saigon, and on an inspection tour. This time he met up with his oldest boy Ronald, a Marine lieutenant, and observed action in Quang Tri, just south of the demilitarized zone.

Then James Lee Barrett rang Stewart late one evening to sound him out on whether he liked the idea of playing a humble cowboy who inherits a bordello. That was the simple notion on which was hung *The Cheyenne Social Club*, an excellent comedy script which Stewart filmed with Henry Fonda in 1969 under Gene Kelly's able direction. Its appeal rested on its two stars, mocking their usual tough, self-reliant attitudes and giving beautifully relaxed, ingratiating performances as two unshaven, unambitious, simple-minded itinerant westerners, voicing James Lee Barrett's flavorsome dialogue. They even perform a song together, "Rolling Stone," as they walk down a Cheyenne street. The leisurely pace of the comedy is indicated by the year it takes a letter to reach Stewart's John O'Hanlon to inform him of the "boarding house" he has inherited and the year he takes to ride from Texas to Cheyenne to collect it, accompanied by his fellow cowpoke, Henry Fonda's Harley O'Sullivan.

The two actors make an amusing double act with Fonda playing even more simple-minded than Stewart. They've been riding together for ten years but Stewart doesn't know why—not that he minds, he'd just like to know why. It's clear he could happily do without Fonda, but Fonda needs him. Stewart rides off to Cheyenne and Fonda follows—it's only a month later that Fonda finally asks where they're headed. Fonda gabs all the time as they ride along and Stewart barely listens, then finally complains: a hundred miles of his talking is all right, but a thousand miles of it is another matter. "I've just been keeping you company," protests Fonda, his feelings hurt. "I appreciate it, Harley," says Stewart, "But if you say another word the rest of the day I'm gonna kill you."

They're an odd couple, a bizarre addition to the cycle of male bonding or buddy movies like *Butch Cassidy and the Sundance Kid*. When they arrive at the Social Club, they even share the same bed on their first night, with Stewart being put out by Fonda practicing his habit of cracking nuts in his hands. At one point in their bickering, the parallel with matrimony is pointed up as Fonda declares that their arguments remind him of when he was married and he doesn't like it. Later Fonda plays the neglected wife, moaning at how inconsiderate Stewart is.

There is an inside joke at the opposing political views of the actors. Stewart was a staunch Republican who had worked for Eisenhower and openly supported Nixon and Reagan. Fonda was a Democrat and liberal in his views. They were close friends but made a point of never discussing controversial issues like the Vietnam War. In the film they kid each other with Stewart mocking Fonda for being a Democrat—look where it's got him—

[171]

but admitting that he also voted Democrat once although he doesn't want it to get out. "There can't be a finer calling in the world than being a Republican businessman," avers Stewart. Fonda inquires if it's all right if he stays a Democrat. "Just so long as you're not seen with me when you're doing it," replies Stewart.

The plot has Stewart embarrassed to discover that the Social Club is really "a whore . . . a whore . . . ," which is as far as he can get in saying whorehouse. Run by Shirley Jones' sweet-mannered Madame, it's a happy place where all the girls love their work. In one extraordinary scene, Stewart embraces the permissive seventies in the form of Elaine Devry, playing the buxom Pauline in a very see-through blouse, who has a friendly wrestle with Stewart on one of the beds and offers him a sample of the services on offer, whereupon there is a discreet fade.

When Shirley Jones is beaten up, Stewart begins to take pride in the establishment and goes out to deal with the man responsible, Corey Bannister (played by Robert Wilke, previously the worst heavy in *Night Passage*). Stewart accuses him of attacking "one of my girls" even though he can't shoot worth a penny and it is only because Fonda inadvertently distracts Wilke at the vital moment that Stewart kills him. They are lucky again in disposing of Wilke's nearby revenge-seeking relatives and Stewart basks in the girls' admiring remarks that he has "enough guts to fill a smokehouse." However, his gallantry fades when the out-of-town relatives of the late and lamented Wilke gather in their thousands and Stewart's final image as a western star is one of prudent retreat. Having started his sagebrush career with *Destry Rides Again*, it seems fitting that he should end it with another spirited comedy western.

During filming, Stewart was hit by news that his son Ronald had been killed in Vietnam. Later he would comment: "People say what a terrible tragedy that he had to die. We never look on it as a tragedy. It's a loss, not a tragedy. He had a useful life. He graduated from college, and his country was at war. He became a Marine and when he got on the battlefield he conducted himself with gallantry. What's tragic about that? What's tragic is boys giving their lives without having a unified country behind them. That's what's tragic." At one political gathering attended by

[172]

Stewart and John Wayne, the Duke was so aggrieved by demonstrators waving a Vietcong banner that he blasted them for the affront to Stewart after the loss he had suffered.

The Cheyenne Social Club was also the last film for Stewart's faithful steed, Pie. "We did it in Santa Fe, New Mexico—I took Pie up but he was getting old and he got sick so I couldn't use him in the whole picture. But unbeknownst to me, Hank Fonda painted a picture of Pie in watercolor—he's an excellent artist—and when we got home he brought the picture to me. And two days later Pie died, and it was a great loss. But I have Pie in our library and I consider him a friend." Fonda had noticed Stewart slipping away after lunch each day with an apple, a carrot or a piece of water melon as a tidbit for Pie and so Fonda spent his Sundays sketching the horse at the stables as a basis for the watercolor which he did when he got home.

Even before *The Cheyenne Social Club* was shot, Stewart had decided on a return to the stage in *Harvey*. He co-starred with Helen Hayes as Veta Louise in a new production directed by Stephen Porter. It opened first at the Mendelssohn Theater on the University of Michigan campus. Stewart noted: "That was when they were having all those, you know, riots and things. But they loved the play and had lots of smart observations about it, things I'd never thought of before."

The production opened on Broadway on February 24, 1970 for a limited ten-week run. Jesse White repeated the part he'd had in the film version as a sanatorium attendant. Stewart was quoted as saying that he now felt better suited to playing Elwood P. Dowd. *Variety*'s critic was able to compare his stage interpretations: "If memory isn't more than normally fallible, the actor is right about what twenty-five years of living have given him for playing this part. He seems a little more relaxed, more real and more humorous, if perhaps a trifle less comic than in retrospect. The main thing is, he's a genuine star, with the presence, projection, feel of an audience and the personal magnetism to take command of a theater. He gives the impression of almost not acting at all." Even more praise was rendered Helen Hayes. Stewart was keen to bring the show to London. "I'd love to do *Harvey* over here," he said while in Britain in 1971, glancing upwards to

[173]

his left, adding: "And Harvey would love it, too." British Equity apparently refused to allow both Stewart and Helen Hayes to come over and there were exploratory talks with Margaret Rutherford as a substitute for Miss Hayes. That would have been a sight to behold.

James Lee Barrett had written another script highly suitable for James Stewart called *Fools' Parade*, an excellent adaptation of a richly idiosyncratic novel by the author of *Night of the Hunter*, Davis Grubb. Stewart helped push it into production at Columbia where Barrett functioned as executive producer and also took a supporting role. Once again Andrew McLaglen directed but the story was rather too intricate and ironic, too varied in mood, and the characterizations really too bizarre to suit his blunt approach to material. The film was not a financial success (in Britain it was retitled *Dynamite Man from Glory Jail* in the hope of improving business), but it is vividly remembered by everyone who saw it for some of its outlandish features.

Stewart played Mattie Appleyard, an old lag with a glass eye— he wore a prosthesis over his own eye, a painful business that limited shooting time—and in the film delights in plucking it out as a magical trick to startle bystanders or confound his enemies. He even converses with it at times of stress. The character he plays is released from West Virginia State Penitentiary in 1935 with two other convicts played by Strother Martin and the young Kurt Russell. He has assiduously saved his prison pay which amounts to $25,452. He plans to go straight and open a general store in partnership with Strother Martin. But the check for his savings can only be cashed in the town from which they've been legally expelled. Furthermore, their prison warder, George Kennedy's Bible-quoting Doc Council, is intent on relieving him of the check and has hired two killers to help him.

Fools' Parade finally boils down to Stewart's stubborn assertion of his right to the money. He first obtains it by threatening to dynamite the bank, is then pursued by Doc and his men, and arrested after he kills Doc with a well-aimed stick of explosive. Put on trial for murder and cleared, he finds he has become a local hero when he once again turns up at the bank but modestly describes himself as "just an American coming into a bank to cash a check." It was a fitting image of quiet heroism for Stewart to conclude his career as a big screen Hollywood star. It recalled the young Senator Jefferson Smith asserting *his* rights all those years ago; it was another stubborn Stewart hero winning through against all odds. It was cast in the more cynical viewpoint of the seventies, but with audiences consisting predominantly of teen-agers, it was almost impossible for the veteran stars to succeed at the box-office. Besides which, as he openly admitted: "There are less and less movie parts—let's face it—because of my age."

And Stewart didn't think much of the kind of films being made: "The trouble is the movies they're making today are the wrong kind of movies, the seamy, depressing, hopeless, semi-pornographic things. At this point, why should I fool around with stuff like that?"

An offer could be wrong in another way. Peter Bogdanovich, riding high from the success of *The Last Picture Show*, approached Stewart with an idea for a western. "We lunched and, well, he didn't have much of an idea, it was all very hazy," said Stewart, "But I said fine, go ahead." Bogdanovich and Larry McMurtry (his collaborator on *The Last Picture Show*) went off and wrote *Streets of Laredo* with the idea of bringing John Wayne, Henry Fonda and James Stewart together in one film. Unfortunately, the three stars found it too consciously rubbing in their age and declining powers. "I read it and I wasn't impressed," said Stewart. "I called Duke and asked him what he thought. He said, 'Jimmy boy, they're trying to make three old fogies out of us.' And he was right. So we all turned it down."

So Stewart went where the work was. Over the years there had been many offers from television. He now let it be known that he was interested in doing a television series, and he was inundated with proposals.

18

The Television Star

IT WAS A SIMPLE FORMAT FOR a half-hour television comedy series, based on the harassed parent image of *Mr. Hobbs Takes a Vacation, Take Her, She's Mine* and *Dear Brigitte*. No pilot was filmed. The story was told that Stewart met NBC network executives who asked him what the show was about. Stewart replied, "It's about half an hour." It was devised by Hal Kanter, who had worked on the last of the three movies, and gave Stewart the part of Jim Howard, a homespun, bicycle-riding professor of anthropology in a small town college setting. It was called *The Jimmy Stewart Show* and featured Jimmy often talking directly to the home audience, who were the same people who had enjoyed Stewart on the big screen when they too were young. As his wife (who is a painter), there was Julie Adams (who, as Julia Adams, had co-starred with him in *Bend of the River*), and the small, bald-pated character actor John McGiver (who had been in two of the Stewart feature comedies) came aboard as a sharp-tongued faculty colleague with a Rolls-Royce. There was a married son who is an insufferable square (Jonathan Daly), a daughter-in-law who's a deft hand at making waffles (Ellen Geer), two rambunctious eight-year-olds (Dennis Larson, Kirby Furlong), one a grandson, the other a late addition to Professor Stewart's own family. As Jimmy confided to the audience: "Twenty-nine years ago I had a son. Eight years ago I had another son. Now you know what's meant by an absent-minded professor." In the first episode he also absent-mindedly burnt down his son's house by leaving a burning cigar lying around, so that his son and family have to crowd into his house.

[177]

He also played his grandfather in a flashback with his real-life wife Gloria playing Grandmother Howard.

Stewart explained the approach: "People are looking for the familiar Jimmy Stewart, and that's largely a question of style. I am consistent, recognizable. The way I figure it, I play Jimmy Stewart with deference to the character in the series. To do something in a completely different way would be a form of self-indulgence. Pointless, as well, because the audience wouldn't like it."

Variety covered the series' debut in September 1971: "Stewart again demonstrated his stock-in-trade warm folksiness—and gave good evidence that his warmth is to be channelled into family domestic comedy of a very familiar stripe . . . He seemed completely at ease in the new medium and registered with unusual sincerity in the episode. There were no signs that the college he teaches in was to resemble the seething schools of real life, however, as the debut's sets, pacing and flavors all point to *Life with Grandpa*."

The second episode focused on the crucial question of whether Stewart should buy a new briefcase. The third featured Stewart and McGiver becoming soused on a trip to San Francisco and tottering into a nudie parlor. Beulah Bondi appeared early in the series as Stewart's mother, for the fifth and last time. The show proved to be only a moderate success, running to twenty-four episodes.

Stewart went on to film *Harvey* again, this time for television with Helen Hayes, John McGiver (as Doctor Chumley), Jesse White (repeating his role from the 1950 screen version as well as from the recent Broadway revival with Helen Hayes), and Madeline Kahn (as the nurse, a distinct casting improvement over Peggy Dow in the previous filming). *Variety*'s reviewer felt that *Harvey* didn't work too well on the home screen with its favoring of close-ups because space and distance were needed to accommodate the giant invisible rabbit and it was suggested that perhaps an actor should have been used in a costume, visible only to the privileged few. It was observed that "Stewart bobbled a few of the familiar lines and on occasion carried his laconic style to an extreme, but generally was in good form."

Hawkins on Murder was the actor's next stab at a television series.

The ninety-minute pilot, shown in 1973, devised for him the character of Billy Jim Hawkins, a down-to-earth West Virginia lawyer ("Just call me Billy Jim") who owed a little to Stewart's success in *Anatomy of a Murder*. Strother Martin was cast as R. J. Hawkins, his cracker-barrel sheriff cousin who does the legwork on investigations. The story displayed Stewart defending Bonnie Bedelia as the heiress accused of triple murder—she is rumored to be insane and admits she hated the victims. It sold the series, which was called simply *Hawkins* and ran to seven more ninety-minute stories that were transmitted from October 1973, interspersed with other shows in the same time slot.

"*Hawkins* was an interesting attempt to plant the old homespun Stewart image . . . squarely in the midst of seamy contemporary situations," observed Joseph McBride. In *Murder in Movieland* Stewart came to Tinsel City to defend a star's husband who admits clubbing another man to death. In *Die, Darling, Die* he defended Julie Harris as a widow accused of murdering her dying husband and he discovered whether she threw away his life-saving medication as an act of mercy or to hasten the day she inherited his fortune. In *A Life for a Life* he defended William Windom as the father accused of murdering a computer analyst he blames for his son's death. In *Blood Feud* he was involved in a murder within the Hawkins clan that is seemingly linked to a century-old dispute with a neighboring family (Lew Ayres guest-starred as a small-town historian). In *Murder in the Slave Trade* Stewart was engaged by the widow of a tyrannical sports czar to defend the down-at-heel football pro accused of murdering her husband. In *Murder on the 13th Floor* the son of an old flame (Teresa Wright) needed his services after being found in a hotel room minutes after a killing has taken place. And in *Candidate for Murder* Stewart took on a case defending a politician's campaign manager accused of murdering a television reporter about to release a smear story.

The series was shot at MGM where Stewart also filmed introductory sequences as one of the star commentators in *That's Entertainment!*, the studio's highly successful musical compilation feature that displayed him nearly forty years younger in his number "Easy to Love" from *Born to Dance*.

Stewart finally made the trip to London to star in *Harvey* on a six-month work permit. Anthony Quayle directed a British supporting cast headed by Mona Washbourne (by this time, alas, Margaret Rutherford was dead). Stewart was splendid—even during a heatwave in the non-air-conditioned theater—and theatergoers loved him although the rest of the cast were little more than adequate. The play opened on April 7, 1975 and audiences invariably gave Stewart a rapturous reception.

19

Cameo Roles

STEWART WAS NOT ENTIRELY LOST to the big screen, as he began making cameo appearances. When in 1976 John Wayne filmed what turned out to be his last movie, *The Shootist*, the story of a cancer-ridden gunfighter John Bernard Books who ends his days with dignity, Stewart participated in the small but significant role of Doctor Hostetler. He dropped all mannerisms and played his key scene in a simple, direct manner as he levels with Wayne, telling him that he can expect to suffer badly and hints at suicide as the sensible way out. There is perhaps just a trace of relish in Stewart's voice as he emphasizes the stark prognosis, suggesting that the Doc feels Wayne has earned his suffering for his wicked past or is jealous of the exciting life he's led—but if so, it's too subtle to be definite. As Stewart stares down at Wayne's dead body in the saloon, there is a look of relief on his features (as well as, just possibly, the superior feeling of out-surviving him).

In *Airport '77*, Stewart played his first figure of fabulous wealth. And, after *The Shootist*, it was his turn to be given a dose of terminal illness as the Paul Getty-like Philip Stevens, owner of a custom-built luxury airliner that he uses to transport guests and works of art to the grand opening of his own private museum. On board the flight are his rebellious daughter (Pamela Bellwood) and her young son, as well as his secretary (Brenda Vaccaro) and the blind piano-player he has hired to entertain his guests so that he can feel they are altogether traveling in style.

However, the plane is hijacked during the journey and crashes into a fog-shrouded oil rig to settle intact (and full of air) on an underwater sandbank. Stewart has to wait in anguish until brave pilot Jack Lemmon manages to surface and radio for help. As the Navy gently raises the plane with all the passengers, Stewart is on hand to be reunited with his daughter and his grandson. It was the second follow-up to the success of 1970's *Airport* and simply offered the expected assortment of varied characters and disaster thrills (with a nod to *The Poseidon Adventure*).

One of the most bizarre and totally unnecessary remakes of all time was Michael Winner's 1978 adaptation of *The Big Sleep* which preposterously relocated the story in present-day England and, despite an amazingly strong cast, lost all the qualities that made the novel and Howard Hawks' original film so memorable. Winner's mania for big names even made him cast a star in the part of General Sternwood, the frail hothouse invalid who hires private eye Philip Marlowe. Brilliantly as the role was played in the 1946 film, it was a small character part and hardly anyone remembers the name of the obscure actor, Charles Waldron, who took it. Now Stewart accepted the role and was seen as another rich, old, dying man, confined to a wheelchair by an accident while steeplechasing, who summons Robert Mitchum's Marlowe to handle a pornographic book dealer who has a hold over his unstable daughter Camilla (Candy Clark).

Charles Waldron played the part with an absolute minimum of movement but Winner directs Stewart into being lively at first before tiring in his initial scene with Mitchum. Later, though, he is seen in bed with his head propped up on pillows, fully justifying Mitchum's comment on leaving that "He looked more like a dead man than most dead men do." Waldron was dead before the first *Big Sleep* opened, but fortunately Stewart's alarmingly fragile appearance was only good acting. (Waldron, incidentally, had played Stewart's father in the 1937 *Navy Blue and Gold*.)

He had an unusual role to follow, appearing in *The Magic of Lassie* with fellow veterans Mickey Rooney and Alice Faye. As he said before filming: "All my career, people have told me that with dogs and young babies you have no chance. Well, Lassie has to be the most famous dog in the world and there are two young children who are going to be terrific and I shall stand around in the background . . ." Which is pretty much what he did most of the time.

He was the northern California vineyard proprietor Clovis Mitchell, who also owns Lassie but has to surrender him to a businessman (Pernell Roberts) with a prior claim of ownership. Taken far away, the dog promptly escapes and sets out for his old home. Kelly (Stephanie Zimbalist), a young girl being raised by the doting Stewart, disappears to search for the pet and Stewart follows searching for her. Everyone is reunited for the happy ending at Thanksgiving.

The film threw in ten songs and Stewart sang two of them, "That Hometown Feeling" and "Thanksgiving Prayer." It was the kind of wholesome family entertainment that no longer attracted audiences—but it didn't have the polish of the old studio-made pictures. Yet Stewart seemed particularly at home with the part, in which once more he exemplified solid rustic values against the devious ways of big businessmen.

From competing with one animal, Stewart went off to Kenya in 1979 to co-star with a whole horde of them. He had been a frequent visitor to Africa and India to enjoy the wildlife for many years and his daughter Kelly had married a British anthropologist, Alexander Harcourt, who specialized in the study of gorilla life (the couple have made wild-life films). Yet Stewart had never done any films with African or Indian settings and the temptation to appear in a movie set in the African bush—even a Japanese one—must have been irresistible—besides which, director Susumu Hani was no stranger to Africa and once had a fair reputation as a film-maker (*He and She, Bride of the Andes*).

The film was *Afurika Monogatari*, titled for the American market *The Green Horizon*. Its very limited amount of dialogue seems to have been spoken in English (none of the characters are Japanese) and Stewart has barely a dozen lines to speak plus a few other moments hugging a chimp and stroking a young serval. Such plot as there is would be considered too elementary for a children's picture book. The film is padded out to an incredible degree with "mood-setting" footage of animals and scenery. Stewart just about takes care of himself (in safari jacket, wide-brimmed hat and white beard, he looks more like John Huston than himself) but the few other performers are awful and the handling of fire and flood sequences totally ineffective.

Stewart plays the Old Man (his name is never revealed) who

lives cut off from civilization in a large hut with his granddaughter, visited only by various animals and nomadic tribesmen. Their pleasant existence is disturbed by the arrival of a pilot whose plane has crashed. Stewart is at first hostile to the man (whose name is also, for no good reason, kept secret) but he gradually relents. The small mystery as to why Stewart lives the way he does is cursorily explained before the camera zooms slowly in on his grizzled features as a prelude to the discovery of him lying on the floor, dead. The granddaughter and the pilot bury him and stay on . . .

From this squib, Stewart returned to accept the Eighth Annual Life Achievement Award of the American Film Institute, presented before the television cameras on February 27, 1980.

20

His Golden Pond?

IT LOOKED AS THOUGH THERE would be few acting challenges left for James Stewart—certainly nothing real, nothing contemporary, nothing *biting* to make us sit up and take notice of him anew.

A young playwright, Richard Lees, had a different idea. In the late seventies, he wrote a tough little play about a couple of elderly people who make a logical decision to do away with themselves. He called it *Right of Way* and he had mental images of Bette Davis and James Stewart as models for his two principal characters as he hammered out the script of his provocative black comedy. It was staged in Minneapolis, then his agent dispatched the play to Bette Davis who took her time to warm to it but eventually passed it on to director George Schaefer as the basis for a television movie she would like to do.

There was little chance that the big American networks would take a subject that dealt sympathetically with suicide for the elderly, or that advertisers would want to be associated with it. The solution proved to be the American cable company Home Box Office which wanted to undertake films that were different from the norm and would command attention. James Stewart was delighted to be offered the part and the chance to co-star with Bette Davis for the first time. *Right of Way* went into production in 1982 as the first television movie made for cable in Hollywood. It cost $2.8 million with Davis and Stewart receiving $250,000 each.

They had to play four years older than themselves as the seventy-eight-year-olds, Mini and Teddy Dwyer, whose plans to end their lives in a joint suicide pact after she contracts a terminal blood disease horrify their thirty-nine-year-old daughter, played by Melinda Dillon. As the brittle, spindly Stewart character puts it to her: "Your mother and I have lived as one. We'll die as one." The picture goes on to deal with the difficulties imposed by a bureaucracy that won't permit the couple to carry out their plan.

Inevitably, the film has evoked comparisons with the teaming of Henry Fonda and Katharine Hepburn for the first time in *On Golden Pond* which also explored the difficult aspects of old age. The circumstances of *Right of Way*'s production rule out the kind of attention that *On Golden Pond* received as a major big-screen feature and at the time of writing (September 1983) it has yet to be seen in the United States. However, it was dispatched to the Montreal Film Festival and entered in competition. There it was reviewed by *Variety*'s Leonard Klady who reported: "Prime weakness of the material is finding the levity in the grim conviction of the couple . . . Nonetheless, both Stewart and Davis fight valiantly to rise above their material with Stewart demonstrating a conviction and sensitivity in his role. Davis fares slightly worse . . . *Right of Way* remains a production of noble intentions which squanders the skills of two accomplished stars. Less cleverness and more attention to detail should have been applied to this material."

Stewart told *Emmy Magazine*'s reporter Elizabeth Mehren that he took a month off to learn his lines . . . "the type of thing I used to do, just to become completely familiar with the part, so that you can work on the actual visual parts and not have to think of the lines." Production took place over twenty days on a specially constructed set rather than on location, just as in the old days of Hollywood.

For Stewart, old age has made its inevitable inroads. On the *Hawkins* television series he didn't have the luxury of a month to learn his lines and he found it difficult coping with dialogue at short notice. He had to reject the idea of the lines being put on cue cards for, as he explained, "I can't *see* the cue cards." His hearing has also caused difficulties. It made him give up flying in 1981 for, as he related to journalist Lesley Salisbury, "I had a Piper Cub that I loved, used to go out every week taking the little thing up into the mountains and landing at tiny strips the ranchers have laid down. But I have a hearing problem and it got so that I couldn't understand communications from the tower. I would have to have them repeat everything. Then I tried putting a loudspeaker in the plane. Only trouble was they could hear me all over the airport but I couldn't understand a thing. So, I just had to give up. I miss it terribly. But I did it for forty-five years. I guess that's long enough. I had a pretty good run . . ." On *Right of Way*, George Schaefer admitted that Stewart's troubles with his hearing aid had occasionally upset the tight production schedule.

There have been trips to the hospital, too—to check on an irregular heart beat in August 1980, for tests in August 1982. But there has been talk of another television series: he would make a two-hour pilot called *His Honor, Doc Potter*, playing a local doctor who doubles as a small town mayor, for a fee of $350,000—then, if its ratings were high enough, it would become a series paying him $40,000 per episode. It hardly matters if he doesn't make it. He has done more than enough.

He has been offered grandfather parts modeled on the irascible character played by Henry Fonda in *On Golden Pond*, and he turns them down. "I look at the script and I find a description of the character—he's 'an old grouch.' I object to this. I don't see why if you're old you have to be grouchy."

More to his liking is a plan to film an old hit play, *The Late Christopher Bean*, probably for American cable television. Stewart would star opposite Carol Burnett in the parts that Lionel Barrymore and Marie Dressler played in a now forgotten 1933 film version.

So Stewart remains active. "Time enough for retirement when I hit eighty," he said in 1970. "The men in our family all lived until they were eighty or ninety and I hope to do the same. While people want me, I am willing to work." On May 20, 1983, he celebrated his seventy-fifth birthday with a party at his birthplace—Indiana, Pennsylvania. Afterwards, he flew to Britain for a reunion with members of his war-time bomb group.

For many years, there have been invitations to attend retrospectives of his work and awards to be accepted. He was one of five artists honored late in 1983 for the sixth annual Kennedy

Center Honors along with Frank Sinatra, Elia Kazan, Katherine Dunham and Virgil Thompson—a prestigious occasion attended by the President and televised. With the revival of his old Hitchcock movies, he has been out meeting the press in New York, London and Paris for their new distributor, Universal.

When he first went into television seriously, he found himself working on soundstages where he had once made films for the big screen. "The movies," he murmured softly, "I used to think they were indestructible."

Of course, the films themselves are. And so are the best actors in them.

"It's a funny thing . . . the things people remember you for," Stewart is apt to say. "A guy came up to me one time. I was making *The Far Country* up in Canada some place . . . and this fella nodded to me and . . . he said how much he'd liked this scene I'd done *years before*. It was a little thing . . . a poem I did in *Come Live with Me*. . . and he remembered it and he said that it was good. He didn't remember the Indians I'd killed or the bridges I'd taken or the bad men I'd run outta town. He just remembered this one little thing. He said, 'I doubt if it *means* much to you . . .' Well, when he told me that, it was the most *moving* . . . I tell you, it was better than getting a fistful of fine notices.

"Did it *mean* anything? Why, it means *everything* to me. When they get around to writing my epitaph, I'll settle for, I'll be happy with, 'He sure gave us a lot of pleasure over the years.' I wouldn't mind that at all—to die knowing . . . knowing you've given people just a little piece of . . . a small piece of *time* they'll never forget."

Filmography

THIS FILMOGRAPHY LISTS THE film work of James Stewart for large screen and for television in the order in which it was first shown (which is not always the same as the order in which it was made). Films which Stewart narrated or introduced, or in which he was interviewed as himself, are listed separately at the end. The release date and the name of the distributor apply to the United States unless otherwise indicated.

ART TROUBLE (1934)

Director: Ralph Staub. Story: Jack Henley, Dolph Singer.

Cast: Harry Gribbon, Shemp Howard, Beatrice Blinn, Leni Stengel, James Stewart.

Production company: Vitaphone Corp. Distributor: Warner Bros. Length: 20 minutes. Release date: 23 June 1934.

A 'Big V Comedy' (No. 18).

THE MURDER MAN (1935)

Director: Tim Whelan. Screenplay: Tim Whelan, John C. Higgins (from a story by Tim Whelan and Guy Bolton). Photographer: Lester White. Art directors: Cedric Gibbons, Eddie Imazu and (set decoration) Edwin B. Willis. Editor: James E. Newcom. Music: William Axt.

Cast: Spencer Tracy (Steve Grey), Virginia Bruce (Mary

Shannon), Lionel Atwill (Captain Cole), Harvey Stephens (Henry Mander), Robert Barrat (Robins), James Stewart (Shorty), William Collier Sr (Pop Grey), Bobby Watson (Carey Booth), William Demarest (Red McGuire), John Sheehan (Maxie Sweeney), Lucien Littlefield (Peter Rafferty), George Chandler (Sol Hertzberger), Fuzzy Knight (Buck Hawkins), Louise Henry (Lillian Hopper), Robert Warwick (Colville), Joe Irving (Tony), Ralph Bushman [Francis` X. Bushman Jr] (Pendleton), Ed Coppo (Fingerprint expert), Heinie Conklin (Warden's secretary), James Pierce (Sing Sing guard), Ben Taggart (Dave, Sing Sing guard), Frank O'Connor (Reporter), John Dilson (Meltzer, City Editor), William Norton Bailey (Welch, police photographer), Harry Tyler (Doc Warren), Jennie Roberts (Mabel), Theodore von Eltz (James Spencer Halford), Irving Bacon (Merry-Go-Round operator), James Flavin (Cop at Merry-Go-Round), Howard Hickman (Howard Jannings), George Guhl (Cop at apartment), Stanley Andrews (Police Commissioner), Cyril Ring (Court official), Robert Warwick (Defense attorney), Bob Murphy (Cop), Charles Delaney (Cop), Matty Roubert (Newsboy), Charles Trowbridge, Jack Cheatham and Larry Steers (Investors), Reginald Pash (Third mate), Robert Frazer (Doctor), James Burtis (Police phone man), Charles Coleman (Hotel doorman).

Producer: Harry Rapf. Production company/distributor: Metro-Goldwyn-Mayer. Length: 70 minutes. Release date: 12 July 1935.

ROSE MARIE (1936)

Director: W. S. Van Dyke II. Screenplay: Frances Goodrich, Albert Hackett, Alice Duer Miller (from the operetta with book and lyrics by Otto A. Harbach and Oscar Hammerstein II, music by Rudolf Friml). Photographer: William Daniels. Art directors: Cedric Gibbons, Joseph Wright and (set decoration) Edwin B. Willis. Editor: Blanche Sewell. Music director: Herbert Stothart.

Cast: Jeanette MacDonald (Marie de Flor), Nelson Eddy (Sergeant Bruce), James Stewart (John Flower), Reginald Owen (Myerson), Allan Jones (Romeo/Mario Cavaradossi), George Regas (Boniface), Robert Greig (Cafe manager), Gilda Gray

(Bella), Una O'Connor (Anna), Lucien Littlefield (Storekeeper), Alan Mowbray (Premier), David Nivens [Niven] (Teddy), Herman Bing (Daniels), James Conlin (Joe), Dorothy Gray (Edith), Mary Anita Loos (Corn Queen), Aileen Carlyle (Susan), Halliwell Hobbes (Mr Gordon), Paul Porcasi (Emil), Edgar Dearing (Mountie), Pat West (Travelling salesman), Milton Owen (Stage manager), David Clyde (Doorman), Russell Hicks (Commandant), Rolfe Sedan and Louis Mercier (Admirers in hall), Jack Pennick (Brawler), David Robel and Rinaldo Alacorn (Dancers), Matty Roubert (Newsboy), Leonard Carey (Louis), Major Sam Harris (Guest), Bert Lindley (Pop), James Mason (Trapper), Ernie Alexander (Elevator attendant), Lee Phelps and John George (Barflies), Fred Graham (Corporal), Agostino Borgato and Adrian Rosley (Opera fans), Delos Jewkes (Butcher at hotel).

Producer: Hunt Stromberg. Production company/distributor: Metro-Goldwyn-Mayer. Length: 113 minutes. Release date: 28 January 1936 (premiere at Miami Beach).

Filming started mid-September 1935. Location work at Lake Tahoe. Retitled *Indian Love Call* for American television screenings to distinguish it from the 1954 MGM production of *Rose Marie*.

NEXT TIME WE LOVE (1936)

Original British release title: **Next Time We Live**

Director: Edward H. Griffith. Screenplay: Melville Baker, (uncredited additions) Doris Anderson (from the story *Say Goodbye Again* by Ursula Parrott) (uncredited adaptation by Preston Sturges). Photographer: Joseph Valentine. Art director: Charles D. Hall. Editor: Ted J. Kent. Music direction: Franz Waxman.

Cast: Margaret Sullavan (Cicely Tyler), James Stewart (Christopher Tyler), Ray Milland (Tommy Abbott), Grant Mitchell (Michael Jennings), Anna Demetrio (Madame Donato), Robert McWade (Frank Carteret), Ronnie Cosbey (Kit aged 8), Florence Roberts (Mrs Talbot), Christian Rub (Otto, Swiss Innkeeper), Charles Fallon (Professor Dindet), Nat Carr (Assistant stage manager), Gottlieb Huber (Swiss porter),

Hattie McDaniel (Hanna), Leonid Kinskey (Designer), John King (Juvenile), Nan Grey (Ingenue), Albert Conti (Charles), Tyler Brooke (Author), John Dilson (Stage manager), Eddie Phillips (Ticket taker), Clark Williams and Clive Morgan (Leading men), Tom Manning and King Baggot (Character actors), Harry C. Bradley (Desk clerk), Jack Daley and Broderick O'Farrell (Conductors), Buddy Williams (Porter), Dutch Hendrian, Philip Morris, Al Hill and Jack Cheatham (Taxi drivers), Emmett Vogan (Bartender), Harry Bowe and Jack Mower (Waiters), Donna Mae Roberts (Cigarette girl), George Davis and Ludwig Lowery (Waiters), Daisy Bufford (Maid), Alfred P. James (Aquarium attendant), Billy Gratton (Kit aged 3), Jacqueline Smylle (Susan), Arthur Aylesworth (Secretary), Julie Carter (Sob sister), Don Roberts (City editor), Paddy O'Flynn (Reporter), Harry Tracy (Valet), Jane Keckley (Nurse), Miki Morita (Dr Ito), Selmer Jackson (Dr Campbell), Teru Shimada (Steward), Otto Fries (Conductor).

Producer: Paul Kohner. Production company/distributor: Universal. Length: 87 minutes. Release date: 30 January 1936 (premiere in New York).

Shooting started 21 October and finished 28 December 1935.

WIFE VS. SECRETARY (1936)

Director: Clarence Brown. Screenplay: Norman Krasna, Alice Duer Miller, John Lee Mahin (from the short story by Faith Baldwin). Photographer: Ray June. Art directors: Cedric Gibbons, William A. Horning and (set decoration) Edwin B. Willis. Editor: Frank E. Hull. Music: Herbert Stothart, Edward Ward.

Cast: Clark Gable (Van Stanhope), Jean Harlow (Helen 'Whitey' Wilson), Myrna Loy (Linda Stanhope), May Robson (Mimi), Hobart Cavanaugh (Joe), James Stewart (Dave), George Barbier (Underwood), Gilbert Emery (Simpson), Margaret Irving (Edna Wilson), William Newell (Tom Wilson), Marjorie Gateson (Eve Merritt), Leonard Carey (Taggart), Charles Trowbridge (Hal Harrington), John M. Qualen (Mr Jenkins), Hilda Howe (Mary Connors), Mary MacGregor (Ellen), Gloria Holden (Joan Carstairs), Tommy Dugan (Finney), Jack Mulhall (Howard), Frank Elliott (Mr Barker),

Greta Meyer (German cook), Aileen Pringle (Mrs Barker), Frank Puglia (Hotel clerk), Myra Marsh (Miss Clark), Holmes Herbert (Frawley), Frederick Burton (Trent), Harold Minjir (Williams), Maurice Cass (Bakewell), Tom Herbert (Businessman), Niles Welch (Tom Axel), Guy D'Ennery (Cuban waiter), Richard Hemingway (Bridegroom), Paul Ellis (Raoul), Tom Rowan (Battleship), Clay Clement (Herbert), Tom Mahoney (Cop), Nina Quartaro (Telephone operator), Charles Irwin (Information clerk), André Cheron (Frenchman), Eugene Borden (Ship's officer), Hooper Atchley (Postal clerk), Lucille Ward (Scrub woman), Clifford Jones (Elevator boy), Helen Shipman, Edward Le Saint.

Producer: Hunt Stromberg. Production company/distributor: Metro-Goldwyn-Mayer. Length: 88 minutes. Release date: 28 February 1936.

Shooting from 26 November 1935 to 13 January 1936.

IMPORTANT NEWS (1936)

Director: Edwin Laurence.

Cast: Chic Sale, James Stewart.

Production company/distributor: Metro-Goldwyn-Mayer. Length: 10 minutes. Release date: 29 February 1936.

An MGM Miniature.

SMALL TOWN GIRL (1936)

Director: William A. Wellman. Screenplay: John Lee Mahin, Edith Fitzgerald, Frances Goodrich and Albert Hackett (from the novel by Ben Ames Williams). Photographer: Charles Rosher. Art directors: Cedric Gibbons, Arnold Gillespie and (set decoration) Edwin B. Willis. Editor: Blanche Sewell. Music: Herbert Stothart, Edward Ward.

Cast: Janet Gaynor (Kay Brannan), Robert Taylor (Bob Dakin), Binnie Barnes (Priscilla), Lewis Stone (Dr Dakin), Elizabeth Patterson (Ma Brannan), Frank Craven (Pa Brannan), Andy Devine (George), James Stewart (Elmer), Douglas Fowley (Chick), Isabel Jewell (Emily), Charley Grapewin (Dr Fabre), Agnes Ayres (Catherine), Nella Walker (Mrs Dakin), Robert Greig (Childers), Edgar Kennedy (Captain Mack), Mary Forbes

(Mrs Hyde), Willie Fung (So So), John Harron (Pat), Nora Lane (Cissie), Walter Johnson (Jim), Drue Leyton (Felicia), Joan Breslau (Martin girl), Joan Russell (June Brannan), Adrian Rosley (Cafe proprietor), Richard Carle (J.P.), James Donlan (Attendant), Frank Sully (Bill), Buster Phelps (Boy), Grace Hayle (Floor nurse), Ethel Wales (Mrs Johnson), Leonard Carey (Concierge), Helen Shipman and Ellen Lowe (Nurses), George Breakston (Little Jimmy), Otto Fries (Cook), Jack Hatfield, William Wayne and Franklin Parker (Reporters), Claire McDowell (Woman in bed), Robert Livingston, Thelma 'Pat' Ryan [Nixon].

Producer: Hunt Stromberg. Production company/distributor: Metro-Goldwyn-Mayer. Length: 90 minutes. Release date: 10 April 1936.

Shooting from 26 December 1935. Retitled *One Horse Town* for American television screenings to distinguish it from the 1953 MGM production *Small Town Girl* (which was not a re-make).

SPEED (1936)

Director: Edwin L. Marin. Screenplay: Michael Fessier (from an original story by Milton Krims and Larry Bachman). Photographer: Lester White. Art directors: Cedric Gibbons, Arnold Gillespie, Paul Crawley and (set decoration) Edwin B. Willis. Editor: Ben Lewis. Music: Edward Ward.

Cast: James Stewart (Terry Martin), Wendy Barrie (Jane Mitchell), Una Merkel (Josephine Sanderson), Weldon Heyburn (Frank Lawson), Ted Healy (Clarence Gadget), Patricia Wilder (Fanny Lane), Ralph Morgan (Mr Dean), Robert Livingston (George Saunders), Charles Trowbridge and William Tannen (Doctors), Walter Kingsford (Uncle Edward Emery), Claudelle Kaye and Barbara Bedford (Nurses), George Chandler (Rustic bystander), Jack Clifford (Master of ceremonies), Don Brodie (Track official), Grace Hale (Dance partner).

Producer: Lucien Hubbard. Production company/distributor: Metro-Goldwyn-Mayer. Length: 72 minutes. Release date: 8 May 1936.

Principal shooting commenced 20 March 1936.

THE GORGEOUS HUSSY (1936)

Director: Clarence Brown. Screenplay: Ainsworth Morgan, Stephen Morehouse Avery (from the novel by Samuel Hopkins Adams). Photographer: George Folsey. Art directors: Cedric Gibbons, William A. Horning and (set decoration) Edwin B. Willis. Editor: Blanche Sewell. Music: Herbert Stothart.

Cast: Joan Crawford (Peggy O'Neal Eaton), Robert Taylor (Bow Timberlake), Lionel Barrymore (Andrew Jackson), Franchot Tone (John Eaton), Melvyn Douglas (John Randolph), James Stewart ('Rowdy' Roderick Dow), Louis Calhern (Professor Sunderland), Alison Skipworth (Mrs Beall), Beulah Bondi (Rachel Jackson), Melville Cooper (Cuthbert), Edith Atwater (Lady Vaughn), Sidney Toler (Daniel Webster), Gene Lockhart (Major O'Neal), Phoebe Foster (Emily Donaldson), Clara Blandick (Louisa Abbot), Frank Conroy (John C. Calhoun), Nydia Westman (Maybelle), Louise Beavers (Aunt Sukey), Charles Trowbridge (Martin Van Bueren), Willard Robertson (Secretary Ingham), Greta Meyer (Mrs Oxenrider), Fred 'Snowflake' Toone (Horatius), William Orlamond (Herr Oxenrider), Tom Herbert (Slave dealer), Lee Phelps (Bartender), Rubye de Remer (Mrs Bellamy), Betty Blythe (Mrs Wainwright), Zeffie Tilbury (Mrs Daniel Beall), George Reed (Braxton), Bert Roach (Majordomo), Else Janssen (Dutch minister's wife), Oscar Apfel (Tompkins), Richard Powell (Doorman), Wade Boteler (Fight starter), Sid Saylor, Lee Harvey and Hooper Atchley (Brawlers), Harry Holman (Auctioneer), Morgan Wallace (Slave buyer), Ward Bond (Officer), Samuel S. Hinds (Commander), Sam McDaniel (Butler), Harry Strang (Navigator), Edward Le Saint (Minister), Frank Reicher (Ship's Captain), Harry Bradley (Secretary).

Producer: Joseph L. Mankiewicz. Production company/distributor: Metro-Goldwyn-Mayer. Length: 102 minutes. Release date: 1 September 1936.

Filming from 27 April 1936.

BORN TO DANCE (1936)

Director: Roy Del Ruth. Screenplay: Jack McGowan, Sid Silvers (from their screen story written with B. G. De Sylva).

Photographer: Ray June. Art directors: Cedric Gibbons, Joseph Wright and (set decoration) Edwin B. Willis. Editor: Blanche Sewell. Music director: Alfred Newman. Songs: Cole Porter.

Cast: Eleanor Powell (Nora Paige), James Stewart (Ted Barker), Virginia Bruce (Lucy James), Una Merkel (Jenny Saks), Sid Silvers (Gunny Saks), Frances Langford (Peppy Turner), Raymond Walburn (Captain Percival Dingby), Alan Dinehart (James McKay), Buddy Ebsen (Mush Tracy), Juanita Quigley (Sally Saks), Reginald Gardiner (Policeman), Georges and Jalna (Dancers – Themselves), Barnett Parker (Floorwalker), John Kelly (Recruiting officer), Helen Troy (Telephone operator), J. Marshall Smith, L. Dwight Snyder, Jay Johnson and Del Porter (The Foursome), Charles Trowbridge (Store demonstrator), William and Joe Mandel, Leona and Naomi Keene (Acrobats), Anita Brown (Maid), Wally Maher, Johnny Tyrrell and Franklin Parker (Reporters), Harry Strang, Fred Graham and Douglas McPhail (Sailors), Dennis O'Keefe (Man at Lonely Hearts club), Fuzzy Knight (Pianist), George King (Assistant stage manager), Jonathan Hale (Hector, columnist), Bobby Watson (Costume designer/assistant stage manager), Charles Coleman (Waiter), James Flavin (Ship's officer), Geraldine Robertson, Mary Dees, Jacqueline Dax, Ginger Wyatt, Gay DeLys and Jean Joyce (Girls), Billy Watson (Newsboy), Sherry Hall (Cameraman), David Horsley.

Producer: Jack Cummings. Production company/distributor: Metro-Goldwyn-Mayer. Length: 108 minutes. Release date: 27 November 1936.

Shooting began in early July 1936.

AFTER THE THIN MAN (1936)

Director: W. S. Van Dyke II. Screenplay: Frances Goodrich, Albert Hackett (from unpublished story material by Dashiell Hammett). Photographer: Oliver T. Marsh. Art directors: Cedric Gibbons, Harry McAfee and (set decoration) Edwin B. Willis. Editor: Robert J. Kern. Music: Herbert Stothart, Edward Ward.

Cast: William Powell (Nick Charles), Myrna Loy (Nora Charles), James Stewart (David Graham), Elissa Landi (Selma

Landis), Joseph Calleia ('Dancer'), Jessie Ralph (Aunt Katherine Forrest), Alan Marshall (Robert Landis), Teddy Hart (Floyd Casper), Sam Levene (Lt. Abrahams), Dorothy McNulty [Penny Singleton] (Polly Byrnes, nightclub singer), Dorothy Vaughn (Charlotte), William Law (Lum Kee), George Zucco (Dr Adolph Kammer), Paul Fix (Phil Byrnes), Harlan Briggs (Burton Forrest), Maude Turner Gordon (Helen), William Burress (General), Thomas Pogue (William), Tom Ricketts (Henry, valet), Joe Caits (Joe), Joe Phillips (Willie the Weeper), Edith Kingdon (Hattie), John T. Murray (Jerry), John Kelly (Harold, chauffeur), Clarence Kolb (Lucius), Zeffie Tilbury (Aunt Lucy), Donald Briggs, Fredric Santly and Jack Norton (Reporters), Baldwin Cooke, Sherry Hall and Jack Raymond (Photographers), George Guhl (San Francisco Police Captain), Edgar Dearing (Bill, San Francisco policeman), Dick Rush (San Francisco detective), Jim Farley (Police sergeant), Guy Usher (Judge), Ray Cook (Newsboy), Lucy Beaumont (Jail matron), Ric Powell (Cop), Mary Gordon (Rose, the cook), Ben Hall (Butcher boy), George H. Reed (Porter), John Butler (Racetrack tout), Harry Tyler (Fingers), Bobby Watson (Crowd leader), Jack Adair (Blonde's escort), Charlie Arnt and Arthur Housman (Drunks), William Gould (Detective), Charles Trowbridge (Police examiner), Alice H. Smith (Emily), George Taylor (Eddie), Murray Alper (Kid), Richard Loo (Head waiter), Eric Wilton (Peter, butler), Vince Barnett (Wrestler's manager), William Benedict (Newsboy), Chester Gan (Waiter), Heinie Conklin (Trainman), Harvey Perry, Monte Vandergrift, Eddie Allen, Jimmy Lucas, Eadie Adams.

Producer: Hunt Stromberg. Production company/distributor: Metro-Goldwyn-Mayer. Length: 112 minutes. Release: 25 December 1936.

Filming began 21 September 1936.

SEVENTH HEAVEN (1937)

Director: Henry King. Screenplay: Melville Baker (from the play by Austin Strong). Photographer: Merritt Gerstad. Art directors: William Darling, David Hall. Editor: Barbara McLean. Music director: Louis Silvers.

Cast: Simone Simon (Diane), James Stewart (Chico), Jean

Hersholt (Father Chevillon), Gregory Ratoff (Boul), Gale Sondergaard (Nana), J. Edward Bromberg (Aristide), John Qualen (Sewer Rat), Victor Kilian (Gobin), Thomas Beck (Brissac), Sig Rumann (Durand), Mady Christians (Marie), Rafaela Ottiano (Madame Frisson), Georges Renavent (Sergeant Gendarme), Edward Keane, John Hamilton and Paul Porcasi (Gendarmes), Will Stanton and Irving Bacon (Young soldiers), Evelyn Selbie (Old slattern), John Picorri (Proprietor), Rollo Lloyd (Mateot), Leonid Snegoff (Officer), Gene Massett (Wounded soldier), Frank Puglia (Postman), John Bleifer (Lamplighter), Adrienne d'Ambricourt (Nurse), Pedro Lara (Wounded man), Constant Franke, Alphonse Martell, Joseph De Stefani, Eugene Borden, Marcelle Corday.

Producer: Darryl F. Zanuck. Associate producer: Raymond H. Griffith. Production company/distributor: 20th Century-Fox. Length: 102 minutes. Release date: 26 March 1937.

Filming commenced 4 December 1936. Charles Farrell played the role of Chico in the 1927 version.

THE LAST GANGSTER (1937)

Director: Edward Ludwig. Screenplay: John Lee Mahin (from a story by William A. Wellman and Robert Carson). Photographer: William Daniels. Art directors: Cedric Gibbons, Daniel B. Cathcart and (set decoration) Edwin B. Willis. Editor: Ben Lewis. Music: Edward Ward.

Cast: Edward G. Robinson (Joe Krozac), James Stewart (Paul North), Rose Stradner (Talya Krozac), Lionel Stander (Curly), Douglas Scott (Joe Krozac Jr/Paul North Jr), John Carradine (Casper), Signey Blackmer (San Francisco editor), Grant Mitchell (Warden), Edward Brophy ('Fats' Garvey), Alan Baxter ('Acey' Kile), Frank Conroy (Sid Gorman), Louise Beavers (Gloria), Moroni Olsen (Danny Shea), Ivan Miller (Wilson), Willard Robertson (Broderick), Donald Barry (Billy Ernst), Ben Welden ('Buckles' Bailey), Horace McMahon (Limpy), Edward Pawley (Brockett), Pierre Watkin (Editor), Douglas McPhail (Reporter), Frederick Vogeding (Ambassador), Walter Miller (Mike Kile), Edward Marr (Frankie Kile), Robert Neil Taylor (The baby at six months), Larry Sims (The baby at three years), Wade Boteler (Turnkey), Priscilla

Dean (Nurse), Esther Muir (Blonde), Martin Turner (Cook on train), Lee Phelps (Guard on train), William Benedict (Bernie, office boy), Cy Kendall (Editor), David Leo Tillotson, Jim Kehner, Billy Smith, Dick Holland and Reggie Streeter (Boys), Arthur Howard, Broderick O'Farrell, Michell Ingraham, Billy Arnold and Cyril Ring (Fathers), Allen Mathews, Eddie Foster, Al Hill, Huey White, Sammy Finn, Charlie Sullivan, Brooks Benedict and Jack Raynold (Prisoners), Eddie Parker and Lee Powell (Federal men), Priscilla Lawson and Shirley Chambers (Girls in dive), Ernest Wood and Phillip Terry (Reporters), Jack Pennick (Convict in mess hall riot), Victor Adams, George Magrill and Jerry Jerome (Gangsters).

Producer: J. J. Cohn. Production company/distributor: Metro-Goldwyn-Mayer. Length: 81 minutes. Release date: 12 November 1937.

Shooting started 23 August 1937.

NAVY BLUE AND GOLD (1937)

Director: Sam Wood. Screenplay: George Bruce (from his novel). Photographer: John Seitz. Art directors: Cedric Gibbons, Urie McCleary and (set decoration) Edwin B. Willis. Editor: Robert J. Kern. Music: Edward Ward.

Cast: Robert Young (Roger Ash), James Stewart (John Carter, alias 'Truck' Cross), Lionel Barrymore (Captain 'Skinny' Dawes), Florence Rice (Patricia Gates), Billie Burke (Mrs Gates), Tom Brown (Richard Gates Jr), Samuel S. Hinds (Richard Gates Sr), Paul Kelly (Tommy Milton), Barnett Parker (Graves), Frank Albertson (Weeks), Minor Watson (Lt. Milburn), Robert Middlemass (Academy Superintendent), Phillip Terry (Kelly), Charles Waldron (Commander Carter), Pat Flaherty (Coach of Southern Institute), Stanley Morner [Dennis Morgan] (Lieutenant of Marines), Matt McHugh (Heckler), Ted Pearson (Harnet), Wilfred Lucas (Ship captain), Gloria Wood.

Producer: Sam Zimbalist. Production company/distributor: Metro-Goldwyn-Mayer. Length: 94 minutes. Release date: 19 November 1937.

Filming from 7 September 1937.

OF HUMAN HEARTS (1938)

Director: Clarence Brown. Screenplay: Bradbury Foote (from the story *Benefits Forgot* by Honore Morrow). Photographer: Clyde DeVinna. Art directors: Cedric Gibbons, Harry Oliver and (set decoration) Edwin B. Willis. Editor: Frank E. Hull. Music: Herbert Stothart.

Cast: Walter Huston (Ethan Wilkins), James Stewart (Jason Wilkins), Beulah Bondi (Mary Wilkins), Guy Kibbee (George Ames), Charles D. Coburn (Dr Charles Shingle), John Carradine (President Lincoln), Ann Rutherford (Annie Hawks), Charley Grapewin (Jim Meaker), Leona Roberts (Sister Clark), Gene Lockhart (Quid), Arthur Aylesworth (Rufus Inchpin), Clem Bevans (Elder Massey), Gene Reynolds (Jason aged 12), Leatrice Joy Gilbert (Annie Hawks aged 10), Sterling Holloway (Chauncey Ames aged 18), Charles Peck (Chauncey Ames aged 13), Robert McWade (Dr Lupus Crumm), Minor Watson [or John Miljan?] (Captain Griggs), Rosina Galli (Mrs Ardsley), Anne O'Neal (Mrs Hawks), Esther Dale (Mrs Cantwell), Brenda Fowler (Mrs Ames), William Stack (Salesman), Ward Bond and Frank McGlynn Jr (Louts), Stanley Fields (Horse owner), Roger Moore (Attendant), Guy Bates Post (Horse buyer), Jack Mulhall (Soldier), Phillip Terry and Joe Forte (Internes), Morgan Wallace (Dr Crandall), Francis X. Bushman Jr (Blacksmith), Barbara Bushman (Youngster).

Producer: John W. Considine Jr. Production company/ distributor: Metro-Goldwyn-Mayer. Length: 105 minutes. Release date: 11 February 1938.

Shooting started 18 October 1937. Location work at Lake Arrowhead North Shore in the San Bernardino Mountains and at the Clarence Brown ranch at Calabasas. Robert McWade died on the set of the film just after completing his scenes with Stewart.

VIVACIOUS LADY (1938)

Director: George Stevens. Screenplay: P. J. Wolfson, Ernest Pagano, (uncredited) Anne Morrison Chapin (from a novelette by I. A. R. Wylie). Photographer: Robert De Grasse. Art directors: Van Nest Polglase, Carroll Clark. Editor: Henry Berman. Music: Roy Webb.

Cast: Ginger Rogers (Frances Brent, alias Francey Larache), James Stewart (Peter Morgan), James Ellison (Keith Beston), Charles Coburn (Dr Morgan), Beulah Bondi (Mrs Morgan), Frances Mercer (Helen), Phyllis Kennedy (Jenny, the maid), Franklin Pangborn (Apartment manager), Grady Sutton (Culpepper), Jack Carson (Waiter captain), Alec Craig (Joseph), Willie Best (Porter), Hattie McDaniel (Maid), Dorothy Moore (Hatcheck girl), Maurice Black (waiter), Frank M. Thomas (Railroad conductor), Spencer Charters and Maude Eburne (Husband and wife), Marvin Jones and Jane Eberling (Boy and girl on bus), Bobby Barber (Italian), Ray Mayer and George Chandler (Passengers on train), Edgar Dearing (Cop), June Johnson (Miss Barton), Floyd Shackelford (Porter), Jack Arnold (Druggist), Ed Mortimer (Publisher), Lloyd Ingraham (Professor Noble), Harry Campbell, Kay Sutton, Phyllis Fraser, Bud Flanagan [Dennis O'Keefe], Helena Grant, Vivian Reid, William Brisbane, Vernon Dent, Katharine Ellis, June Horne, Dorothy Johnson, Phoebe Terbell, Robert Wilson, Stanley Blystone, Barbara Pepper.

Producer: Pandro S. Berman. Production company/distributor: RKO Radio. Length: 90 minutes. Release date: 13 May 1938.

Filming began 17 December 1937.

THE SHOPWORN ANGEL (1938)

Director: H. C. Potter. Screenplay: Waldo Salt, (uncredited) Howard Estabrook (from the story *Private Pettigrew's Girl* by Dana Burnet). Photographer: Joseph Ruttenberg. Art directors: Cedric Gibbons, Joseph C. Wright and (set decoration) Edwin B. Willis. Editor: W. Donn Hayes. Music: Edward Ward.

Cast: Margaret Sullavan (Daisy Heath), James Stewart (Bill Pettigrew), Walter Pidgeon (Sam Bailey), Hattie McDaniel (Martha, the maid), Nat Pendleton ('Dice'), Alan Curtis ('Thin Lips'), Sam Levene ('Leer'), Eleanor Lynn (Sally, the waitress), Charles D. Brown (McGonigle, the stage manager), Charley Grapewin (Wilson, the caretaker), Jimmy Butler (Elevator boy), William Stack (Minister), Hudson Shotwell (Jack, soldier), John Merton (Speaker), Wesley Giraud (Bellboy), Harry Tyler (Eddy, stagehand), Mary Howard and Virginia Grey (Chorus girls), Wade Boteler (Irish cop), James Flavin (Guard), George

Chandler (Soldier), Grace Hayle (Mistress of ceremonies), Jack Murphy (Sailor), Frank McGlynn Jr (Motorcyclist), Edward Keane (Captain), Eddy Chandler (Corporal), Paul Spiegel (Stage manager), Don Brodie (Attendant), Jack Hutchinson (Army officer), Roger Converse (Hotel clerk), Francesco Maran (Headwaiter), Paul Kruger (Riveter), Dorothy Granger (Dancer), Mary Dees, Joan Mitchell and Frances Millen (Babes).

Producer: Joseph L. Mankiewicz. Production company/ distributor: Metro-Goldwyn-Mayer. Length: 85 minutes. Release date: 15 July 1938.

Filmed 28 March to 6 May 1938. Gary Cooper played Stewart's role (then called William Tyler) in the 1928 version for Paramount.

YOU CAN'T TAKE IT WITH YOU (1938)

Director: Frank Capra. Screenplay: Robert Riskin (from the stage play by George S. Kaufman and Moss Hart). Photographer; Joseph Walker. Art directors: Stephen Goosson, Lionel Banks. Editor: Gene Havlick. Music: Dimitri Tiomkin.

Cast: Jean Arthur (Alice Sycamore), Lionel Barrymore (Martin Vanderhof), James Stewart (Tony Kirby), Edward Arnold (Anthony P. Kirby), Mischa Auer (Kolenkhov), Ann Miller (Essie Carmichael), Spring Byington (Penny Sycamore), Samuel S. Hinds (Paul Sycamore), Donald Meek (Poppins), H. B. Warner (Ramsey), Halliwell Hobbes (DePinna), Dub Taylor (Ed Carmichael), Mary Forbes (Mrs Kirby), Lillian Yarbo (Rheba), Eddie Anderson (Donald), Clarence Wilson (John Blakely), Josef Swickard (Professor), Ann Doran (Maggie O'Neill), Christian Rub (Jensen), Bodil Rosing (Mrs Jensen), Charles Lane (Henderson), Harry Davenport (Judge), Pierre Watkin (Attorney), Edwin Maxwell (Attorney), Russell Hicks (Attorney), Byron Foulger (Kirby's assistant), Ian Wolfe (Kirby's secretary), Irving Bacon (Henry), Chester Clute (Hammond), James Flavin (Jailer), Edward Keane (Board member), Pat Kelton (Inmate), Dick Curtis (Strongarm man), Kit Guard (Inmate), James Burke (Detective), Ward Bond (Detective), Edward Hearn (Court attendant), Robert Greig (Diner), John Hamilton (Diner), John Ince and Edward Peil (Neighbors).

Producer: Frank Capra. Production company/distributor: Columbia. Length: 127 minutes. Release date: 28 September 1938.

Shooting commenced 25 April 1938.

MADE FOR EACH OTHER (1939)

Director: John Cromwell. Screenplay: Jo Swerling (joke contributor: Frank Ryan) (from a story idea by Rose Franken). Photographer: Leon Shamroy. Production designer: William Cameron Menzies. Art director: Lyle Wheeler. Editors: James E. Newcom, (supervision) Hal C. Kern. Music: Lou Forbes.

Cast: Carole Lombard (Jane Mason), James Stewart (Johnny Mason), Charles Coburn (Judge Joseph Doolittle), Lucile Watson (Mrs Mason), Harry Davenport (Dr Healy), Ruth Weston (Eunice Doolittle), Donald Briggs (Carter), Eddie Quillan (Conway), Esther Dale (Annie, the cook), Renee Orsell (Hilda, the second cook), Louise Beavers (Lily, the third cook), Alma Kruger (Sister Madeline), Fred Fuller (Doolittle's brother), Edwin Maxwell (Messerschmidt), Harry Depp (Hutch), Mickey Rentschler (Office boy), Jackie Taylor (John Mason Jr at age one), Robert Emmett O'Connor (Elevator starter), Milburn Stone (Sam), Bonnie Belle Barber (John Mason Jr newly born), Olin Howland (Farmer), Robert Strange, Perry Ivans and Gladden James (Doctors), Ward Bond (Jim Hatton), Russell Hopton (Collins), Harlan Briggs (Judge), Arthur Hoyt (Jury foreman), Fern Emmett (Farmer's wife), Ivan Simpson (Simon), Jack Mulhall, Gary Owen, Carlyle Moore, Russ Clark, Mike Killian, John Austin and Arthur Gardner (Radio operators), Tom London and Lane Chandler (Rangers), Mary Field (Indianapolis lab assistant), Wilhelmina Morris, Nella Walker, Marjory Wood and Ethel Marical (Nurses).

Producer: David O. Selznick. Production company: Selznick International. Distributor: United Artists. Length: 90 minutes. Release date: 10 February 1939.

Filming from late August 1938.

THE ICE FOLLIES OF 1939 (1939)

Director: Reinhold Schunzel. Screenplay: Leonard Praskins,

Florence Ryerson, Edgar Allan Woolf (from a screen story by Leonard Praskins). Photographers: Joseph Ruttenberg, (Technicolor sequence) Oliver T. Marsh. Art directors: Cedric Gibbons, Eddie Imazu, (scenic effects) Merrill Pye, and (set decoration) Edwin B. Willis. Editor: W. Donn Hayes. Incidental music: Franz Waxman.

Cast: Joan Crawford (Mary McKay), James Stewart (Larry Hall), Lew Ayres (Eddie Burgess), Lewis Stone (Douglas Tolliver Jr), Bess Ehrhardt (Kitty Sherman), Lionel Stander (Mort Hodges), Charles D. Brown (Barney), Truman Bradley (Paul Rodney), Marie Blake (Effie Lane), Ray Shipstad, Eddie Shipstad and Oscar Johnson (of 'The International Ice Follies'), Charles Williams (Max Norton), Eddy Conrad (Hal Gibbs), Arthur Loft (Director), Mary Forbes (Lady Hilda), James Flavin (Doorman), Joe Manz (Tolliver's chauffeur), Hal K. Dawson (Publicity man), Louis Adlon (Dress designer), Charles Judels (Make-up man), Wade Boteler (Cop), Libby Taylor (Maid), Marrison Greene (Agent), Adolphe Hebert and Larry Jackson (Skating Horse), Carl Switzer (Small boy), Darla Hood (Sister), James McNamara and Eddie Kane (Politicians), Truman Bradley (Voice of announcer), Edward Earle.

Producer: Harry Rapf. Production company/distributor: Metro-Goldwyn-Mayer. Length: 82 minutes. Release date: 10 March 1939.

Shooting began 6 October 1938.

IT'S A WONDERFUL WORLD (1939)

Director: W. S. Van Dyke II. Screenplay: Ben Hecht (from a screen story by Ben Hecht and Herman J. Mankiewicz). Photographer: Oliver T. Marsh. Art directors: Cedric Gibbons, Paul Groesse. Editor: Harold F. Kress. Music: Edward Ward.

Cast: Claudette Colbert (Edwina Corday), James Stewart (Guy Johnson), Guy Kibbee (Capt. Streeter), Nat Pendleton (Sgt. Koretz), Frances Drake (Vivian Tarbel), Edgar Kennedy (Lt. Miller), Ernest Truex (Willie Heyward), Richard Carle (Major Willoughby), Cecilia Callejo (Dolores Gonzales), Sidney Blackmer (Al Mallon), Andy Clyde (Gimpy), Cliff Clark (Capt. Haggerty), Cecil Cunningham (Madame Chambers), Leonard

Kilbrick (Herman Plotka), Hans Conried (Stage manager), Grady Sutton (Lupton Peabody).

Producer: Frank Davis. Production company/distributor: Metro-Goldwyn-Mayer. Length: 86 minutes. Release date: 19 May 1939.

Filming began 22 February 1939.

MR. SMITH GOES TO WASHINGTON (1939)

Director: Frank Capra. Screenplay: Sidney Buchman (from the story *The Gentleman from Montana* by Lewis R. Foster). Photographer: Joseph Walker. 2nd unit director: Charles Vidor. Art director: Lionel Banks. Editors: Gene Havlick, Al Clark. Music: Dimitri Tiomkin.

Cast: Jean Arthur (Clarissa Saunders), James Stewart (Jefferson Smith), Claude Rains (Senator Joseph Paine), Edward Arnold (Jim Taylor), Guy Kibbee (Governor Hubert Hopper), Thomas Mitchell (Diz Moore), Eugene Pallette (Chick McGann), Beulah Bondi (Ma Smith), H. B. Warner (Senator Fuller), Harry Carey (President of the Senate), Astrid Allwyn (Susan Paine), Ruth Donnelly (Emma Hopper), Grant Mitchell (Senator Mac-Pherson), Porter Hall (Senator Monroe), Pierre Watkin (Senator Barnes), Charles Lane (Nosey), William Demarest (Bill Griffith), Dick Elliott (Carl Cook), H. V. Kaltenborn (Broad-caster), Kenneth Carpenter (Announcer), Jack Carson (Sweeney), Joe King (Summers), Paul Stanton (Flood), Russell Simpson (Ken Allen), Stanley Andrews (Senator Hodges), Walter Soderling (Senator Pickett), Frank Jaquet (Senator Byron), Ferris Taylor (Senator Carlisle), Carl Stockdale (Senator Burdette), Alan Bridge (Senator Dwight), Edmund Cobb (Senator Gower), Frederick Burton (Senator Dearhorn), Vera Lewis (Mrs Edwards), Dora Clemant (Mrs McGann), Laura Treadwell (Mrs Taylor), Ann Doran (Paine's secretary), Douglas Evans (Francis Scott Key), Allan Cavan (Ragner), Maurice Costello (Diggs), Lloyd Whitlock (Schultz), Myonne Walsh (Jane Hopper), Billy Watson, Delmar Watson, John Russell, Harry Watson, Garry Watson, Baby Dumpling [Larry Simms] (The Hopper boys), Frederick Hoose (Senator), Byron Foulger (Hopper's secretary), Fred 'Snowflake' Toone and Charles Moore (Porters), Dickie Jones (Senate page boy),

Margaret Mann (Nun), Frances Gifford, Lorna Gray, Adrian Booth and Linda Winters [Dorothy Comingore] (Girls), Clyde Dilson, William Newell, George Chandler, Evalyn Knapp, Dub Taylor, Jack Gardner, Donald Kerr, Eddie Kane, George McKay, Gene Morgan, Matt McHugh, William Arnold, Hal Cooke, James McNamara, Jack Egan and Eddy Chandler (Reporters), Eddie Fetherston, Ed Randolph, Milton Kibbee, Vernon Dent, Craig Stevens, Ed Brewer, Anne Cornwall, James Millican, Mabel Forrest, Nick Copeland and Dulce Daye (Senate reporters), Lafe McKee (Tourist), Frank Puglia and Erville Alderson (Handwriting experts), Arthur Loft (Senate clerk).

Producer: Frank Capra. Production company/distributor: Columbia. Length: 126 minutes. Release date: 19 October 1939.

Began shooting on 3 April 1939. Extract in *Land of Liberty* (1940). Fess Parker played Jefferson Smith in the 1962 television series, *Mr Smith Goes to Washington*, and Tom Laughlin played the character (renamed Billy Jack) in an updated version, *Billy Jack Goes to Washington* (1978).

DESTRY RIDES AGAIN (1939)

Director: George Marshall. Screenplay: Felix Jackson, Gertrude Purcell, Henry Myers (from a screen story by Felix Jackson derived from the novel by Max Brand). Photographer: Hal Mohr. Art directors: Jack Otterson, Martin Obzina. Editor: Milton Carruth. Music: Frank Skinner.

Cast: Marlene Dietrich (Frenchy), James Stewart (Thomas Jefferson Destry Jr), Mischa Auer (Boris Callahan), Charles Winninger (Washington Dimsdale), Brian Donlevy (Kent), Allen Jenkins (Gyp Watson), Warren Hymer (Bugs Watson), Irene Hervey (Janice Tyndall), Una Merkel (Lily Belle Callahan), Billy Gilbert (Loupgerou, the bartender), Samuel S. Hinds (Hiram J. Slade), Jack Carson (Jack Tyndall), Tom Fadden (Lem Claggett), Virginia Brissac (Sophie Claggett), Edmund MacDonald (Rockwell), Lillian Yarbo (Clara), Joe King (Sheriff Joseph Keogh), Dickie Jones (Eli Whitney Claggett), Ann Todd (Claggett girl), Harry Cording (Rowdy cowboy), Dick Alexander and Bill Steele Gettinger (Cowboys), Minerva Urecal (Mrs DeWitt), Bob McKenzie (Doctor), Billy Bletcher

(Pianist), Lloyd Ingraham (Turner, the Express Agent), Harry Tenbrook (Stage rider), Bud McClure (Stage driver), Chief John Big Tree (Indian in saloon), Philo McCullough (Bartender), Alex Voloshin (Assistant bartender), Carmen D'Antonio (Dancer), Bill Cody Jr (Small boy), Loren Brown and Harold De Carro (Jugglers), Dora Clemant, Mary Shannon, Robert Keith, Duke York.

A Joe Pasternak production. Associate producer: Islin Auster. Production company/distributor: Universal. Length: 94 minutes. Release date: 29 December 1939.

Filming started 7 September 1939. Tom Mix played Stewart's role in the 1932 production while Audie Murphy played it in the 1955 version simply called *Destry*. *Frenchie* (1950) was also suggested by the same story.

THE SHOP AROUND THE CORNER (1940)
Director: Ernst Lubitsch. Screenplay: Samson Raphaelson, (uncredited) Ben Hecht (from the play *Perfumerie* [*Illatszertar*] by Nikolaus Laszlo [Miklos Laszlo]). Photographer: William Daniels. Art directors: Cedric Gibbons, Wade B. Rubottom. Editor: Gene Ruggiero. Music: Werner R. Heymann.

Cast: Margaret Sullavan (Klara Novak), James Stewart (Alfred Kralik), Frank Morgan (Hugo Matuschek), Joseph Schildkraut (Ferencz Vadas), Sara Haden (Flora), Felix Bressart (Pirovitch), William Tracy (Pepi Katona), Inez Courtney (Ilona), Sarah Edwards and Gertrude Simpson (Customers), Edwin Maxwell (Doctor), Charles Halton (Detective), Charles Smith (Rudy), Charles Arnt (Policeman), William Edmunds (Waiter), Mary Carr (Grandmother), Mabel Colcord (Aunt Anna), Grace Hayle (Plump woman), Renie Riano, Claire DuBrey, Ruth Warren, Joan Blair and Mira McKinney (Other customers).

Producer: Ernst Lubitsch. Production company/distributor: Metro-Goldwyn-Mayer. Length: 97 minutes. Release date: 12 January 1940.

Shooting from 2 November 1939. Van Johnson took the Stewart role in the 1949 musical re-make, *In the Good Old Summertime*.

THE MORTAL STORM (1940)
Director: Frank Borzage. Screenplay: Claudine West, Andersen

Ellis, George Froeschel (from the novel by Phyllis Bottome). Photographer: William Daniels. Art directors: Cedric Gibbons, Wade B. Rubottom. Editor: Elmo Vernon. Music: Edward Kane, Eugene Zador.

Cast: Margaret Sullavan (Freya Roth), James Stewart (Martin Breitner), Robert Young (Fritz Marberg), Frank Morgan (Professor Victor Roth), Robert Stack (Otto Von Rohn), Bonita Granville (Elsa), Irene Rich (Mrs Roth), William T. Orr (Erich Von Rohn), Maria Ouspenskaya (Mrs Breitner), Gene Reynolds (Rudi), Russell Hicks (Rector), William Edmunds (Lehman), Thomas Ross (Professor Werner), Ward Bond (Franz), Esther Dale (Marta), Fritz Leiber (Oppenheim), Dan Dailey Jr (Holl), Robert O. Davis (Hartman), Granville Bates (Professor Berg), Sue Moore (Theresa), Harry Depp, Julius Tannen and Gus Glassmire (Colleagues), Dick Rich and Ted Oliver (Guards), William Tannen (Concentration camp official), Lloyd Corrigan (Postman), Lucien Prival and Dick Elliott (Passport officials), Henry Victor and John Stark (Gestapo officials), Tom Drake (Class student), William Irving (Waiter), Kurt Katch (Passport Inspector on train), Bert Roach (Fat man in cafe), Max Davidson (Old man), Bob Stevenson (Gestapo guard), Howard Lang, Bodil Rosing, Hans Schumm, James Millican.

Producers (uncredited): Frank Borzage, Victor Saville. Production company/distributor: Metro-Goldwyn-Mayer. Length: 100 minutes. Release date: 14 June 1940.

NO TIME FOR COMEDY (1940)

Director: William Keighley. Screenplay: Julius J. and Philip G. Epstein (from the play by S. N. Behrman). Photographer: Ernest Haller. Art director: John Hughes. Editor: Owen Marks. Music: Heinz Roemheld.

Cast: James Stewart (Gaylord Esterbrook), Rosalind Russell (Linda Paige), Genevieve Tobin (Amanda Swift), Charlie Ruggles (Philo Swift), Allyn Joslin (Morgan Carrell), Clarence Kolb (Richard Benson), Louise Beavers (Clementine), J. M. Kerrigan (Jim), Lawrence Grosmith (Frank), Robert Greig (Robert), Robert Emmett O'Connor (Desk sergeant), James Burke (Desk sergeant), Edgar Dearing (Sweeney), Frank Faylen (Cab driver), Herbert Heywood (Doorman), Arthur Housman

(Drunk), Olaf Hytten (Swift's butler), John Ridgely (Cashier), Selmer Jackson (Firstnighter), Herbert Anderson (Actor), Pierre Watkins and Nella Walker (Theatergoers).

Producer: Hal B. Wallis. Associate producer: Robert Lord. Production company/distributor: Warner Bros. Length: 93 minutes. Release date: 14 September 1940.

THE PHILADELPHIA STORY (1940)

Director: George Cukor. Screenplay: Donald Ogden Stewart, (uncredited contribution) Waldo Salt (from the play by Philip Barry). Photographer: Joseph Ruttenberg. Art directors: Cedric Gibbons, Wade B. Rubottom. Editor: Frank Sullivan. Music: Franz Waxman.

Cast: Cary Grant (C. K. Dexter Haven), Katharine Hepburn (Tracy Lord), James Stewart (Macaulay Connor), Ruth Hussey (Elizabeth Imbrie), John Howard (George Kittredge), Roland Young (Uncle Willie), John Halliday (Seth Lord), Virginia Weidler (Dinah Lord), Mary Nash (Margaret Lord), Henry Daniell (Sidney Kidd), Lionel Pape (Edward), Rex Evans (Thomas), Russ Clark (John), Hilda Plowright (Librarian), Lita Chevret (Manicurist), Lee Phelps (Bartender), Dorothy Fay, Florine McKinney, Helene Whitney and Hillary Brooke (Mainliners), Claude King (Uncle Willie's butler), Robert de Bruce (Dr Parsons), Veda Buckland (Elsie), David Clyde (Mac).

Producer: Joseph L. Mankiewicz. Production company/distributor: Metro-Goldwyn-Mayer. Length: 112 minutes. Release date: 26 December 1940.

Filmed 5 July to August 1940. Re-made as a musical comedy *High Society*, in 1956 with Frank Sinatra in the Stewart role.

COME LIVE WITH ME (1941)

Director: Clarence Brown. Screenplay: Patterson McNutt (from an original story by Virginia Van Upp). Photographer: George Folsey. Art directors: Cedric Gibbons, Randall Duell. Editor: Frank E. Hull. Music: Herbert Stothart.

Cast: James Stewart (Bill Smith), Hedy Lamarr (Johanna Janns alias Johnny Jones), Ian Hunter (Barton Kendrick), Verree

Teasdale (Diana Kendrick), Donald Meek (Joe Darsie), Barton MacLane (Barney Grogan), Edward Ashley (Arnold Stafford), Ann Codee (Yvonne), King Baggot (Doorman), Adeline de Walt Reynolds (Grandma), Frank Orth (Jerry), Si Jenks (Farmhand), Fritz Feld (Headwaiter), Dewey Robinson (Chef), Joe Yule (Sleeping neighbor), Tom Fadden (Hired hand), Horace MacMahon (Taxi driver), Greta Meyer (Frieda), Frank Faylen (Waiter), George Watts (Waiter).

Producer: Clarence Brown. Production company/distributor: Metro-Goldwyn-Mayer. Length: 86 minutes. Release date: 29 January 1941 (joint New York/Los Angeles premiere).

Started shooting on 7 October 1940 (Stewart completed his role on 26 November 1940).

POT O' GOLD (1941)
British release title: **The Golden Hour**

Director: George Marshall. Screenplay: Walter De Leon (from a screen story by Monte Brice, Andrew Bennison and Harry Tugend based on a story idea by Haydn Roth Evans and Robert Brilmayer). Dance director: Larry Ceballos. Photographers: Hal Mohr, (dance) Harry Jackson. Art director: Hans Peters. Editor: Lloyd Nosler. Musical director: Lou Forbes. Songs: Mack David and Vee Lawnhurst, Hy Heath and Fred Rose, Dave Franklin, Lou Forbes and Henry Sullivan.

Cast: James Stewart (James Hamilton Haskel), Paulette Goddard (Molly McCorkle), Horace Heidt and his Musical Knights (Themselves), Charles Winninger (C. J. Haskel), Mary Gordon (Ma McCorkle), Frank Melton (Jasper), Jed Prouty (Mr Louderman), Dick Hogan (Willie McCorkle), James Burke (Lt. Grady), Charlie Arnt (Parks), Donna Wood (Donna McCorkle), Larry Cotton (Himself), Henry Rocquemore (Samson), William Gould (Chalmers), Aldrich Bowker (Judge Murray), Victor Potel (Ole Svenson), Mary Ruth (Mary Simmons), Beverly Andre (Alice), Jay Ward (Boyfriend), James Flavin (Bud Connolly), Master Stan Worth (Tommy), Edgar Dearing (McGinty), Nestor Paiva (Guide), Purnell Pratt (Thompson).

Producer: James Roosevelt. Production company: Globe. Distributor: United Artists. Length: 86 minutes. Release date: 3 April 1941.

[210]

Shooting began on 11 December 1940 (Stewart arrived on 13 December 1940).

ZIEGFELD GIRL (1941)

Director: Robert Z. Leonard. Screenplay: Marguerite Roberts, Sonya Levien (from a story by William Anthony McGuire). Musical numbers director: Busby Berkeley. Photographer: Ray June. Art directors: Cedric Gibbons, Daniel B. Cathcart. Editor: Blanche Sewell. Incidental music: Herbert Stothart.

Cast: James Stewart (Gilbert Young), Judy Garland (Susan Gallagher), Hedy Lamarr (Sandra Kolter), Lana Turner (Sheila Regan), Tony Martin (Frank Merton), Jackie Cooper (Jerry Regan), Ian Hunter (Geoffrey Collis), Charles Winninger ('Pop' Gallagher), Edward Everett Horton (Noble Sage), Philip Dorn (Franz Kolter), Paul Kelly (John Slayton), Eve Arden (Patsy Dixon), Dan Dailey Jr (Jimmy Walters), Al Shean (Al), Fay Holden (Mrs Regan), Felix Bressart (Mischa), Rose Hobart (Mrs Merton), Bernard Nedell (Nick Capalini), Ed McNamara (Officer Regan), Mae Busch (Jenny), Joyce Compton (Miss Sawyer), Renie Riano (Annie), Ruth Tobey (Betty Regan), Sergio Orta (Native dancer), Reed Hadley (Geoffrey's friend), Bess Flowers (Casino patron), Antonio and Rosario (Specialty dancers), Armand Kaliz (Pierre), Georgia Carroll, Myrna Dell, Patricia Dane, Virginia Curzon, Lorraine Gettman [Leslie Brooks], Jean Wallace, Madeleine Martin, Harriet Bennett, Vivien Mason, Louise La Planche, Nina Bissell, Anya Taranda, Alaine Brandeis, Irma Wilson and Frances Gladwin (Ziegfeld girls), Claire James (Hopeful), Josephine Whittell (Perkins), George Lloyd (Saloon waiter), Fred Santley (Floorwalker), Six Hits and a Miss (Singers), Elliott Sullivan, Al Hill and James Flavin (Truckers), Ray Teal (Jeweler), Roscoe Ates (Theater janitor), Anne O'Neal (Woman in elevator).

Producer: Pandro S. Berman. Production company/distributor: Metro-Goldwyn-Mayer. Length: 131 minutes. Release date: 25 April 1941.

Production started 4 November 1940. Stewart was not available until 27 November 1940 and completed his role on 12 December 1940.

IT'S A WONDERFUL LIFE (1947)

Director: Frank Capra. Screenplay: Frances Goodrich, Albert Hackett, Frank Capra, (uncredited contributions) Michael Wilson, Clifford Odets (additional scenes: Jo Swerling) (from the short story *The Greatest Gift* by Philip Van Doren Stern). Photographers: Joseph Walker, Joseph Biroc. Art director: Jack Okey. Editor: William Hornbeck. Music: Dimitri Tiomkin.

Cast: James Stewart (George Bailey), Donna Reed (Mary Hatch), Lionel Barrymore (Dr Potter), Thomas Mitchell (Uncle Billy), Henry Travers (Clarence), Beulah Bondi (Mrs Bailey), Ward Bond (Bert), Frank Faylen (Ernie), Gloria Grahame (Violet Bick), H. B. Warner (Mr Gower), Todd Karns (Harry Bailey), Frank Albertson (Sam Wainwright), Samuel S. Hinds (Pa Bailey), Mary Treen (Cousin Millie), Virginia Patton (Ruth Dakin), Charles Williams (Cousin Eustace), Sara Edwards (Mrs Hatch), Bill Edmunds (Mr Martini), Lillian Randolph (Annie), Argentina Brunetti (Mrs Martini), Bobby Anderson (Little George), Ronnie Ralph (Little Sam), Jean Gale (Little Mary), Jeanine Anne Roose (Little Violet), Danny Mummert (Little Marty Hatch), Georgie Noaks (Little Harry Bailey), Sheldon Leonard (Nick), Frank Hagney (Potter's bodyguard), Ray Walker (Joe, at luggage shop), Charles Lane (Real estate salesman), Carol Coombs (Janie Bailey), Karolyn Grimes (Zuzu Bailey), Larry Simms (Pete Bailey), Jimmy Hawkins (Tommy Bailey), Carl 'Alfalfa' Switzer (Freddie), Hal Landon (Marty Hatch), Harry Holman (High School principal), Charles Halton (Carter, bank examiner), Ed Featherstone (Bank teller), Stanley Andrews (Mr Welch), J. Farrell MacDonald (House owner), Marion Carr (Mrs Wainwright), Max Wagner (Bartender), Gary Owen (Bill poster), Harry Cheshire (Dr Campbell), Bobby Scott (Mickey), Ellen Corby (Mrs Davis), Alan Bridge (Deputy with summons), Tom Fadden (Watchman), Almira Sessions, Lee Frederick, Bert Moorhouse, Harry Rosenthal, Max Wagner, Frank Fenton, Dick Elliott, Ernie Adams, Sam Flint.

Producer: Frank Capra. Production company: Liberty Films. Distributor: RKO Radio. Length: 129 minutes. Release date: January 1947.

Shooting started 8 April 1946. James Stewart repeated his role in a one-hour radio version for NBC Radio Theatre in 1949.

Remade for television as *It Happened One Christmas* (1977) with actress Marlo Thomas playing the Stewart role and Wayne Rogers as her husband George Hatch.

MAGIC TOWN (1947)

Director: William A. Wellman. Screenplay: Robert Riskin (from a screen story by Robert Riskin and Joseph Krumgold). Photographer: Joseph F. Biroc. Production designer: Lionel Banks. Editors: Sherman Todd, Richard Wray. Music: Roy Webb.

Cast: James Stewart (Lawrence 'Rip' Smith), Jane Wyman (Mary Peterman), Kent Smith (Hoopendecker), Ned Sparks (Ike Sloan), Wallace Ford (Lou Dicketts), Regis Toomey (Ed Weaver), Ann Doran (Mrs Weaver), Donald Meek (Mr Twiddle), E. J. Ballentine (Moody), Ann Shoemarker (Ma Peterman), Mickey Kuhn (Hank Nickleby), Howard Freeman (Richard Nickleby), Harry Holman (Mayor), Mary Currier (Mrs Frisby), Mickey Roth (Bob Peterman), Frank Fenton (Birch), George Irving (Senator Wilton), Selmer Jackson (Charlie Stringer), Robert Dudley (Dickey, the reporter), Julia Dean (Mrs Wilton), Joel Friedkin (Dingle), Paul Scardon (Hodges), George Chandler (Bus driver), Frank Darien (Quincy), Larry Wheat (Sam Fuller), Jimmy Crane (Shorty), Richard Belding (Junior Dicketts), Danny Mummert (Benny), Emmett Vogan (Reverend), Anna Q. Nilsson (Swedish housekeeper), Peter Stackpole and Roy Craft (Reporters), Griff Barnett (Henry), Edna Holland (Secretary), Eddie Parks (Bookkeeper), Lee 'Lasses' White (Oldtimer), Wheaton Chambers (Electrician), Eddy Waller (Newcomer), Paul Maxey (Fat man), Edgar Dearing, Snub Pollard.

Producer: Robert Riskin. Production company: Robert Riskin Productions. Distributor: RKO Radio. Length: 103 minutes. Release date: 12 October 1947.

Filming commenced late October 1946.

CALL NORTHSIDE 777 (1948)
Director: Henry Hathaway. Screenplay: Jerome Cady, Jay Dratler (adaptation by Leonard Hoffman and Quentin Reynolds) (from newspaper articles by James P. McGuire).

Photographer: Joe MacDonald. Art directors: Lyle Wheeler, Mark-Lee Kirk. Editor: J. Watson Webb Jr. Music: Alfred Newman.

Cast: James Stewart (P. J. – James – McNeal), Richard Conte (Frank Wiecek), Lee J. Cobb (Brian Kelly), Helen Walker (Laura McNeal), Betty Garde (Wanda Skutnik), Kasia Orzazewski (Tillie), Joanne de Bergh (Helen Wiecek-Rayska), Howard Smith (Palmer), Moroni Olsen (Parole Board chairman), John McIntire (Sam Faxon), Paul Harvey (Martin J. Burns), J. M. Kerrigan (Sullivan, the bailiff), Samuel S. Hinds (Judge Charles Moulton), George Tyne (Tomek Zaleska), Richard Bishop (Warden), Otto Waldis (Boris), Michael Chapin (Frank Jr), John Bleifer (Jan Gruska), Addison Richards (John Albertson), Richard Rober (Larson), Eddie Dunn (Patrolman), Percy Helton (William Decker, the mailman), Charles Lane (Prosecuting attorney), E. G. Marshall (Rayska), Norman McKay and Walter Greaza (Detectives), William Post Jr (Police sergeant), George Melford, Charles Miller, Joe Forte and Dick Ryan (Parole Board members), Lionel Stander (Corrigan), Jonathan Hale (Robert Winston), Lew Eckels (Policeman), Freddie Steele and George Turner (Hold-up men), Jane Crowley (Anna Felczak), Robert Karnes (Spitzer, the photographer), Larry Blake and Robert Williams (Technicians), Leonarde Keeler and Bill Vendetta (Themselves), Thelma Ritter (Police photo lab receptionist), Cy Kendall (Bartender – Bill's Place), Edward Peil Jr and Buck Harrington (Bartenders), Robert Adler (Cab driver), Helen Foster (Secretary), Truman Bradley (Narrator).

Producer: Otto Lang. Production company/distributor: 20th Century-Fox. Length: 111 minutes. Release date: February 1948.

Shooting began in late September 1947 and was completed on 15 November 1947. Locations in Chicago and at Stateville Prison near Joliet, Illinois.

ON OUR MERRY WAY (1948)

* indicates some of the participants in the James Stewart episode

Directors: King Vidor, Leslie Fenton, (uncredited) *John

Huston, *George Stevens. Screenplay: Laurence Stallings, Lou Breslow, *John O'Hara (from a story by Arch Oboler). Photographers: John Seitz, Ernest Laszlo, Joseph Biroc. Art directors: Duncan Cramer, Ernst Fegté. Editor: James Smith. Music: Heinz Roemheld.

Cast: Paulette Goddard (Martha Pease), *Burgess Meredith (Oliver Pease), *James Stewart (Slim), *Henry Fonda (Lank), Dorothy Lamour (Gloria Manners), Victor Moore (Ashton Carrington), Fred MacMurray (Al), William Demarest (Floyd), Hugh Herbert (Elisha Hobbs), *Eduardo Ciannelli (Maxim), Charles D. Brown (An editor), *Dorothy Ford (Lola Maxim), Betty Caldwell (Cynthia), *Carl Switzer (Zoot), Frank Moran (A bookie), Eilene Janssen (Peggy Thorndyke), David Whorf (Sniffles Dugan), Tom Fadden (Deputy sheriff), Paul Hurst (Another deputy), *Harry James (Himself), Nana Bryant (Housekeeper), John Qualen (Mr Atwood), Chester Clute (Bank teller), Walter Baldwin (Man at livery stable), Leo Kaye (Bartender), Almira Sessions (Mrs Cotton), Daniel Haight (Squirt), Max Wagner, George Davis and George Lloyd (Movers), Joe Devlin and Peggy Norman (Parents), Greta Grandstedt (Secretary), Charles Tony Hughes and Jack Cheatham (Cops), Dewey Robinson (Bailiff), Damian O'Flynn (Smallwood, the film director).

Producers: Benedict Bogeaus, Burgess Meredith. Production company: Miracle Productions. Length: 107 minutes. Release date: 13 February 1948.

Also known as *A Miracle Can Happen*. A Charles Laughton sequence was filmed late in 1946 but deleted.

ROPE (1948)

Director: Alfred Hitchcock. Screenplay: Arthur Laurents, (uncredited) Ben Hecht (adaptation by Hume Cronyn) (from the play by Patrick Hamilton). Photographers (Technicolor): Joseph Valentine, William V. Skall. Art director: Perry Ferguson. Editor: William H. Ziegler. Music: Leo F. Forbstein (from a theme by Poulenc).

Cast: James Stewart (Rupert Cadell), Farley Granger (Philip), John Dall (Shaw Brandon), Joan Chandler (Janet Walker), Sir

Cedric Hardwicke (Mr Kentley), Constance Collier (Mrs Atwater), Edith Evanson (Mrs Wilson), Douglas Dick (Kenneth Lawrence), Dick Hogan (David Kentley).

Producers: Sidney Bernstein, Alfred Hitchcock. Production company: Transatlantic Pictures. Distributor: Warner Bros. Length: 81 minutes. Release date: 25 September 1948.

Production started mid-January 1948. Reissued by Metro-Goldwyn-Mayer circa 1963 for a limited period, and by Universal in 1984.

YOU GOTTA STAY HAPPY (1948)

Director: H. C. Potter. Screenplay: Karl Tunberg (from a serialised magazine story by Robert Carson). Photographer: Russell Metty. 2nd unit director: Jack Hively. Production designer: Alexander Golitzen. Editor: Paul Weatherwax. Music: Daniele Amfitheatrof.

Cast: Joan Fontaine (Dee Dee Dillwood), James Stewart (Marvin Payne), Eddie Albert (Bullets Baker), Roland Young (Ralph Tutwiler), Willard Parker (Henry Benson), Percy Kilbride (Mr Racknell), Porter Hall (Mr Caslon), Marcy McGuire (Georgia Goodrich), Arthur Walsh (Milton Goodrich), William Bakewell (Dick Hebert), Paul Cavanagh (Dr Blucher), Halliwell Hobbes (Martin), Stanley Prager (Jack Samuels), Mary Forbes (Aunt Martha), Edith Evanson (Mrs Racknell), Peter Roman (Barnabas), Houseley Stevenson (Jud Tavis), Emory Parnell (Bank watchman), Don Kohler (Ted), Bert Conway (Neil), Hal K. Dawson (Night clerk), Vera Marshe (Mae), Jimmie Dodd (Curly), Robert Rockwell (Eddie), Bill Clauson (Simon), Eddie Ehrhart (Thaddeus), Beatrice Roberts (Maid), Edward Gargan (Detective), Frank Jenks (Man in checkered suit), Arthur Hohl (Man at cemetery), Myron Healey (Day clerk), David Sharpe (Motorcycle rider), Frank Darien (Old man), Chief Yowlachie (Indian), Isabel Withers (Maid), Al Murphy (Mechanic), Joe Cook Jr and Don Garner (Bellhops), Hal Melone and Frank White (Elevator operators), Fritz Feld (Small man), Don Shelton (Minister), George Carleton (Portly man), Harland Tucker (Mr Thrush), Al Murphy (Mechanic), Donald Dewar (Boy), Tiny Jones (Pedestrian), William H. O'Brien (Waiter).

Producer: Karl Tunberg. Production company: Rampart, presented by William Dozier. Distributor: Universal-International. Length: 100 minutes. Release date: November 1948 (premiere engagements).

Filming began early in May 1948. Stewart and Fontaine recorded their roles for a radio version of *You Gotta Stay Happy* on Lux Radio Theatre, transmitted 17 January 1949.

THE STRATTON STORY (1949)

Director: Sam Wood. Screenplay: Douglas Morrow, Guy Trosper, (uncredited) George Wells (from a screen story by Douglas Morrow). Photographer: Harold Rosson. Art directors: Cedric Gibbons, Paul Groesse. Editor: Ben Lewis. Music: Adolph Deutsch. Technical adviser: Monty Stratton.

Cast: James Stewart (Monty Stratton), June Allyson (Ethel Stratton), Frank Morgan (Barney Wile), Agnes Moorehead (Ma Stratton), Bill Williams (Eddie Dibson), Bruce Cowling (Ted Lyons), Cliff Clark (Josh Higgins), Mary Lawrence (Dot), Eugene Bearden (Western All-Stars Pitcher), Bill Dickey and Jimmy Dykes (Themselves), Dean White (Luke Appling), Robert Gist (Ernie), Mervyn Shea (White Sox Catcher), Pat Flaherty (Western Manager), Capt. F. G. Somers (Giants Manager), Mitchell Lewis (Conductor), Michael Ross (Pitcher), Florence Lake (Mrs Appling), Anne Nagel (Mrs Piet), Barbara Woodell (Mrs Shea), William Basset (Baby), Gino Corrado (Waiter serving oysters), Lee Tung Foo (Waiter), Fred Millican (All-Star Catcher), John Kerr (Yankee Coach), Kenneth Tobey (Detroit player), Roy Partee (Western Pitcher), Charles B. Smith (Theatre usher), Holmes Herbert (Doctor), Alphonse Martel (Head Waiter), James Nolan and Peter Crouse (Reporters), Pat Orr, John 'Ziggy' Sears, Jack Powell and Joe Rue (Umpires), Dwight Adams, George Vico and Louie Novikoff (Detroit ballplayers), Robert Graham and Eugene Persson (Boys), Syd Saylor, George Melford, George Ovey, Cy Stevens, William Bailey, Polly Bailey, Vangie Beilby, Mabel Smaney and Jessie Arnold (People at cinema).

Producer: Jack Cummings. Production company/distributor: Metro-Goldwyn-Mayer. Length: 106 minutes. Release date: July 1949.

Shooting started late October 1948.

MALAYA (1949)

British release title: **East of the Rising Sun**

Director: Richard Thorpe. Screenplay: Frank Fenton (from an original story by Manchester Boddy). Photographer: George Folsey. Art directors: Cedric Gibbons, Malcolm Brown. Editor: Ben Lewis. Music: Bronislau Kaper.

Cast: Spencer Tracy (Carnahan), James Stewart (John Royer), Valentina Cortesa (Luana), Sydney Greenstreet (The Dutchman), John Hodiak (Kellar), Lionel Barrymore (John Manchester), Gilbert Roland (Romano), Roland Winters (Bruno Gruber), Richard Loo (Col. Genichi Tomura), Ian MacDonald (Carlos Tassuma), Tom Helmore (Matisson), Frank Wilcox, Joseph Crehan and Russell Hicks (Officer in train conference), William Haade (Naval officer), Robert B. Williams (Guard in railway yard), James Todd (Carson), Anna Q. Nilsson (Secretary), Herbert Heywood (Bartender), Carli Elinor (Waiter), Luther Crockett (Naval officer), Ben Haggerty (Sub-officer), Matt Moore (Prison official), Spencer Chan (Master of ship), Roque Espiritu (Malay servant), Leon Stewart (Piano player), Weaver Levy and Eddie Lee (Tomura's aides), David Fresco (Barracuda Ed), Jack Davis (Captain), DeForest Kelley (Lt. Glenson), Jack Shea (Interne), James Somers (Army transport captain), Joel Allen (Federal agent), Paul Kruger (Official), Leonard Strong (Malay), Charles Meredith, Anthony Jochim, George Carleton, Victor Groves, Bismark Auelua, George Khoury, Peter Mamakos, James O'Gatty, Kula Tutiama, Carl Deloro, Uluao Letuli, Alex Pope, William Self, Leon Lontoc, Paul Singh, Silan Chan.

Producer: Edwin H. Knopf. Production company/distributor: Metro-Goldwyn-Mayer. Length: 98 minutes. Release date: 27 December 1949 (world premiere at Greensboro, North Carolina).

Shooting started 21 February 1949.

WINCHESTER '73 (1950)

Director: Anthony Mann. Screenplay: Robert L. Richards,

Borden Chase (from a story by Stuart N. Lake). Photographer: William Daniels. Art directors: Bernard Herzbrun, Nathan Juran. Editor: Edward Curtiss. Music director: Joseph Gershenson.

Cast: James Stewart (Lin McAdam), Shelley Winters (Lola Manners), Dan Duryea (Waco Johnny Dean), Stephen McNally (Dutch Henry Brown, really Matthew McAdam), Millard Mitchell ('High-Spade' Frankie Wilson), Charles Drake (Steve Miller), John McIntire (Joe Lamont), Will Geer (Wyatt Earp), Jay C. Flippen (Sgt. Wilkes), Rock Hudson (Young Bull), John Alexander (Jack Riker), Steve Brodie (Wesley), James Millican (Wheeler), Abner Biberman (Latigo Means), Anthony [Tony] Curtis (Trooper Doan), James Best (Trooper Crater), Gregg Martell (Mossman), Frank Chase (Cavalryman), Chuck Roberson (Long Tom), Carol Henry (Dudeen), Ray Teal (Marshal Noonan), Virginia Mullens (Mrs Jameson), John Doucette (Roan Daley), Steve Darrell (Bat Masterson), Chief Yowlachie (Indian at rifle shoot), Frank Conlan (Clerk), Ray Bennett (Charles Bender), Guy Wilkerson (Virgil Earp), Bob Anderson (Bassett), Larry Olsen, Tim Hawkins and Bill McKenzie (Boys at rifle shoot), Edmund Cobb (Target watcher), Forrest Taylor (Target clerk), Ethan Laidlaw (Station master), Gary Jackson (Bunny Jameson), Bonnie Kay Eddy (Benny Jameson), Jennings Miles (Stagecoach driver), John War Eagle (Indian interpreter), Norman Kent (Buffalo hunter), Norman Olestad (Stable boy), Mel Archer (Bartender), Bud Osborne, Duke York, Tony Taylor.

Producer: Aaron Rosenberg. Production company/distributor: Universal-International. Length: 92 minutes. Release date: 12 July 1950.

Shooting started 14 February 1950. Location filming in southern Arizona. Story re-made as a 1967 television movie of the same title with Tom Tryon in the Lin McAdam role (much altered).

BROKEN ARROW (1950)

Director: Delmer Daves. Screenplay: Michael Blankfort (from the novel *Blood Brother* by Elliott Arnold). Photographer (Technicolor): Ernest Palmer. Art directors: Lyle Wheeler,

Albert Hogsett. Editor: J. Watson Webb Jr. Music: Hugo Friedhofer.

Cast: James Stewart (Tom Jeffords), Jeff Chandler (Cochise), Debra Paget (Sonseeahray), Basil Ruysdael (General Howard), Will Geer (Ben Slade), Joyce MacKenzie (Terry), Arthur Hunnicutt (Mel Duffield), Raymond Bramley (Col. Bernall), Jay Silverheels (Goklia, later Geronimo), Argentina Brunetti (Nalikadeya), Jack Lee (Boucher), Robert Adler (Lonergan), Harry Carter (Miner), Robert Griffin (Lowrie), Bill Wilkerson (Juan), Mickey Kuhn (Chip Slade), Iron Eyes Cody (Teese), John Doucette (Mule driver), Trevor Bardette (Stage passenger), Edwin Rand (Sergeant), Chris Willow Bird (Nochalo), J. W. Cody (Pionsenay), John War Eagle (Nahilzay), Charles Soldani (Skinyea), Robert Foster Dover (Machogee), John Marston (Maury), Richard Van Opel (Adjutant), Nacho Galindo (Barber), Peter Brocco (Townsman).

Producer: Julian Blaustein. Production company/distributor: 20th Century-Fox. Length: 93 minutes. Release date: 1 August 1950.

Shooting started 6 June 1949. Filmed almost entirely on location in northern Arizona, near Sedona. The 1956–1958 television series of the same name was based on the film and starred John Lupton.

THE JACKPOT (1950)

Director: Walter Lang. Screenplay: Phoebe and Henry Ephron (from a magazine article by John McNulty). Photographer: Joseph La Shelle. Art directors: Lyle Wheeler, Joseph C. Wright. Editor: J. Watson Webb Jr. Music: Lionel Newman.

Cast: James Stewart (Bill Lawrence), Barbara Hale (Amy Lawrence), James Gleason (Harry Summers), Fred Clark (Andrew J. Woodruff), Alan Mowbray (Leslie), Patricia Medina (Hilda Jones), Natalie Wood (Phyllis), Tommy Rettig (Tommy), Robert Gist (Pete Spooner), Lyle Talbot (Fred Burns), Charles Tannen (Al Vogel), Bigelow Sayre (Capt. Sullivan), Dick Cogan (Mr Brown), Jewel Rose (Mrs Brown), Eddie Firestone (Mr McDougall), Estelle Etterre (Mrs McDougall), Claud Stroud (Herman Wertheim), Caryl Lincoln (Susan Wertheim), Valerie Mark (Mary Vogel), Joan Miller (Mabel Spooner), Walter

Baldwin (Watch buyer), Syd Saylor (Ernie, mailman), John Qualen (Mr Ferguson), Fritz Feld (Pianist), Kathryn Sheldon (Mrs Simpkins), Robert Dudley (Mr Simpkins), Minerva Urecal (Strange woman), Milton Parsons (Piano player), Kim Spaulding (Mr Dexter), Dulce Daye (Mrs Dexter), Andrew Tombes (Pritchett), Peggy O'Connor and Dorothy Adams (Salesgirls), Franklin 'Pinky' Parker (Poker player), Bill Nelson (Truck driver), Billy Wayne (Flashlight Joe), Phillip van Zandt (Flick Morgan), Ann Doran (Miss Bowen), Billy Lechner (Johnny, office boy), Jerry Hausner (Al Stern), Frances Budd (Saleslady), George Conrad and Sam Edwards (Parking lot attendants), Jack Roper, Dick Curtis and Guy Way (Removal men), Marjorie Holliday and Carol Savage (Telephone operators), Robert Bice, John Day and John Roy (Policemen), Tudor Owen (Jailer), John Bleifer (Bald man), Jack Mather and Jay Barney (Detectives), Harry Hines (Elevator man), June Evans (Washerwoman), Harry Carter, Colin Ward and Ken Christy (Players in card game), Elizabeth Flournoy.

Producer: Samuel G. Engel. Production company/distributor: 20th Century-Fox. Length: 87 minutes. Release date: November 1950.

Shooting started 19 June 1950.

HARVEY (1950)

Director: Henry Koster. Screenplay: Mary Chase, Oscar Brodney (from the play by Mary Chase). Photographer: William Daniels. Art directors: Bernard Herzbrun, Nathan Juran. Editor: Ralph Dawson. Music: Frank Skinner.

Cast: James Stewart (Elwood P. Dowd), Josephine Hull (Veta Louise Simmons), Peggy Dow (Miss Kelly), Charles Drake (Dr Sanderson), Cecil Kellaway (Dr Chumley), Victoria Horne (Myrtle Mae), Jesse White (Wilson), William Lynn (Judge Gaffney), Wallace Ford (Lofgren), Nana Bryant (Mrs Chumley), Grace Mills (Mrs Chauvenet), Clem Bevans (Herman), Ida Moore (Mrs McGiff), Richard Wessel (Cracker), Pat Flaherty (Policeman), Norman Leavitt (Cab driver), Maudie Prickett (Elvira), Ed Max (Salesman), Grace Hampton (Mrs Strickleberger), Almira Sessions (Mrs Halsey), Ruth Elma Stevens (Miss LaFay), Minerva Urecal (Nurse Dunphy), Anne

O'Neal (Nurse), Eula Guy (Mrs Johnson), Sam Wolfe (Minninger), William Val (Chauffeur), Polly Bailey (Mrs Krausmeyer), Sally Corner (Mrs Cummings), Gino Corrado (Eccentric man), Don Brodie (Mailman), Harry Hines (Meegels), Aileen Carlyle (Mrs Tewksbury).

Producer: John Beck. Production company/distributor: Universal-International. Length: 104 minutes. Release date: December 1950.

Shooting commenced 17 April 1950. Stewart played the role of Elwood P. Dowd on stage both before and after making this film as described in the text. He also made a television version – see 1972 in this listing of his work.

NO HIGHWAY IN THE SKY (1951)

British release title: **No Highway**

Director: Henry Koster. Screenplay: R. C. Sherriff, Oscar Millard, Alec Coppel (from the novel *No Highway* by Nevil Shute). 2nd unit director: Herbert Mason. Photographer: Georges Périnal. Art director: C. P. Norman. Editor: Manuel Del Campo.

Cast: James Stewart (Theodore Honey), Marlene Dietrich (Monica Teasdale), Glynis Johns (Marjorie Corder), Jack Hawkins (Denis Scott), Janette Scott (Elspeth Honey), Ronald Squire (Sir John), Elizabeth Allan (Shirley Scott), Niall MacGinnis (Capt. Samuelson), Kenneth More (Dobson), Jill Clifford (Peggy), David Hutcheson (Bill Penworthy), Wilfrid Hyde White (Fisher), Maurice Denham (Major Pearl), Dora Bryan (Rosie), Hugh Wakefield (Sir David Moon), Hector McGregor (First engineer), Basil Appleby (Second engineer), Peter Murray (Radio operator), Michael Kingsley (Navigator), Felix Aylmer (Sir Philip), Karel Stepanek (Mannheim), Wilfrid Walter (Tracy), John Salew (Symes), Marcel Poncin (Scientist), Cyril Smith (Airport officer), Tom Gill (R.A.F. pilot), Hugh Gross (Director's secretary), Philip Ray (Burroughs), Roy Russell (Butler), Diana Bennett (Stewardess), Michael McCarthy (Bus conductor), Arthur Lucas, Dodd Mehan, Maxwell Foster, Gerald Kent, John Lennox and Douglas Bradley Smith (Staff at Farnborough), Stuart Nichol and Philip

Vickers (Control officers), Robert Lickens and Catherine Leach (Autograph hunters), Bessie Love.

Producer: Louis D. Lighton. Production supervisor: Robert E. Dearing. Production company/distributor: 20th Century-Fox. Length: 99 minutes. Release dates: 2 August 1951 (British premiere), 27 August 1951 (British general release), October 1951 (American release).

Shooting commenced 11 September 1950. Location filming at Blackbushe Airport, Hampshire.

THE GREATEST SHOW ON EARTH (1952)

Director: Cecil B. DeMille. Screenplay: Fredric M. Frank, Barré Lyndon, Theodore St John (from a screen story by Fredric M. Frank, Theodore St John and Frank Cavett). 2nd unit director: Arthur Rosson. Photographers (Technicolor): George Barnes, (additional photography:) J. Peverell Marley, Wallace Kelley. Art directors: Hal Pereira, Walter Tyler. Circus and dance numbers: John Murray Anderson. Editor: Anne Bauchens. Music: Victor Young.

Cast: Betty Hutton (Holly), Cornel Wilde (Sebastian), Charlton Heston (Brad), Dorothy Lamour (Phyllis), Gloria Grahame (Angel), James Stewart (Buttons), Lyle Bettger (Klaus), Henry Wilcoxon (F.B.I. man), Lawrence Tierney (Henderson), Emmett Kelly, Cucciola, Antoinette Concello and John Ringling North (Themselves), John Kellogg (Harry), John Ridgely (Jack Steelman), Frank Wilcox (Circus doctor), Bob Carson (Thompson – Ringmaster), Lillian Albertson (Buttons' mother), Julia Faye (Birdie), Tuffy Genders (Tuffy), John Parrish (Jack Lawson), Keith Richards (Keith), Brad Johnson (Reporter), Adele Cook Johnson (Mable), Lydia Clarke (Circus girl), John Merton (Chuck), Lane Chandler (Dave), Bradford Hatton (Osborne), Herbert Lytton (Foreman), Norman Field (Truesdale), Everett Glass (Board member), Lee Aaker (Boy), Ethan Laidlaw (Hank), Edmond O'Brien (Midway barker), William Boyd (Hopalong Cassidy), Bing Crosby, Bob Hope, Mona Freeman, Nancy Gates, Bess Flowers and Clarence Nash (Spectators), Gloria Drew (Ann), Anthony Marsh (Tony), Bruce Cameron (Bruce), Noel Neill (Noel), Charmienne Harker (Charmienne), Dorothy Crider (Dorothy), Patricia Michon

(Patricia), Vicki Bakken (Vicki),Gay McEldowney (Gay), Hugh Prosser (Hugh), Rus Conklin (Rus), John Crawford (Jack), Claude Dunkin (Claude), Rosemary Dvorak (Rosemary), Lorna Jordan (Lorna), Mona Knox (Mona), Gertrude Messinger (Gertrude), William Hall (Bill), William J. Riley and Robert W. Rushing (Policemen), Howard Negley (Truck boss), Syd Saylor and Lester Door (Circus barkers), Milton Kibbee (Townsman), Fred Kohler Jr (Fireman), Dale van Sickel (Man in train wreck), Beverly Washburn, Erik Nielsen, Kathleen Freeman, Mary Field, Greta Grandstedt, Ross Bagdasarian, Dolores Hall, Robert St Angelo, Davidson Clark, Dorothy Adams, Ottola Nesmith, David Newell, Joseph Whitell, Stanley Andrews, Queenie Smith, Lou Jacobs, Felix Adler, Liberty Horses, Paul Jung, The Maxellos.

Producer: Cecil B. DeMille. Associate producer: Henry Wilcoxon. Production company/distributor: Paramount. Length: 153 minutes. Release date: January 1952.

Shooting started 31 January 1950. Location filming at Sarasota, Florida.

BEND OF THE RIVER (1952)

British release title: **Where the River Bends**

Director: Anthony Mann. Screenplay: Borden Chase (from the novel *Bend of the Snake* by Bill Gulick). Photographer (Technicolor): Irving Glassberg. Art directors: Bernard Herzbrun, Nathan Juran. Editor: Russell Schoengarth. Music: Hans J. Salter.

Cast: James Stewart (Glyn McLyntock), Arthur Kennedy (Emerson Cole), Julia Adams (Laura Baile), Rock Hudson (Trey Wilson), Lori Nelson (Marjie Baile), Jay C. Flippen (Jeremy Baile), Chubby Johnson (Captain Mello), Henry 'Harry' Morgan (Shorty), Royal Dano (Long Tom), Frances Bavier (Mrs Prentiss), Howard Petrie (Tom Hendricks), Stepin Fetchit (Adam), Jack Lambert (Red), Frank Ferguson (Don Grundy), Cliff Lyons (Wullie), Jennings Miles (Lock), Frank Chase (Wasco), Lillian Randolph (Aunt Tildy), Britt Wood (Roustabout), Gregg Barton and Manuel Thomas Golemis (Miners), Hugh Prosser (Johnson), Donald Kerr and Harry Arnie (Barkers), Philo McCullough and George Taylor (Prospectors).

Producer: Aaron Rosenberg. Associate producer: Frank Cleaver. Production company/distributor: Universal-International. Length: 91 minutes. Release date: 23 January 1952 (Oregon world premiere).

Shooting started 25 July 1951. Exteriors shot at Mount Hood in Oregon and along the Sandy and Columbia rivers. The film was retitled for British release to avoid confusion with the 1947 British production *The End of the River* which had the same British distributor (General Film Distributors).

CARBINE WILLIAMS (1952)

Director: Richard Thorpe. Screenplay: Art Cohn (from a non-fiction magazine piece by David Marshall Williams). Photographer: William Mellor. Art directors: Cedric Gibbons, Eddie Imazu. Editor: Newell P. Kimlin. Music: Conrad Salinger.

Cast: James Stewart (Marsh Williams), Jean Hagen (Maggie Williams), Wendell Corey (Capt. H. T. Peoples), Carl Benton Reid (Claude Williams), Paul Stewart ('Dutch' Kruger), Otto Hulett (Mobley), Rhys Williams (Redwick Karson), Herbert Heyes (Lionel Daniels), James Arness (Leon Williams), Porter Hall (Sam Markley), Fay Roope (District Attorney), Ralph Dumke (Andrew White), Leif Erickson (Feder), Henry Corden (Bill Stockton), Frank Richards (Truex), Howard Petrie (Sheriff), Stuart Randall (Tom Vennar), Dan Riss (Jesse Rimmer), Bobby Hyatt (David Williams), Willis Bouchey (Joseph Mitchell), Emile Meyer (Head guard), Robert Foulk (Torchy), Harry Cheshire (Judge), Lillian Culver (Laura Williams), Marlene Lyden (Mary Eloise Williams), Norma Jean Cramer (Mary Ruth Williams), Robert Van Orden (Bob Williams), Jordan Corenweth (Will Williams), Harry Macklin (John Williams), Jon Gardner (Mac Williams), Bob Alden (Messenger), Fiona O'Shiel (Mrs Rimmer), James Harrison (Trusty), Erik Nielsen (Child at wedding), Bert LeBaron, Duke York and Richard Reeves (Guards), Sam Flint, Nolan Leary, Marshall Bradford and George Pembroke (Board members), Emmett Vogan (Swanson), Gene Roth (Railroad foreman), Robert Wilke, Charles Horvath.

Producer: Armand Deutsch. Production company/distributor:

Metro-Goldwyn-Mayer. Length: 91 minutes. Release date: May 1952.

Shooting started 10 December 1951.

THE NAKED SPUR (1952)

Director: Anthony Mann. Screenplay: Sam Rolfe, Harold Jack Bloom. Photographer: William Mellor. Art directors: Cedric Gibbons, Malcolm Brown. Editor: George White. Music: Bronislau Kaper.

Cast: James Stewart (Howard Kemp), Robert Ryan (Ben Vandergroat), Janet Leigh (Lina Patch), Ralph Meeker (Roy Anderson), Millard Mitchell (Jesse Tate).

Producer: William H. Wright. Production company/distributor: Metro-Goldwyn-Mayer. Length: 91 minutes. Release date: February 1953.

Shooting started 21 May 1952. Exteriors filmed in the Durango area of the Colorado Rockies.

THUNDER BAY (1953)

Director: Anthony Mann. Screenplay: Gil Doud, John Michael Hayes, (uncredited) Borden Chase (from a screen story by John Michael Hayes based on an idea by George W. George and George F. Slavin). Photographer (Technicolor): William Daniels. Art directors: Alexander Golitzen, Richard H. Riedel. Editor: Russell Schoengarth. Music: Frank Skinner.

Cast: James Stewart (Steve Martin), Joanne Dru (Stella Rigaud), Gilbert Roland (Teche Bossier), Dan Duryea (Johnny Gambi), Marcia Henderson (Francesca Rigaud), Jay C. Flippen (Kermit MacDonald), Antonio Moreno (Dominique Rigaud), Robert Monet (Philippe Bayard), Henry 'Harry' Morgan (Rawlings), Fortunio Bonanova (Sheriff), Mario Siletti (Louis Chighizola), Antonio Filauri (Joe Sephalu), Frank Chase (Radio technician), Allen Pinson, Dale Van Sickel and Ted Mapes (Oilmen), Ben Welden, Jean Hartelle, Jack Tesler, Adrine Champagne and Donald Green (Fishermen), Laurie Vining (Technician), Emanuel Russo (Radio man).

Producer: Aaron Rosenberg. Production company/distributor:

Universal-International. Length: 102 minutes. Release date: August 1953.

Shooting started 24 September 1952. Location work at Morgan City, Louisiana.

THE GLENN MILLER STORY (1953)

Director: Anthony Mann. Screenplay: Valentine Davies, Oscar Brodney. Photographer (Technicolor): William Daniels. Art directors: Bernard Herzbrun, Alexander Golitzen. Editor: Russell Schoengarth. Technical consultant: Chummy Mac-Gregor. Music arranger (uncredited): Henry Mancini. Music direction: Joseph Gershenson.

Cast: James Stewart (Glenn Miller), June Allyson (Helen Burger), Henry 'Harry' Morgan (Chummy MacGregor), Charles Drake (Don Haynes), George Tobias (Si Schribman), Barton MacLane (General Arnold), Sig Ruman (W. Kranz), Irving Bacon (Mr Miller), James Bell (Mr Burger), Kathleen Lockhart (Mrs Miller), Katharine Warren (Mrs Burger), Frances Langford, Louis Armstrong, Ben Pollack, Gene Krupa, The Modernaires, The Archie Savage Dancers, Barney Bigard, James Young, Marty Napoleon, Arvell Shaw, Cozy Cole and Babe Russil (Themselves), Dayton Lummis (Col. Spaulding), Marion Ross (Polly Haynes), Phil Garris (John Becker), Deborah Sydes (Jonnie Dee), Anthony Sydes (Herbert), Ruth Hampton (Girl singer), Damian O'Flynn (Col. Baker), Carleton Young (Adjutant General), William Challee (Dispatch clerk), Steve [Gaylord] Pendleton (Lt. Col. Baessell), Harry Harvey Sr (Doctor), Leo Mostovoy (Dr Schillinger), Dick Ryan (Garage man), Hal K. Dawson (Used car salesman), Lisa Gaye and Cicily Carter (Bobbysoxers), Nino Tempo (Wilbur Schwartz), Carl Vernell (Music cutter), Bonnie Eddy (Irene), Robert A. Davis and Kevin Cochran (Boys), The Mello Men (Singing foursome), The Rolling Robinsons (Skating act), Rickey Powell (Child).

Producer: Aaron Rosenberg. Production company/distributor: Universal-International. Length: 116 minutes. Release date: 10 December 1953 (Hollywood premiere).

Shooting started 4 June 1953.

[227]

REAR WINDOW (1954)

Director: Alfred Hitchcock. Screenplay: John Michael Hayes (from the short story by Cornell Woolrich). Photographer (Technicolor): Robert Burks. Art directors: Hal Pereira, Joseph McMillan Johnson. Editor: George Tomasini. Music: Franz Waxman.

Cast: James Stewart (L. B. Jeffries), Grace Kelly (Lisa Fremont), Wendell Corey (Thomas J. Doyle), Thelma Ritter (Stella), Raymond Burr (Lars Thorwald), Judith Evelyn (Miss Lonely-hearts), Ross Bagdasarian (Songwriter), Georgine Darcy (Miss Torso), Sara Berner (Woman on fire escape), Frank Cady (Man on fire escape), Jesslyn Fax (Miss Hearing Aid), Rand Harper and Harris Davenport (Honeymooners), Irene Winston (Mrs Thorwald), Marla English and Kathryn Grandstaff [Grant] (Girls at party), Alan Lee (Landlord), Anthony Warde (Detective), Benny Bartlett (Miss Torso's friend), Iphigenie Castiglioni (Bird woman), Ralph Smiley (Carl, the waiter), Bess Flowers (Woman with poodle), Jerry Antes (Dancer), Barbara Bailey (Choreographer), Alfred Hitchcock (Man at clock), Harry Landers, Dick Simmons.

Producer: Alfred Hitchcock. Production company: Patron. Distributor: Paramount. Length: 112 minutes. Release date: September 1954. (Reissued 1983 by Universal.)

Shooting began 23 November 1953.

THE FAR COUNTRY (1955)

Director: Anthony Mann. Screenplay: Borden Chase. Photographer (Technicolor): William Daniels. Art directors: Bernard Herzbrun, Alexander Golitzen. Editor: Russell Schoengarth. Music: Hans J. Salter.

Cast: James Stewart (Jeff Webster), Ruth Roman (Ronda Castle) Corinne Calvet (Renée Vallon), Walter Brennan (Ben Tatem), John McIntire (Mr Gannon), Jay C. Flippen (Rube Marsh), Henry 'Harry' Morgan (Ketchum), Steve Brodie (Ives), Royal Dano (Luke), Connie Gilchrist (Hominy), Kathleen Freeman (Grits), Bob Wilke (Bert Madden), Chubby Johnson (Dusty), Jack Elam (Frank Newberry), Eddy C. Waller (Yukon Sam), Eugene Borden (Dr Vallon), Robert Foulk (Kingman), Angeline

Engler (Mrs Kingman), Paul Bryar (Sheriff), Gregg Barton (Rounds), Allan Ray (Bosun), Connie Van (Molasses), Guy Wilkerson (Tanana Pete), Stuart Randall (Capt. Benson), Chuck Roberson (Latigo), Jack Williams (Shep), William J. Williams (Gant), John Doucette (Aggressive miner), Damian O'Flynn (Second mate), Terry Frost (Joe Merin), Edwin Parker (Carson), Don C. Harvey (Tom Kane), John Halloran (Bartender), Carl Harbaugh (Sourdough), Charles Sweetlove (Porcupine Smith), Ted Mapes, Len MacDonald and Jack Dixon (Deputies), Robert Bice, Paul Savage, James W. Horan, Gerard Baril, Ted Kemp, John Mackin, Dick Taylor, Harry Wilson and Dick Dickinson (Miners), Marjorie Stapp and Gina Holland (Girls), Andy Brennan.

Producer: Aaron Rosenberg. Production company/distributor: Universal-International. Length: 97 minutes. Release date: February 1955.

Shooting started 19 August 1953 in Canada where location work was done at Jasper National Park.

THE WINDMILL (1955) (for TV)

Cast: James Stewart (Joe Newman), Barbara Hale (Ellen Newman), Donald MacDonald (Tom), Cheryl Callaway (Mary), John McIntire (Lane McKersher), Walter Sande (Mason), James Millican (Chet), Edgar Buchanan (Buckskin).

Length: 30 minutes (with commercials). First transmission: 24 April 1955 (on CBS network *G. E. Theater* series).

STRATEGIC AIR COMMAND (1955)

Director: Anthony Mann. Screenplay: Valentine Davies, Beirne Lay Jr (from a screen story by Beirne Lay Jr). Photographer (Technicolor, VistaVision): William Daniels (aerial photographers: Thomas Tutwiler, Paul Mantz). Art directors: Hal Pereira, Earl Hedrick. Editor: Eda Warren. Music: Victor Young.

Cast: James Stewart (Lt. Col. Robert R. 'Dutch' Holland), June Allyson (Sally Holland), Frank Lovejoy (General Ennis Hawkes), Barry Sullivan (Lt. Col. Rocky Samford), Alex Nicol (Capt. Ike Knowland), James Millican (Major General 'Rusty'

Castle), Bruce Bennett (Col. Joe Espy), Jay C. Flippen (Tom Doyle), James Bell (Rev. Thorne), Rosemary De Camp (Mrs Thorne), Richard Shannon (Aircraft Commander), John R. McKee (Capt. Symington), Henry Morgan (Sgt. Bible), David Vaile (Capt. Brown), Don Haggerty (Major Patrol Commander), Glenn Denning (Radio operator), Anthony Warde (Colonel), Vernon Rich (Capt. Johnson, medical examiner), Helen Brown (Baby's nurse), Strother Martin (Airman clerk offering cigars), Harlan Warde (Duty officer), William Hudson (Forecaster), Robert House Peters Jr (Air Force Captain), Max Power (Reporter), Len Hendry (General's aide), Henry Richard Lupino, William August Pullen, Stephen E. Wyman.

Producer: Samuel J. Briskin. Production company/distributor: Paramount. Length: 114 minutes. Release date: April 1955.

Shooting commenced 22 March 1954. Location work at Tampa, Florida.

THE MAN FROM LARAMIE (1955)

Director: Anthony Mann. Screenplay: Philip Yordan, Frank Burt (from the magazine serial/novel by Thomas T. Flynn). Photographer (Technicolor, CinemaScope): Charles Lang. Art director: Cary Odell. Editor: William Lyon. Music: George Duning. Title song: Lester Lee, Ned Washington.

Cast: James Stewart (Will Lockhart), Arthur Kennedy (Vic Hansbro), Donald Crisp (Alec Waggoman), Cathy O'Donnell (Barbara Waggoman), Alex Nicol (Dave Waggoman), Aline MacMahon (Kate Canaday), Wallace Ford (Charley O'Leary), Jack Elam (Chris Boldt), John War Eagle (Frank Darrah), James Millican (Sheriff Tom Quigby), Gregg Barton (Fritz), Boyd Stockman (Spud Oxton), Frank de Kova (Padre), Eddy Waller (Doctor), Frank Cordell, Jack Carry, William Catching and Frosty Royse (Mule skinners).

Production company: William Goetz Productions. Distributor: Columbia. Length: 104 minutes. Release date: August 1955.

Shooting started late September 1954.

THE MAN WHO KNEW TOO MUCH (1956)

Director: Alfred Hitchcock. Screenplay: John Michael Hayes,

Angus McPhail (from a story by Charles Bennett and D. B. Wyndham-Lewis). Photographer (Technicolor, VistaVision): Robert Burks. Art directors: Hal Pereira, Henry Bumstead. Editor: George Tomasini. Music: Bernard Herrmann.

Cast: James Stewart (Ben McKenna), Doris Day (Jo McKenna), Brenda de Banzie (Mrs Drayton), Bernard Miles (Mr Drayton), Ralph Truman (Buchanan), Daniel Gelin (Louis Bernard), Mogens Wieth (Ambassador), Alan Mowbray (Val Parnell), Hillary Brooke (Jan Peterson), Christopher Olsen (Hank McKenna), Reggie Nalder (Rien, the assassin), Richard Wattis (Assistant manager), Noel Willman (Woburn), Alix Talton (Helen Parnell), Yves Brainville (Police Inspector), Carolyn Jones (Cindy Fontaine), Alexi Bobrinskoy (Foreign Prime Minister), Abdelhaq Chraibi (Arab), Betty Baskcomb (Edna), Leo Gordon (Chauffeur), Patrick Aherne (English handyman), Louis Mercier and Anthony Warde (French police), Lewis Martin (Detective), Gladys Holland (Bernard's girl friend), Peter Camlin (Head waiter), Ralph Neff (Henchman), Eric Snowden (Special Branch officer), Mahin Shahrivar (Arab woman), Milton Frome (Guard), Frank Atkinson and John Barrard (Workers at taxidermist's premises), Richard Wordsworth (Ambrose Chappell Jr), Nadia Buckingham (Lady in audience), John Marshall (Butler), Lou Krugman (Arab), Alfred Hitchcock (Moroccan street vendor pushing cart), Richard Goolden.

Producer: Alfred Hitchcock. Associate producer: Herbert Coleman. Production company: Filwite. Distributor: Paramount. Length: 120 minutes. Release date: June 1956.

Filming commenced 12 May 1955. Location work in French Morocco and London (Brixton, Camden Town, Royal Albert Hall etc.). Re-make of Hitchcock's 1934 production in which Leslie Banks played the Stewart role, then called Bob Lawrence.

THE TOWN WITH A PAST (1957) (for TV)

Cast: James Stewart, Fredd Wayne, Walter Sande, Ted Mapes. Introduced by Ronald Reagan.

Length: 30 minutes (with commercials). First transmission: 10 February 1957 (on CBS network G. E. *Theater* series).

[231]

THE SPIRIT OF ST LOUIS (1957)

Director: Billy Wilder. Screenplay: Billy Wilder, Wendell Mayes (adaptation by Charles Lederer) (from the book by Charles A. Lindbergh). Photographers (WarnerColor, CinemaScope): Robert Burks, J. Peverell Marley (technical photographic adviser: Ted McCord) (aerial photographer: Thomas Tutwiler). Art director: Art Loel. Editor: Arthur P. Schmidt. Music: Franz Waxman.

Cast: James Stewart (Charles A. Lindbergh), Murray Hamilton (Bud Gurney), Patricia Smith (Mirror girl), Barlett Robinson (Frank Mahoney), Marc Connelly (Father Hussman), Arthur Space (Donald Hall), Charles Watts (O. W. Schultz), Robert Cornthwaite (Knight), David Orrick (Harold Bixby), Robert Burton (Major Lambert), James L. Robertson Jr (William Robertson), Maurice Manson (E. Lansing Ray), James O'Rear (Earl Thompson), Carleton Young (Inspecting officer), Harlan Warde (Boedecker), Dabbs Greer (Goldsborough), Paul Birch (Blythe), David McMahon (Lane), Herb Lytton (Casey Jones), Richard Deacon (Levine), Sheila Bond (Model – dancer), Griff Barnett (Farmer), John Lee (Jess, the cook), Roy Gordon (Associate producer), Olin Howlin (Salesman), Aaron Spelling (Mr Pearless), Virginia Christine (Secretary), Syd Saylor (Photographer), Ann Morrison (Mrs Pearless), William Neff and William White (Cadets).

Producer: Leland Hayward. Associate producer: Doane Harrison. Production company/distributor: Warner Bros. Length: 135 minutes. Release date: 20 April 1957.

Filmed between August 1955 and March 1956. Location work at Santa Monica Airport, Guyancourt (near Versailles, France), Long Island, Manhattan, and along the Great Circle flight course.

NIGHT PASSAGE (1957)

Director: James Neilson. Screenplay: Borden Chase (from the novel by Norman A. Fox). Photographer (Technicolor, Technirama): William Daniels. 2nd unit director: James Havens. Special photography: Clifford Stine. Art directors: Alexander Golitzen, Robert Clatworthy. Editor: Sherman

Todd. Music: Dimitri Tiomkin. Songs: Ned Washington, Dimitri Tiomkin.

Cast: James Stewart (Grant McLaine), Audie Murphy (The Utica Kid), Dan Duryea (Whitey Harbin), Dianne Foster (Charlotte Drew), Elaine Stewart (Verna Kimball), Brandon de Wilde (Joey Adams), Jay C. Flippen (Ben Kimball), Herbert Anderson (Will Renner), Robert J. Wilke (Concho), Hugh Beaumont (Jeff Kurth), Jack Elam (Shotgun), Tommy Cook (Howdy Sladen), Paul Fix (Clarence Feeney), Olive Carey (Miss Vittles), James Flavin (Tim Riley), Donald Curtis (Jubilee), Ellen Corby (Mrs Feeney), John Day (Latigo), Kenny Williams (O'Brien), Frank Chase (Trinidad), Harold Goodwin (Pick Gannon), Harold Tommy Hart (Shannon), Jack C. Williams (Dusty), Boyd Stockman (Torgenson), Henry Wills (Poche), Chuck Roberson (Roan), Willard Willingham (Click), Polly Burson (Rosa), Patsy Novak (Linda), Ted Mapes (Leary), William 'Bill' Phipps (Barney the blacksmith), Ben Welden (Pete the lunchroom proprietor).

Producer: Aaron Rosenberg. Production company/distributor: Universal. Length: 90 minutes. Release date: May 1957.

Shooting started 14 September 1956.

THE TRAIL TO CHRISTMAS (1957) (for TV)

Director: James Stewart. Screenplay: (from a radio adaptation by Frank Burt of *A Christmas Carol* by Charles Dickens).

Cast: James Stewart (Bart), Richard Eyer (Johnny Carterville), John McIntire (Ebenezer Scrooge), Sam Edwards (Bob Cratchit), Will Wright (Jake Marley), Kevin Hagen (Ghost), Sally Frazier (Belle), Mary Laurence (Mrs Cratchit), Dennis Holmes (Tiny Tim).

Length: 30 minutes (with commercials). First transmission: 15 December 1957 (on CBS network *G. E. Theater* series).

VERTIGO (1958)

Director: Alfred Hitchcock. Screenplay: Alec Coppel, Samuel Taylor (from the novel *D'Entre Les Morts/From Among the Dead* by Pierre Boileau and Thomas Narcejac). Photographer

(Technicolor, VistaVision): Robert Burks. Art directors: Hal Pereira, Henry Bumstead. Editor: George Tomasini. Music: Bernard Herrmann. Title design: Saul Bass.

Cast: James Stewart (John 'Scottie' Ferguson), Kim Novak (Madeleine Elster/Judy Barton), Barbara Bel Geddes (Midge), Tom Helmore (Gavin Elster), Henry Jones (The Coroner), Raymond Bailey (The Doctor), Ellen Corby (Hotel manageress), Konstantin Shayne (Pop Leibel), Lee Patrick (Woman using car mistaken for Madeleine), Paul Bryar (Capt. Hansen), Margaret Brayton (Saleswoman), William Remick (Jury foreman), Sara Taft (Nun), Julian Petruzzi (Flower seller), Fred Graham (Policeman on roof), Mollie Dodd (Beauty operator), Buck Harrington (Gateman), John Benson (Salesman), Nina Shipman (Young woman mistaken for Madeleine), Roxann Delmar (Model), Alfred Hitchcock (Pedestrian), Jack Ano.

Producer: Alfred Hitchcock. Associate producer: Herbert Coleman. Production company: Alfred J. Hitchcock Productions. Distributor: Paramount. Length: 128 minutes. Release date: May 1958. (Reissued 1983 by Universal.)

Shooting commenced 30 September 1957. Location filming in San Francisco and at Watsonville, California.

BELL, BOOK AND CANDLE (1958)

Director: Richard Quine. Screenplay: Daniel Taradash (from the play by John Van Druten). Photographer (Technicolor): James Wong Howe. Art director: Cary Odell. Editor: Charles Nelson. Music: George Duning.

Cast: James Stewart (Shepherd Henderson), Kim Novak (Gillian Holroyd), Jack Lemmon (Nicky Holroyd), Ernie Kovacs (Sidney Redlitch), Hermione Gingold (Mrs De Pass), Elsa Lanchester (Queenie), Janice Rule (Merle Kittridge), Howard McNear (Andy White), Bek Nelson (Shep's secretary), Philippe Clay (French singer), Wolfe Barzell (Proprietor), The Brothers Candoli (Musicians), Joe Barry (Exterminator), Gail Bonney (Merle's maid), Monty Ash (Herb store owner), Ollie O'Toole (Elevator operator), Don Brodie and John Truex (Cab drivers), James Lanphier (Waldo), Ted Mapes, Dick Crockett, Pyewacket the Cat.

Producer: Julian Blaustein. Production company: Phoenix. Distributor: Columbia. Length: 103 minutes. Release date: December 1958.

Filming started 3 February 1958.

ANATOMY OF A MURDER (1959)

Director: Otto Preminger. Screenplay: Wendell Mayes (from the novel by Robert Traver, i.e. Justice John D. Voelker). Photographer: Sam Leavitt. Production designer: Boris Leven. Editor: Louis R. Loeffler. Music: Duke Ellington. Title design: Saul Bass.

Cast: James Stewart (Paul Biegler), Lee Remick (Laura Manion), Ben Gazzara (Lt. Frederick Manion), Joseph N. Welch (Judge Weaver), Kathryn Grant (Mary Pilant), Arthur O'Connell (Parnell McCarthy), Eve Arden (Maida Rutledge), George C. Scott (Claude Dancer), Brooks West (Mitch Lodwick), Orson Bean (Dr Smith), John Qualen (Sulo the guard), Murray Hamilton (Alphonse Paquette), Russ Brown (Mr Lemon), Don Ross (Duane Miller), Jimmy Conlin (Clarence Madigan), Ned Weaver (Dr Raschid), Ken Lynch (Sgt. Durgo), Joseph Kearns (Mr Lloyd Burke), Howard McNear (Dr Dompierre), Royal Beal (Sheriff), Duke Ellington (Pie Eye), James Waters (Army Sergeant), Lloyd LeVasseur (Court employee), Alexander Campbell (Dr Harcourt), Irving Kupcinet (Distinguished gentleman), Mrs Joseph N. Welch (Juror).

Producer: Otto Preminger. Production company: Carlyle. Distributor: Columbia. Length: 160 minutes. Release date: 1 July 1959.

Filmed entirely in upper Michigan, in and around Marquette and Ishpeming, from 23 March 1959 to 16 May 1959.

THE FBI STORY (1959)

Director: Mervyn LeRoy. Screenplay: Richard L. Breen, John Twist (from the book by Don Whitehead). Photographer (Technicolor): Joseph Biroc. Art director: John Beckman. Editor: Philip W. Anderson. Music: Max Steiner.

Cast: James Stewart (Chip Hardesty), Vera Miles (Lucy

Hardesty), Murray Hamilton (Sam Crandall), Larry Pennell (George Crandall), Nick Adams (Jack Graham), Diane Jergens (Jennie as an adult), Jean Willes (Anna Sage), Joyce Taylor (Anne as an adult), Victor Millan (Mario), Parley Baer (Harry Dakins), Fay Roope (Dwight McCutcheon), Ed Prentiss (U.S. Marshal), Robert Gist (Medicine salesman), Buzz Martin (Mike as an adult), Kenneth Mayer (Casket salesman), Paul Genge (Whitey, the suspect), Forrest Taylor (Wedding minister), Ann Doran (Mrs Ballard), Scott Peters (John Dillinger), William Phipps (Baby Face Nelson), John Damler (Interrogator), Paul Smith (Albert Taylor), Eleanor Audley (Mrs Graham), Sam Flint (Doctor), Burt Mustin (Schneider), Harry Harvey (Neighbor), Guy Wilkerson (Cliff), Grandon Rhodes (Minister), Nesdon Booth (Sandy), Ray Montgomery (Cabby), Dorothy Neumann (Landlady), Kimberly Beck (Chip's daughter, aged three), J. Edgar Hoover, Lori Martin, William Challee.

Producer: Mervyn LeRoy. Production company/distributor: Warner Bros. Length: 149 minutes. Release date: October 1959.

Shooting commenced 12 August 1958. Location work in New York City and Washington D.C.

CINDY'S FELLA (1959) (for TV)

Director: Gower Champion. Screenplay: James Brewer (from a radio script by Frank Burt). Color.

Cast: James Stewart (Azel Dorsey), George Gobel (Drifter), Lois Smith (Cindy), James Best (Duke), Mary Wickes (Myrtle), Kathie Browne (Phyllis), Alice Backes (Esther), George Keymas (Zack Riney), Mark Allen (Swaney Rivers), Maurice Kelly (Bartender).

Production company: Hubbell Robinson. Length: 53 minutes. First transmission: 15 December 1959 (in NBC's Lincoln-Mercury *Startime* television series).

THE MOUNTAIN ROAD (1960)

Director: Daniel Mann. Screenplay: Alfred Hayes (from the novel by Theodore H. White). Photographer: Burnett Guffey. Art director: Cary Odell. Editor: Edward Curtiss. Music: Jerome Moross.

Cast: James Stewart (Major Baldwin), Lisa Lu (Sue-Mei Hung), Glenn Corbett (Collins), Henry 'Harry' Morgan (Michaelson), Frank Silvera (General Kwan), James Best (Niergaard), Rudy Bond (Miller), Mike Kellin (Prince), Frank Maxwell (Ballo), Eddie Firestone (Lewis), Alan Baxter (General Loomis), P. C. Lee (Chinese General), Bill Quinn (Col. Magnusson), Leo Chen (Col. Li), Peter Chong (Chinese Colonel).

Producer: William Goetz. Production company: William Goetz Productions. Distributor: Columbia. Length: 102 minutes. Release date: June 1960.

Filming started 9 June 1959.

TWO RODE TOGETHER (1961)

Director: John Ford. Screenplay: Frank Nugent (from the magazine serial and novel *Comanche Captives* by Will Cook). Photographer (Eastman Color by Pathé): Charles Lawton Jr. Art director: Robert Peterson. Editor: Jack Murray. Music: George Duning.

Cast: James Stewart (Guthrie McCabe), Richard Widmark (Lt. Jim Gary), Shirley Jones (Marty Purcell), Linda Cristal (Elena de la Madriaga), Andy Devine (Sgt. Darius P. Posey), John McIntire (Major Frazer), Paul Birch (Edward Purcell), Willis Bouchey (Henry J. Wringle), Henry Brandon (Quanah Parker), Harry Carey Jr (Ortho Clegg), Olive Carey (Abby Frazer), Ken Curtis (Greeley Clegg), Chet Douglas (Ward Corbey), Annelle Hayes (Belle Aragon), David Kent (Running Wolf), Anna Lee (Mrs Malaprop), Jeannette Nolan (Mrs McCandless), John Qualen (Ole Knudsen), Ford Rainey (Henry Clegg), Woody Strode (Stone Calf), O. Z. Whitehead (Officer), Cliff Lyons (William McCandless), Mae Marsh (Hannah Clegg), Frank Baker (Capt. Malaprop), Ted Knight (Lt. Upton), Major Sam Harris (Post doctor), Jack Pennick (Sergeant), Bill Henry (Gambler), Bob Kenneally and Ed Sweeney (Officers), Big John Hamilton (Settler), Chuck Roberson (Comanche), Dan Borzage, Chuck Hayward, Edward Brophy, Ruth Clifford.

Producer: Stan Shpetner. Production companies: John Ford Productions, Shpetner Productions. Distributor: Columbia. Length: 109 minutes. Release date: 26 July 1961 (New York premiere).

Shooting started 17 October 1960. Filmed in southwest Texas, including the Alamo Village, Brackettville.

THE MAN WHO SHOT LIBERTY VALANCE (1962)

Director: John Ford. Screenplay: Willis Goldbeck, James Warner Bellah (from the short story by Dorothy M. Johnson). Photographer: William H. Clothier. Art directors: Hal Pereira, Eddie Imazu. Editor: Otho Lovering. Music: Cyril J. Mockridge (theme from *Young Mr Lincoln* by Alfred Newman).

Cast: James Stewart (Ransom Stoddard), John Wayne (Tom Doniphon), Vera Miles (Hallie Stoddard), Lee Marvin (Liberty Valance), Edmond O'Brien (Dutton Peabody), Andy Devine (Link Appleyard), Ken Murray (Doc Willoughby), John Carradine (Major Cassius Starbuckle), Jeanette Nolan (Nora Ericson), John Qualen (Peter Ericson), Willie Bouchey (Jason Tully), Carleton Young (Maxwell Scott), Woody Strode (Pompey), Denver Pyle (Amos Carruthers), Strother Martin (Floyd), Lee Van Cleef (Reese), Robert F. Simon (Handy Strong), O. Z. Whitehead (Herbert Carruthers), Paul Birch (Mayor Winder), Joseph Hoover (Hasbrouck), Jack Pennick (Bartender), Anna Lee (Widow in stage hold-up), Charles Seel (President of Election Council), Shug Fisher (Drunk), Earle Hodgins (Clue Dumphries), Stuart Holmes, Dorothy Phillips, Buddy Roosevelt, Gertrude Astor, Eva Novak, Slim Talbot, Monty Montana, Bill Henry, John B. Whiteford, Helen Gibson, Major Sam Harris, Ted Mapes, Jack Kenny, Myron Cook, Tom Hennessy, Slim Hightower, Adele Von, Charles Morton, Ed Jauregui, Leonard Baker, Robin Varga.

Producer: Willis Goldbeck. Production company: John Ford Productions. Distributor: Paramount. Length: 122 minutes. Release date: 22 April 1962.

Filmed from 5 September to early November 1961.

MR. HOBBS TAKES A VACATION (1962)

Director: Henry Koster. Screenplay: Nunnally Johnson (from the novel *Mr Hobbs' Vacation* by Edward Streeter). Photographer (color by DeLuxe, CinemaScope): William C. Mellor. 2nd unit director: William Witney. Art directors: Jack Martin

Smith, Malcolm Brown. Editor: Marjorie Fowler. Music: Henry Mancini.

Cast: James Stewart (Roger Hobbs), Maureen O'Hara (Peggy Hobbs), Fabian (Joe), Lauri Peters (Katey), Lili Gentle (Janie), John Saxon (Byron), John McGiver (Martin Turner), Marie Wilson (Emily Turner), Reginald Gardiner (Reggie McHugh), Valerie Varda (Marika), Natalie Trundy (Susan Carver), Josh Peine (Stan Carver), Michael Burns (Danny Hobbs), Minerva Urecal (Brenda), Richard Collier (Mr Kagle), Peter Oliphant (Peter Carver), Tom Lowell (Freddie), Stephen Mines (Carl), Dennis Whitcomb (Dick), Michael Sean (Phil), Sherry Alberoni and True Ellison (Girls in dormitory), Ernie Gutierrez (Pizza maker), Barbara Mansell (Receptionist), Maida Severn (Secretary), Doris Packer (Hostess), Harry Carter (Cab driver), Arthur Tovey (Dance extra), Darryl Duke.

Producer: Jerry Wald. Associate producer: Marvin A. Gluck. Production company: Jerry Wald Productions. Distributor: 20th Century-Fox. Length: 116 minutes. Release date: 15 June 1962 (premiere in New York).

Filming started 21 November 1961. Location work at Carillo Beach and Zuma Beach.

FLASHING SPIKES (1962) (for TV)

Director: John Ford. Screenplay: Jameson Brewer (from a novel by Frank O'Rourke). Photographer: William H. Clothier. Art director: Martin Obzina. Editors: Richard Belding, Tony Martinelli. Music: Johnny Williams.

Cast: James Stewart (Slim Conway), Jack Warden (Commissioner), Pat Wayne (Bill Riley), Edgar Buchanan (Crab Holcomb), Tige Andrews (Gaby Lasalle), Carleton Young (Rex Short), Willis Bouchey (Mayor), Don Drysdale (Gomer), Stephanie Hill (Mary Riley), Charles Seel (Judge), Bing Russell (Hogan), Harry Carey Jr (Man in dugout), Vin Scully (Announcer), Walter Reed and Larry Blake (Reporters), Sally Hughes (Nurse), Charles Morton and Art Passarella (Umpires), Bill Henry (Commissioner's assistant), John Wayne (Drill sergeant in Korea), Vern Stephens, Ralph Volkie, Earl Gilpin, Bud Harden and Whitey Campbell (Baseball players), Cy Malis, Fred Astaire (Host).

Associate producer: Frank Baur. Production company: Avista. Length: 53 minutes. First transmission: 4 October 1962 (in *Alcoa Premiere* American television series).

HOW THE WEST WAS WON (1962)

*indicates some of the participants in the James Stewart episode, *The Rivers*

Directors: John Ford, *Henry Hathaway, George Marshall, (uncredited) Richard Thorpe. Screenplay: James R. Webb, (uncredited) John Gay. Photographers (Metrocolor, [three camera] Cinerama): Joseph LaShelle, *Charles Lang Jr, William Daniels, Milton Krasner, Harold Wellman. Art directors: George W. Davis, William Ferrari, Addison Hehr. Editor: Harold F. Kress. Music: Alfred Newman, Ken Darby.

Cast: *Carroll Baker (Eve Prescott), Lee J. Cobb (Marshal Lou Ramsey), Henry Fonda (Jethro Stuart), Carolyn Jones (Julie Rawlings), *Karl Malden (Zebulon Prescott), Gregory Peck (Cleve Van Valen), George Peppard (Zeb Rawlings), Robert Preston (Roger Morgan), Debbie Reynolds (Lilith Prescott), *James Stewart (Linus Rawlings), Eli Wallach (Charley Gant), John Wayne (General William T. Sherman), Richard Widmark (Mike King), *Brigid Bazlen (Dora), *Walter Brennan (Col. Hawkins), David Brian (Lilith's lawyer), Andy Devine (Corporal Peterson), Raymond Massey (Abraham Lincoln), *Agnes Moorehead (Rebecca Prescott), Henry (Harry) Morgan (General Ulysses S. Grant), Thelma Ritter (Aggie Clegg), Mickey Shaughnessy (Deputy Stover), Russ Tamblyn (Deserter), Rodolfo Acosta, Dean Stanton, Jack Lambert and Chuck Roberson (Gant henchmen), Lee Van Cleef (Marty), Kim Charney (Sam Prescott), Bryan Russell (Zeke Prescott), Karl Swenson (Train conductor), Christopher Dark (Poker player), Jay C. Flippen (Huggins), Gene Roth (Poker player on riverboat), Joe Sawyer (Ship's officer), Clinton Sundberg (Hylan Seabury), James Griffith (Poker player), Walter Burke (Poker player – wagon), John Larch (Grimes), Edward J. McKinley (Auctioneer), Barry Harvey (Angus), Jamie Ross (Bruce), Mark Allen (Colin), Craig Duncan (James Marshall), Charles Briggs (Barker), Paul Bryar (Auctioneer's assistant), Tudor Owen (Parson Harvey), Beulah Archuletta (Jim's wife),

Lou Krugman (Gambler), Willis Bouchey (Surgeon), Claude Johnson (Jeremiah Rawlings), Ken Curtis (Ben–Union corporal), Walter Reed (Army medic), John Damler (Lawyer), Jerry Holmes (Railroad clerk), Ben Black Elk Sr (Indian chief), Jack Pennick (Corporal Murphy), Bob Nash (Lawyer), Tom Greenway (Gambler), Cliff Osmond (Investor), Kem Dibbs (Blacksmith), Carleton Young, Boyd 'Red' Morgan, John Anderson, Dennis Cole, Loren James, Gil Perkins, Robert P. Lieb, Lew Smith, Harvey Perry, Henry Willis, Gregg Martell, Don Rhodes, Chief Weasel, Red Cloud, Red Perkins, Bill Henry, Chuck Hayward, Spencer Tracy (Narrator).

Producer: Bernard Smith. Production companies: Metro-Goldwyn-Mayer, Cinerama. Distributor: Metro-Goldwyn-Mayer. Length: 162 minutes. Release date: 1 November 1962 (world premiere in London).

Shooting began 28 May 1961 and lasted to mid-November. Location work for Stewart's sequence, *The Rivers*, along the Ohio river around Battery Rock, Illinois.

TAKE HER, SHE'S MINE (1963)

Director: Henry Koster. Screenplay: Nunnally Johnson (from the play by Phoebe and Henry Ephron). Photographer (color by DeLuxe, CinemaScope): Lucien Ballard. Art directors: Jack Martin Smith, Malcolm Brown. Editor: Marjorie Fowler. Music: Jerry Goldsmith.

Cast: James Stewart (Frank Michaelson), Sandra Dee (Mollie Michaelson), Audrey Meadows (Anne Michaelson), Robert Morley (Pope-Jones), Philippe Forquet (Henri Bonnet), John McGiver (Hector G. Ivor), Robert Denver (Alex), Monica Moran (Linda), Cynthia Pepper (Adele), Jenny Maxwell (Sarah), Maurice Marsac (M. Bonnet), Irene Tsu (Miss Wu), Charla Doherty (Liz Michaelson), Marcel Hilaire (First policeman), Charles Robinson (Stanley), Janine Grandel (Mme Bonnet), Eddie Quillan (Airline clerk), Francesca Bellini (Mollie's room-mate in Paris), Bobs Watson.

Producer: Henry Koster. Production company/distributor: 20th Century-Fox. Length: 98 minutes. Release date: 13 November 1963 (premiere in New York).

Filming started 23 April 1963.

CHEYENNE AUTUMN (1964)

Director: John Ford. Screenplay: James R. Webb (from the novel by Mari Sandoz). Photographer (Technicolor, Super Panavision 70): William H. Clothier. 2nd unit director: Ray Kellogg. Art director: Richard Day. Editor: Otho Lovering. Music: Alex North.

Cast (*indicates participants in the James Stewart episode): Richard Widmark (Capt. Thomas Archer), Carroll Baker (Deborah Wright), Karl Malden (Capt. Wessels), Sal Mineo (Red Shirt), Dolores Del Rio (Spanish woman), Ricardo Montalban (Little Wolf), Gilbert Roland (Dull Knife), *Arthur Kennedy (Doc Holliday), *James Stewart (Wyatt Earp), Edward G. Robinson (Carl Schurz), Patrick Wayne (2nd Lt. Scott), *Elizabeth Allen (Miss Guinevere Plantagenet), *John Carradine (Major Jeff Blair), Victor Jory (Tall Tree), *Judson Pratt (Mayor John Dog Kelly), Mike Mazurki (Top Sgt. Stanislas Wichowsky), Carmen D'Antonio (Pawnee woman), John Qualen (Svenson), Sean McClory (O'Carberry), *Ken Curtis (Joe), George O'Brien (Major Braden), *Shug Fisher (Trail boss), Nancy Hsueh (Little Bird), Walter Baldwin (Jeremy Wright), *Chuck Roberson (Cowpoke), Harry Carey Jr (Trooper Smith), Ben Johnson (Trooper Plumtree), Jim O'Hara and Chuck Hayward (Troopers), Lee Bradley and Frank Bradley (Cheyennes), Walter Reed (Lt. Peterson), Willis Bouchey (Colonel), Carleton Young (Schurz' aide), Denver Pyle (Senator Henry), Nanomba 'Moonbeam' Morton (Running Deer), Dan Borzage, Dean Smith, David Humphreys Miller and Bing Russell (Troopers), *Dan M. White (Saloon patron), William Henry (Infantry Captain), Major Sam Harris (Townsman), Louise Montana, Kevin O'Neal.

Producer: Bernard Smith. Production company: Ford-Smith Productions. Distributor: Warner Bros. Length: 161 minutes. Release date: 3 October 1964 (premiere at Cheyenne, Wyoming).

Shooting commenced 23 September 1963. Location filming in Utah and Colorado including the Monument Valley Navajo Tribal Park. Running time quoted is that of original British release. A 170 minute version is said to have existed as well as other versions cut as short as 145 minutes.

DEAR BRIGITTE (1965)

Director: Henry Koster. Screenplay: Hal Kanter, (uncredited) Nunnally Johnson (from the novel *Erasmus with Freckles* by John Haase). Photographer: (color by DeLuxe, CinemaScope): Lucien Ballard. Art directors: Jack Martin Smith, Malcolm Brown. Editor: Marjorie Fowler. Music: George Duning.

Cast: James Stewart (Prof. Robert Leaf), Fabian (Kenneth), Glynis Johns (Vina Leaf), Cindy Carol (Pandora Leaf), Billy Mumy (Erasmus Leaf), John Williams (Peregrine Upjohn), Jack Kruschen (Dr Volker), Ed Wynn (The Captain), Charles Robinson (George), Howard Freeman (Dean Sawyer), Jane Wald (Terry), Alice Pearce (Unemployment office clerk), Jesse White (Argyle), Gene O'Donnell (Lt. Rink), Brigitte Bardot (Herself), Orville Sherman (Von Schlogg), Maida Severn (Schoolteacher), Pitt Herbert (Bank manager), Adair Jameson (Saleslady), Marcel de la Brosse (Taxi driver), Susan Cramer (Blonde doll), Harry Fleer (T-Man), Jack Daly (Ticket seller), William Henry (Cashier), Gloria Clark (Prof. Burns), Robert Fitzpatrick, James Brolin, Clive Clerk and John Stevens (Students), Dick Lane (Sports announcer), Ted Mapes (Postman), Percy Helton (Small man in computer room), Bob Biheller, Arthur Tovey.

Producer: Henry Koster. Production company: Fred Kohlmar Productions. Distributor: 20th Century-Fox. Length: 100 minutes. Release date: 21 January 1965 (premiere in New York).

Shooting began mid-May 1964 with location work in Paris.

SHENANDOAH (1965)

Director: Andrew V. McLaglen. Screenplay: James Lee Barrett. Photographer (Technicolor): William H. Clothier. Art directors: Alexander Golitzen, Alfred Sweeney. Editor: Otho Lovering. Music: Frank Skinner.

Cast: James Stewart (Charlie Anderson), Doug McClure (Sam), Glenn Corbett (Jacob Anderson), Patrick Wayne (James Anderson), Rosemary Forsyth (Jennie Anderson), Phillip Alford (Boy Anderson), Katharine Ross (Ann Anderson), Charles Robinson (Nathan Anderson), James McMullan (John

Anderson), Tim McIntire (Henry Anderson), Eugene Jackson Jr (Gabriel), George Kennedy (Col. Fairchild), Strother Martin (Train engineer), Bob Steele (Guard at train), Paul Fix (Dr Tom Witherspoon), Denver Pyle (Pastor Bjoerling), James Best (Carter), Tim Simcox (Lt. Johnson), Berkeley Harris (Capt. Richards), Harry Carey Jr (Jenkins), Kevin Hagen (Mule), Dabbs Greer (Abernathy), Kelly Thordsen (Carroll), Warren Oates (Billy Packer), Edward Faulkner (Union Sergeant), Peter Wayne (Confederate Corporal), Gregg Palmer (Union guard), James Heneghan Jr (First picket), Pae Miller (Negro woman), Rayford Barnes (Horace, a marauder), Dave Cass (Ray), Hoke Howell (Crying prisoner), Chuck Roberson (Officer tending cow), Lane Bradford (Tinkham), Shug Fisher (Confederate soldier), John Cliff (Horse buyer), John Daheim (Osborne), Joe Yrigoyen (Marshal), Henry Wills, Buzz Henry, James Carter and Leroy Johnson (Riders).

Producer: Robert Arthur. Production company/distributor: Universal. Length: 105 minutes. Release date: 3 June 1965 (premiere in Houston).

Shooting began 11 August 1964. Location work done near Eugene, Oregon.

THE FLIGHT OF THE PHOENIX (1965)

Director: Robert Aldrich. Screenplay: Lukas Heller (from the novel by Elleston Trevor). 2nd unit director: Oscar Rudolph. Photography (color by DeLuxe): Joseph Biroc. Aerial sequences: Paul Mantz. Art director: William Glasgow. Editor: Michael Luciano. Music: De Vol.

Cast: James Stewart (Frank Towns), Richard Attenborough (Lew Moran), Peter Finch (Capt. Harris), Hardy Kruger (Heinrich Dorfmann), Ernest Borgnine (Trucker Cobb), Ian Bannen (Crow), Ronald Fraser (Sgt. Watson), Christian Marquand (Dr Renaud), Dan Duryea (Standish), George Kennedy (Bellamy), Gabriele Tinti (Gabriele), Alex Montoya (Carlos), Peter Bravos (Tasso), William Aldrich (Bill), Barrie Chase (Farida), Mike Ragan and Ralph Volkie (Oil-riggers).

Producer: Robert Aldrich. Associate producer: Walter Blake. Production company: The Associates & Aldrich. Distributor:

20th Century-Fox. Length: 147 minutes. Release date: 15 December 1965 (premiere in New York).

Shooting started 29 April 1965 following three days of rehearsals. Locations work done near Yuma, Colorado.

THE RARE BREED (1966)

Director: Andrew V. McLaglen. Screenplay: Ric Hardman. Photographer (Technicolor, Panavision): William H. Clothier. Art directors: Alexander Golitzen, Alfred Ybarra. Editor: Russell F. Schoengarth. Music: Johnny Williams.

Cast: James Stewart (Sam 'Bulldog' Burnett), Maureen O'Hara (Martha Evans), Brian Keith (Alexander Bowen), Juliet Mills (Hilary Evans), Don Galloway (Jamie Bowen), David Brian (Charles Ellsworth), Jack Elam (Deke Simons), Ben Johnson (Jeff Harter), Harry Carey Jr (Ed Mabry), Perry Lopez (Juan), Larry Domasin (Alberto), Alan Caillou (John Taylor), Silvia Marino (Conchita), Gregg Palmer (Rodenbush), Barbara Werle (Gert), Joe Ferrante (Estaban), Jim O'Hara (Sagamon), Bob Gravage (Cattle buyer), Tex Armstrong (Barker), Ted Mapes (Liveryman), Larry Blake (Auctioneer), Charles Lampkin (Porter), Kent McConnell (Cattle herder).

Producer: William Alland. Production company/distributor: Universal. Length: 97 minutes. Release date: 2 February 1966 (premiere at Fort Worth, Texas).

Shooting began 4 February 1965.

FIRECREEK (1968)

Director: Vincent McEveety. Screenplay: Calvin Clements. Photographer (Technicolor, Panavision): William H. Clothier. Art director: Howard Hollander. Editor: William Ziegler. Music: Alfred Newman.

Cast: James Stewart (Johnny Cobb), Henry Fonda (Larkin), Inger Stevens (Evelyn Pittman), Gary Lockwood (Earl), Dean Jagger (Whittier), Ed Begley (Preacher Broyles), Jay C. Flippen (Mr Pittman), Jack Elam (Norman), James Best (Drew), Barbara Luna (Meli), Jacqueline Scott (Henrietta Cobb), Brooke Bundy (Leah), J. Robert Porter (Arthur), Morgan Woodward (Willard),

John Qualen (Hall), Louise Latham (Dulcie), Athena Lorde (Mrs Littlejohn), Henry 'Slim' Duncan (Fyte), Kevin Tate (Aaron), Christopher Shea (Franklin).

Producer: Philip Leacock. Production company: Philip Leacock – John Mantley. Distributor: Warner Bros – Seven Arts. Length: 104 minutes. Release date: 24 January 1968 (premiere at El Paso, Texas). Filming started 5 December 1966.

BANDOLERO! (1968)

Director: Andrew V. McLaglen. Screenplay: James Lee Barrett (from a screen story by Stanley L. Hough). Photographer (colour by DeLuxe, Panavision): William H. Clothier. Art directors: Jack Martin Smith, Alfred Sweeney Jr. Editor: Folmar Blangsted. Music: Jerry Goldsmith.

Cast: James Stewart (Mace Bishop), Dean Martin (Dee Bishop), Raquel Welch (Maria Stoner), George Kennedy (Sheriff Johnson), Andrew Prine (Roscoe Bookbinder), Will Geer (Pop Chaney), Clint Ritchie (Babe), Denver Pyle (Muncie Carter), Tom Heaton (Joe Chaney), Rudy Diaz (Angel Muñoz), Sean McClory (Robbie), Harry Carey (Cort Hayjack), Donald Barry (Jack Hawkins), Guy Raymond (Ossie Grimes), Perry Lopez (Frisco), Jock Mahoney (Stoner), Dub Taylor (Bathhouse attendant), Big John Hamilton (Bank clerk), Bob Adler (Ross Harper), John Mitchum (Bathhouse customer), Joseph Patrick Cranshaw (Bank clerk), Roy Barcroft (Bartender).

Producer: Robert L. Jacks. Production company/distributor: 20th Century-Fox. Length: 106 minutes. Release date: 18 June 1968 (premiere in Dallas).

Shooting started 2 October 1967. Locations included Bracket-ville, Texas.

THE CHEYENNE SOCIAL CLUB (1970)

Director: Gene Kelly. Screenplay: James Lee Barrett. Photographer (Technicolor, Panavision): William H. Clothier. Production designer: Gene Allen. Editor: Adrienne Fazan. Music: Walter Scharf. Songs: Walter Scharf, Al Kasha, Joel Hirschhorn.

Cast: James Stewart (John O'Hanlan), Henry Fonda (Harley

O'Sullivan), Shirley Jones (Jenny), Sue Ane Langdon (Opal Ann), Elaine Devry (Pauline), Robert Middleton (Barman at Great Plains Saloon), Arch Johnson (Marshal Anderson), Dabbs Greer (Willowby), Jackie Russell (Carrie Virginia), Jackie Joseph (Annie Jo), Sharon de Bord (Sara Jean), Richard Collier (Nathan Potter), Charles Tyner (Charlie Bannister), Jean Willes (Alice). Robert J. Wilke (Corey Bannister), Carl Reindel (Pete Dodge), J. Pat O'Malley (Dr Foy), Jason Wingreen (Dr Farley Carter), John Dehner (Clay Carroll), Hal Baylor (Barman at Lady of Egypt), Charlotte Stewart (Mae), Alberto Morin (Ranch foreman), Myron Healey (Deuter), Warren Kemmerling (Kohler), Dick Johnstone (Mr Yancey), Phil Mead (Cook), Hi Roberts (Scared man), Ed Pennybacker (Teamster), Red Morgan (Hansen), Dean Smith, Bill Hicks, Bill Davis, Walter Davis and John Welty (Bannister gang).

Producer: Gene Kelly. Executive producer: James Lee Barrett. Production company/distributor: National General. Length: 103 minutes. Release date: 12 June 1970 (premiere in Chicago).

Filming began 10 July 1969. Location work around Santa Fe, New Mexico.

FOOLS' PARADE (1971)

British release title: **Dynamite Man from Glory Jail**

Director: Andrew V. McLaglen. Screenplay: James Lee Barrett (from the novel by Davis Grubb). Photographer (Eastman color): Harry Stradling Jr. Art director: Alfred Sweeney. Editors: David Bretherton, Robert Simpson. Music: Henry Vars.

Cast: James Stewart (Mattie Appleyard), George Kennedy ('Doc' Council), Anne Baxter (Cleo), Strother Martin (Lee Cottrill), Kurt Russell (Johnny Jesus), William Windom (Roy K. Sizemore), Mike Kellin (Steve Mystic), Kathy Cannon (Chanty), Morgan Paull (Junior Kilfong), Robert Donner (Willis Hubbard), David Huddleston (Homer Grindstaff), Dort Clark (Enoch Purdy), James Lee Barrett (Sonny Boy), Kitty Jefferson Doepken (Clara), Dwight McConnell (Station Master), Richard Carl (Police Chief), Arthur Cain (Prosecuting Attorney), Paul Merriman (Fireman), Walter Dove (Engineer), Peter Miller

(Trusty), George Metro (Train dispatcher), Suzann Stoehr (Bank teller), John Edwards (Bank clerk).

Producer: Andrew V. McLaglen. Executive producer: James Lee Barrett. Associate producer: Harry Bernsen. Production companies: Stanmore/Penbar. Distributor: Columbia. Length: 98 minutes. Release date: July 1971.

Filming started 22 September 1970. Location work in West Virginia.

THE JIMMY STEWART SHOW (1971) (for TV)

Director/screenplay: Hal Kanter. Photographer (color): Harold Stine. Music: Van Alexander.

Cast: James Stewart (Prof. James K. Howard), Julie Adams (Martha Howard), Jonathan Daly (Peter Howard), Ellen Geer (Wendy Howard), Kirby Furlong (Jake Howard), Dennis Larson (Teddy Howard), John McGiver (Prof. Luther Quince), Gloria Stewart (Grandma Howard), Richard Annis, Melissa Newman.

Producer: Hal Kanter. Production company: Warner Bros Television. Length: 30 minutes (with commercials). First transmission: Sunday 19 September 1971 (on NBC network at 8:30 pm sponsored by Proctor & Gamble).

Continued weekly for twenty-three more episodes.

HARVEY (1972) (for TV)

Director: Fielder Cook. Television adaptation: Jacqueline Babbin, Audrey Gellen Maas (from the play by Mary Chase).

Cast: James Stewart (Elwood P. Dowd), Helen Hayes (Veta Louise Simmons), Marian Hailey (Myrtle Mae Simmons), John McGiver (Dr Chumley), Richard Mulligan (Dr Sanderson), Jesse White (Duane Wilson), Arlene Francis (Mrs Chumley), Madeline Kahn (Miss Kelly), Martin Gabel (Judge Gaffney), Fred Gwynne (Cab driver), Dorothy Blackburn (Mrs Chauvenet).

Producer: David Susskind. Production companies: Talent Associates Norton Simon / Foote, Cone & Belding/NBC.

Length: 90 minutes (with commercials). First transmission: Wednesday 22 March 1972 (on *Hallmark Hall of Fame* series).

HAWKINS ON MURDER (1973) (for TV)

Director: Jud Taylor. Screenplay: David Karp. Photographer (color): Earl Rath. Art director: Joseph R. Jennings. Editor: Henry Berman. Music: Jerry Goldsmith.

Cast: James Stewart (Billy Jim Hawkins), Strother Martin (R. J. Hawkins), Bonnie Bedelia (Edith Dayton-Thomas), Kate Reid (Julia Dayton), David Huddleston (Joseph Harrelson), Dana Elcar (Dr Aaronson), Antoinette Bower (Vivian Vincent), Charles McGraw (Capt. Bates), Robert Webber (Carl Vincent), Margaret Markov (Theresa Ruth Colman), Ivan Bonar (Judge), Don Diamond, Tim Hallick, Inez Pedroza, Dennis Robertson, Bill Robles, Virginia Hawkins.

Executive producer: Norman Felton. Producer: David Karp. Production companies: Arena/Leda. Distributor: Metro-Goldwyn-Mayer. Length: 90 minutes (with commercials). First transmission: 13 March 1973 (on CBS network).

Subsequently retitled *Death and the Maiden* when re-run as part of a series on 6 November 1973.

HAWKINS – MURDER IN MOVIELAND (1973) (for TV)

Director: Jud Taylor. Screenplay: David Karp.

Cast: James Stewart (Billy Jim Hawkins), Sheree North (Debbie Lane), Cameron Mitchell (Jake Parkins), Strother Martin (R. J. Hawkins), William Smithers (Sam Drummond), Kenneth Mars (Lester De Ville), Maggie Wellman (Kate Parkins), Thaao Penghlis (Assistant manager), Robert Hamner (Prosecutor), Deborah Newman (Waitress), Justin Smith (Director).

Length: 90 minutes (with commercials). First transmission: 2 October 1973.

Also known as *Murder in Hollywood*.

HAWKINS – DIE, DARLING, DIE (1973) (for TV)

Director: Paul Wendkos. Screenplay: Gene L. Coon.

Cast: James Stewart (Billy Jim Hawkins), Julie Harris (Janet Hubbard), Mayf Nutter (Jeremiah Stocker), Diana Douglas (Clara Guilfoyle), Murray Hamilton (Frank Guilfoyle), Henry Jones (George Davis), Sam Elliott (Luther Wilkes), Judson Morgan (Judge).

Length: 90 minutes (with commercials). First transmission: 23 October 1973.

HAWKINS – A LIFE FOR A LIFE (1973) (for TV)

Director: Jud Taylor. Screenplay: David Karp.

Cast: James Stewart (Billy Jim Hawkins), William Windom (Joe Hamilton), John Ventantonio [Venantonia?] (Jeff Compton), James Hampton (Earl Coleman), Noam Pitlik (Prof. Hastings), Tyne Daly (Ellen Hamilton), Jeanne Cooper (Mrs Hamilton), Joe Maross (Prosecutor).

Length: 90 minutes (with commercials). First transmission: 13 November 1973.

HAWKINS – BLOOD FEUD (1973) (for TV)

Director: Paul Wendkos. Screenplay: David Karp.

Cast: James Stewart (Billy Jim Hawkins), Lew Ayres (Gus Bitterman), Strother Martin (R. J. Hawkins), Richard Kelton (Don Morrison), Mayf Nutter (Jeremiah Stocker), James Best (John Early), Diana Ewing (Connie Hawkins), Jeanette Nolan (Tessie Hawkins).

Length: 90 minutes (with commercials). First transmission: 4 December 1973.

HAWKINS – MURDER IN THE SLAVE TRADE (1974) (for TV)

Director: Paul Wendkos. Screenplay: Robert Hamner.

Cast: James Stewart (Billy Jim Hawkins), Mayf Nutter (Jeremiah Stocker), Ellen Weston (Ellen Vincent), Peter Mark Richman (Paul Forbes), James Luisi (Andy Tyler), Joseph Hindy (Victor Colletta), Dick Gautier (Frank Scotti), Warren Kemmerling (Ernie Fiske), Robert Sampson (Neal Carlson), Clark Howat (Elliott Wolcott), Stephen McNally (Vincent), Stacy Keach Sr (Coroner).

Length: 90 minutes (with commercials). First transmission: 22 January 1974.

HAWKINS – MURDER ON THE 13TH FLOOR (1974) (for TV)

Director: Jud Taylor. Screenplay: David Karp.

Cast: James Stewart (Billy Jim Hawkins), Strother Martin (R. J. Hawkins), Teresa Wright (Jenny Burke), Andrew Parks (David Burke), Albert Paulsen (Teddy Osterman), Herb Edelman (Lt. Horowitz), Signe Hasso (Madame Carrazza), Kurt Kasznar (John Carrazza), Jeff Corey (Julian Maynard), Maxine Stuart (Mrs Constantine), Lezlie Dalton (Victoria Cannon).

Length: 90 minutes (with commercials). First transmission: 5 February 1974.

HAWKINS – CANDIDATE FOR MURDER (1974) (for TV)

Director: Robert Scheerer. Screenplay: Robert Hamner.

Cast: James Stewart (Billy Jim Hawkins), Strother Martin (R. J. Hawkins), Paul Burke (Fred Wyatt), Diana Hyland (Jennifer Pearson), Andrew Prine (Peter Vail), John Ericson (Frank Pearson), Mark Gordon (Simon Kovac), Pernell Roberts (Senator Griffith), John Larch (Herb Talley), Rick Gates (Charlie Hendricks).

Length: 90 minutes (with commercials). First transmission: 5 March 1974.

THE SHOOTIST (1976)

Director: Don Siegel. Screenplay: Miles Hood Swarthout, Scott Hale (from the novel by Glendon Swarthout). Photographer (Technicolor): Bruce Surtees. Production designer: Robert Boyle. Editor: Douglas Stewart. Music: Elmer Bernstein.

Cast: John Wayne (John Bernard Books), Lauren Bacall (Bond Rogers), Ron Howard (Gillom Rogers), James Stewart (Dr Hostetler), Richard Boone (Mike Sweeney), Hugh O'Brian (Pulford), Bill McKinney (Cobb), Harry Morgan (Marshal Thibido), John Carradine (Beckum), Sheree North (Serepta), Richard Lenz (Sam Dobkins), Scatman Crothers (Moses), Gregg Palmer (Burly man), Alfred Dennis (Barber), Dick

Winslow (Streetcar driver), Melody Thomas (Girl on streetcar), Kathleen O'Malley (Schoolteacher).

Producers: M. J. Frankovich, William Self. Production company: Dino De Laurentiis. Distributor: Paramount. Length: 100 minutes. Release date: August 1976.

Shooting began 13 January 1976 with location work at Carson City, Nevada.

AIRPORT '77 (1977)

Director: Jerry Jameson. Screenplay: Michael Scheff, David Spector (from a screen story by H. A. L. Craig and Charles Kuenstle inspired by the film *Airport* based on the novel by Arthur Hailey). Photographer (Technicolor, Panavision): Philip Lathrop. 2nd Unit director: Michael Moore. Production designer: George C. Webb. Editors: J. Terry Williams, Robert Watts. Music: John Cacavas.

Cast: Jack Lemmon (Don Gallagher), Lee Grant (Karen Wallace), Brenda Vaccaro (Eve Clayton), Joseph Cotten (Nicholas St Downs III), Olivia de Havilland (Emily Livingston), Darren McGavin (Stan Buchek), Christopher Lee (Martin Wallace), George Kennedy (Patroni), James Stewart (Philip Stevens), Robert Foxworth (Chambers), Robert Hooks (Eddie), Monte Markham (Banker), Kathleen Quinlan (Julie), Gil Gerard (Frank Powers), James Booth (Ralph Crawford), Monica Lewis (Anne), Maidie Norman (Dorothy), Pamela Bellwood (Lisa), Arlene Golonka (Mrs Jane Stern), Tom Sullivan (Steve), M. Emmet Walsh (Dr Williams), Michael Richardson (Walker), Michael Pataki (Wilson), George Furth (Gerald Lucas), Richard Venture (Cmdr. Guay), Ross Bickell (Johnson), Peter Fox (Lt. Norris), Beverly Gill (Stewardess), Charles Macaulay (Admiral Corrigan), Tom Rosqui (Hunter), Arthur Adams (Cmdr. Reed), Anthony Battaglia (Benjy), Elizabeth Cheshire (Bonnie), Charlotte Lord (Stewardess), Paul Tuerpe (Deck officer), Dar Robinson (Larry), Ted Chapman (Chef), Jim Arnett, Ron Burke, Chuck Hayward, Janet Brady, Johana De Winter, George Whiteman and Jean Coulter (Passengers), John Clavin (F.A.A. Supervisor), John Kerry (Lt. Commander), James Ray Weeks (Pilot), Chris Lemmon and William Whitaker (Radiomen), Mary Nancy Burnett (Radar controller), Bill Jelliffe and

Rick Sorenson (Controllers), Peter Greene and Asa Teeter (Frogmen).

Producer: William Frye. Executive producer: Jennings Lang. Production company/distributor: Universal. Length: 114 minutes. Release date: March 1977.

Spare or additional footage was subsequently added to create a television version of approximately 177 minutes.

THE BIG SLEEP (1978)

Director/screenplay: Michael Winner (from the novel by Raymond Chandler). Photographer (color by DeLuxe): Robert Paynter. Production designer: Harry Pottle. Art director: John Graysmark. Editor: Freddie Wilson. Music: Jerry Fielding.

Cast: Robert Mitchum (Philip Marlowe), Sarah Miles (Charlotte Regan), Richard Boone (Lash Canino), Candy Clark (Camilla Sternwood), Joan Collins (Agnes Lozelle), Edward Fox (Joe Brody), John Mills (Inspector Jim Carson), James Stewart (General Guy de Brisai Sternwood), Oliver Reed (Eddie Mars), Harry Andrews (Vincent Norris), Colin Blakely (Harry Jones), Richard Todd (Commander Barker), Diana Quick (Mona Mars), James Donald (Inspector Gregory), John Justin (Arthur Gwynn Geiger), Simon Turner (Karl Lundgren), Martin Potter (Owen Taylor), David Saville (Rusty Regan), Dudley Sutton (Lanny), Don Henderson (Lou), Nik Forster (Croupier), Joe Ritchie (Taxi driver), Patrick Durkin (Reg), Derek Deadman (Customer in bookshop), Roy Evans (Man in overalls), Mike Lewin (Detective Waring), David Jackson (Inspector Willis), David Millett (Detective), Clifford Earl (Police doctor), Michael Segal (Barman), Norman Lumsden (Lord Smethurst), Judy Buxton (Receptionist at Cheval Club).

Producers: Elliott Kastner, Michael Winner. Associate producer: Bernard Williams. Production company: Winkast. Distributor (U.K.): ITC. Length: 99 minutes. Release date: March 1978 (U.S.A.), 28 September 1978 (U.K.).

THE MAGIC OF LASSIE (1978)

Director: Don Chaffey. Screenplay: Jean Holloway, Richard M. Sherman, Robert B. Sherman (from a screen story by Richard

M. Sherman and Robert B. Sherman). Photographer (color): Michael Margulies. Art director: George Troast. Editor: John C. Horger. Music: Irwin Kostal. Songs: Richard M. Sherman, Robert B. Sherman.

Cast: James Stewart (Clovis Mitchell), Mickey Rooney (Gus), Pernell Roberts (Jamison), Stephanie Zimbalist (Kelly), Michael Sharrett (Chris), Alice Faye (Alice), Gene Evans (Sheriff Andrews), Mike Mazurki (Apollo), Robert Lussier (Finch), Lane Davies (Allan Fogerty), William Flatley (Truck driver), James V. Reynolds (Officer Wilson), Rayford Barnes (Reward seeker), W. D. Goodman (Mighty Manuel), Hank Metheney (Referee), Buck Young (TV announcer), David Himes (Father), Ron Honthaner (Official), Ed Vasgersian (Lee), Bob Cashell (Ed), Robin Cawiezell (Girl in casino), Gary Davis (Motorcycle officer), Ralph Garrett (Kennelman), Pete Kellett (Security guard), Klause Hense (Helicopter pilot), Carl Nielsen (Mr Kern), Regina Waldon (Mrs Kern), Roger Jenkins Jr, Maureen Smith, Nanci Bergman, Lynda Chase, Eddie D'Angelo, Mark McGee and Mary Bennett (The Mike Curb Congregation).

Producers: Bonita Granville Wrather, William Beaudine Jr. Executive producer: Jack Wrather. Production company: Lassie Productions. Distributor: International Picture Show. Length: 99 minutes. Release date: August 1978.

THE GREEN HORIZON (1981)
Japanese title: **Afurika Monogatari**

Directors: Susumu Hani, Simon Trevor. Screenplay: Shintaro Tsuji (from a screen story by Shuji Terayama). Photographers (color by DeLuxe): Simon Trevor, (2nd unit) Tsuguzo Matsumae. Editors: Nobuhiko Hosaka, Numazaki Henshushitsu, (English version) Terence Anderson. Music director: Naozumi Yamamoto.

Cast: James Stewart (Old man), Philip Sayer (Young man), Kathy [Cathleen McOsker] (Maya), Eleonora Vallone (Erica), Hakuta Simba (Elder), Michael Clark (First guide), Mike Simochelo (Second guide), Oliver Lintondo (Nomad).

Producers: Terry Ogisu, Yoichi Matsue. Executive in charge o English production: Ken Kawarai. Production company: Sanri(

Communications. Lengths: 120 minutes (Japan), 87 minutes (U.S.A.). Release dates: May 1981 (Japan), 7 November 1981 (U.S.A., premiere on ShowTime Cable television outlets).

Production started 10 December 1979 in Kenya. Also known as *A Tale of Africa*. Only released in Britain on video cassette (by Skyline Video through CBS/Fox Video).

RIGHT OF WAY (1983)

Director: George Schaefer. Screenplay: Richard Lees (from his play). Photographer (color): Howard Schwartz. Production designer: Jack Chilberg. Editor: Sid Katz. Music: Brad Fiedel.

Cast: Bette Davis (Mini Dwyer), James Stewart (Teddy Dwyer), Melinda Dillon (Ruda Dwyer), Priscilla Morrill (Louise Finter), John Harkins (G. Clayburn), Louis Schaefer (Kahn), Jacque Lynn Colton (Mrs Belkin), Charles Walker (Kahn's assistant), Jane Kaczmarek (TV reporter), Philip Littell (Cashier), Paco Vela (TV cameraman), Edith Fields (Saleswoman), Mark Taylor (Para-Medic), John Ratzenberger (Policeman), Archie Lang (Motel desk clerk), East Carlo (Gardener), Jodi Hicks, Erin Karpf and Bobby Jacoby (Mrs Belkin's children), Michael Murphy (Process server).

Producers: George Schaefer, Philip Parslow. Executive producer: Merrill H. Karpf. Production companies: Schaefer/Karpf, Post-Newsweek Video, Home Box Office. Length: 106 minutes. Release date: 23 August 1983 (Montreal Film Festival showing) (American Pay-TV screenings scheduled to start November 1983).

Production began 11 October 1982 in Los Angeles.

ADDENDA

James Stewart also narrated or appeared as himself in the following films.

FELLOW AMERICANS (1942). Documentary dramatizing the implications of the Japanese attack on Pearl Harbor. Director: Garson Kanin. Screenplay: Robert W. Russell. For the Office of Emergency Management. 10 minutes.

WINNING YOUR WINGS (1942). Short about the Army Air Corps. Produced by the Office of War Information.

THE AMERICAN CREED (1946). (British release title: **American Brotherhood Week**). Producer: David O. Selznick.

THUNDERBOLT (1947). Introduced by James Stewart, a documentary about fighter plane support of ground troops. Director: William Wyler. Technicolor. 44 minutes.

10,000 KIDS AND A COP (1948). Documentary.

HOW MUCH DO YOU OWE? (1949). Documentary for the Disabled American Veterans. Distributor: Columbia. 9 minutes.

AND THEN THERE WERE FOUR (1950). Documentary about road safety. Director: Frank Strayer. Production company: Roland Reed Productions for Socony-Vacuum Oil Company. 27 minutes.

AMBASSADORS WITH WINGS (1958). Production company: Robert J. Enders Inc. for the Ex-Cello Corp. 25 minutes.

X-15 (1961). Missile base drama starring David McLean, Charles Bronson, Ralph Taeger, Brad Dexter, Mary Tyler Moore, Patricia Owens, and narrated by Stewart. Director: Richard Donner. Distributor: United Artists. 106 minutes.

DIRECTED BY JOHN FORD (1971). Interview with Stewart for documentary on Ford. Director: Peter Bogdanovich. Production company: The American Film Institute.

THE AMERICAN WEST OF JOHN FORD (1971). More of the same. For CBS.

PAT NIXON: PORTRAIT OF A FIRST LADY (1972). Personal look at Mrs Richard M. Nixon during her years as First Lady. Narrated by Stewart. Producer: Ed Spiegel. Production company: David Wolper for the Republican Party.

THAT'S ENTERTAINMENT! (1974). Musical compilation with Stewart among the star narrators seen at the MGM Studio introducing an extract from *Born to Dance* featuring himself, and other sequences. Director/screenplay/producer: Jack Haley Jr. Production company/distributor: Metro-Goldwyn-Mayer. Length: 127 minutes.

SENTIMENTAL JOURNEY (1976). Commemorating the 40th anniversary of the DC-3 aircraft. Director/producer: Ferde Grofé. Length: 20 minutes.

MR KRUEGER'S CHRISTMAS (1980). Sponsored by the Mormons. Featured Stewart and the Mormon Tabernacle Choir. Director: Keith Merrill. Length: 30 minutes.

Bibliography

Allyson, June (with Frances Spatz Leighton), *June Allyson,* (New York, G. P. Putnam's Sons, 1982).

Beaver, Jim, "James Stewart," *Films in Review* (October 1980).

Bogdanovich, Peter, *Picture Shows: Peter Bogdanovich on the Movies* (London, George Allen & Unwin, 1975). Features essay "Th' Respawnsibility of bein' J . . . Jimmy Stewart" from *Esquire,* an entertaining and most useful piece.

Capra, Frank, *The Name Above the Title: An Autobiography* (New York, Macmillan, 1972).

Castell, David (Editor), "James Stewart: 40 Years a Star" (interview/story), *Films Illustrated* (March 1972). Reprinted in: Castell, David (Editor), *Cinema '76* (London, Independent Magazines [Publishing], 1975).

Culhane, John, "Dear Mr. Stewart:", part of "A James Stewart Album," *American Film* (March 1980).

Davidson, Bill, "Wal, you see, I'm an actor: Besides the money's good, so Jimmy Stewart is in television—every week," *TV Guide* (October 2, 1971).

Ford, Dan, *The Unquiet Man: The Life of John Ford* (London, William Kimber, 1982).

Grady, Billy, *The Irish Peacock: The Confessions of a Legendary Talent Agent* (New Rochelle, New York, Arlington House, 1972).

Hall, Dennis John, "Box Office Drawl" (three-part career survey), *Films and Filming* (December 1972, January and February 1973).

Hayward, Brooke, *Haywire* (New York, Alfred A. Knopf, 1977).

Higham, Charles, *Marlene: The Life of Marlene Dietrich* (New York, W. W. Norton, 1977).

Hotchner, A. E., *Doris Day: Her Own Story* (New York, Morrow, 1976).

Kitses, Jim, "The Rise and Fall of the American West" (interview with Borden Chase), *Film Comment* (Winter 1970-71).

Kobal, John, *The Art of the Great Hollywood Portrait Photographers 1925-1940* (New York, Alfred A. Knopf, 1980).

Logan, Joshua, *Josh: My Up and Down, In and Out Life* (New York, Delacorte, 1976).

McBride, Joseph, "Aren't You . . . Jimmy Stewart?", *American Film* (June 1976).

Mehren, Elizabeth, "Davis and Stewart: Together at Last," *Emmy Magazine* (March/April 1983).

Missiaen, Jean-Claude, "A Lesson in Cinema" (interview with Anthony Mann), *Cahiers du Cinéma in English* (No. 12, 1967). Unfortunately, a somewhat cumbersome translation from the French rather than Mann's original English.

Newquist, Roy, *Conversations with Joan Crawford* (Secaucus, New Jersey, The Citadel Press, 1980).

Ostroff, Roberta, "Henry Fonda" (interview), *Take One* (Vol. 3, No. 10, 1973).

Parish, James Robert, and Stanke, Don E., *The All-Americans* (New Rochelle, New York, Arlington House, 1977). Contains a lengthy chapter on James Stewart together with a very detailed filmography of which I have made some use while checking closely for factual accuracy and omissions—certainly the most substantial coverage of Stewart's career prior to this present volume.

Salisbury, Lesley, "When a superstar went to war" (about Stewart's war-time experiences), *TV Times* (March 20-26, 1982).

Spoto, Donald, *The Life of Alfred Hitchcock: The Dark Side of Genius* (Boston, Little-Brown, 1983).

Stewart, James, "One Hat's Enough for Me" (uncredited interview), *Films and Filming* (April 1966).

Teichmann, Howard, *Fonda: My Life as Told to Howard Teichmann* (New York, New American Library, 1981).

Truffaut, François, *Hitchcock* (New York, Simon and Schuster, 1969).

Vallance, Tom, "A Conversation with June Allyson" (*Films and Filming*, July 1982).

Westmore, Frank (with Muriel Davidson), *The Westmores of Hollywood* (New York, J. B. Lippincott, 1976).

Wicking, Chris, and Pattison, Barrie, "Interviews with Anthony Mann" (*Screen*, July-October 1969). A really thorough and entertaining piece, quoted extensively in this book.

Willis, Donald C., *The Films of Frank Capra* (Metuchen, New Jersey, Scarecrow Press, 1974).

Index

[263]